Emotion, Thought and Therapy

Emotion, Thought & Therapy

A Study of Hume and Spinoza and the Relationship of Philosophical
Theories of the Emotions to Psychological Theories of Therapy

Jerome Neu

UNIVERSITY OF CALIFORNIA PRESS
Berkeley and Los Angeles 1977

University of California Press
Berkeley and Los Angeles, California

ISBN: 0-520-03288-8
Library of Congress Catalog Card Number: 76-20010

Printed in Great Britain

For Stuart and Renee Hampshire

Contents

Acknowledgments   ix

Introduction   1

I   Hume

 1   Impressions of Reflexion   7
 2   Pride and Double Association   8
 3   'Limitations'   10
 4   Association: Resemblance and Simplicity   11
 5   Association: Simplicity and the Essential   16
 6   Impressions of Pleasure and Pleasant Impressions   20
 7   Self and the Idea of Self   24
 8   Emotion and Object   26
 9   Object and Effect   28
10   Object and Cause   32
11   Thought-Dependence   36
12   Sympathy and Knowledge of Other Minds   46
13   Calm Passions   53
14   Thought, Turbulence, and Action   56
     Hume's Classification of the Passions (diagram)   68

II   Spinoza

 1   *Conatus* and Unconscious Desire   71
 2   Pleasure and Pain and the Spinozist Analysis of Love   76
 3   Active/Passive and the Intellectual Love of God   79
 4   More Adequate Ideas and Activity   81
 5   Transforming Emotions   84
 6   Intellectual or Social Emotions   92
 7   Active Emotion and Action   97

III Thought, Theory and Therapy

1	Non-Analytical Therapies	107
2	Behaviour Therapy and 'Effectiveness'	108
3	Lévi-Strauss and Quesalid	112
4	Consensus and Curing	114
5	Structuralist Explanation: Coherence and Correspondence and Curing	117
6	Psychoanalysis and Shamanism: The 'Same Forces'?	122
7	Little Hans and Little Albert, Psychoanalysis and Behaviour Therapy: On Aetiology and Displacement	124
8	Nosology and Anthropology	128
9	Psychoanalysis and Behaviour Therapy: The Effectiveness of Interpretations	133
10	Insight Is Not Enough	135
11	Freud's 'Theory' of the Emotions	139
12	Unconscious Fantasy and Emotion	143
13	Spinoza: 'The Philosopher of Psychoanalysis'	146

In Summary   152

Appendix A: On Objects and Causes   157

Appendix B: On Thoughts and Emotions   165

Appendix C: On a Humean View of Fantasy   169

Notes   175

Bibliography   181

Index   189

Acknowledgments

At various points, in a variety of ways, a number of people have helped to make this book possible. I would like especially to thank Rogers Albritton, Stanley Cavell, Patrick Gardiner, Pam Matz, Pat Patterson, and David Pears.

Part III includes material previously published in *Man: The Journal of the Royal Anthropological Institute* (Vol. X) and *Psychoanalysis and Contemporary Science* (Vol. IV).

Preparation of the manuscript was assisted by Faculty Research Funds granted by the University of California, Santa Cruz.

Jerome Neu

Introduction

The world of feeling and the world of thought are not unrelated. How they are related, however, is a matter of dispute. I will be discussing Hume and Spinoza as the best and most systematic representatives of two different traditions of argument about their relation. Hume and those who follow him treat emotions as essentially feelings ('affects' or 'impressions') with thoughts incidentally attached. Spinoza and those who follow him, on the other hand, treat emotions as essentially thoughts ('beliefs' or 'ideas') with feelings incidentally attached. I think that strong arguments can be produced to show that the Spinozists are closer to the truth, that is, that thoughts are of greater importance than feelings (in the narrow sense of felt sensations) in the classification and discrimination of emotional states. Spinoza can, for example, account for ranges of intellectuality among emotions and within particular emotions that Hume has difficulty even in recognizing. It is no part of these arguments to deny the importance of affects or feelings or other elements constituting emotions, but rather to understand how these elements fit together and to bring out the special importance of thoughts in discriminating mental states one from another. To say that thoughts are 'essential' is to say, for example, that what is most distinctive about my anger is the belief (roughly) that someone has caused me harm, and that without that belief or something like it my state could not be one of 'anger'. The point here is more than the general linguistic one that one could not mark the difference between apples and oranges if one lacked separate labels for them, that one might not be able to notice the difference if one had no way to describe it – in that case there would none the less be apples and oranges (one just might suffer from an unfortunate tendency to confuse them, in ordering over the telephone and so on, under the heading of 'fruit'). But in the case of emotions, without appropriate beliefs one lacks not only the capacity for discriminating emotions, but also the emotions themselves. Appropriate beliefs (whether conscious or unconscious) constitute an essential part of what it means to have an emotion. If one has no ground for ascribing the appropriate type of belief – to oneself or to another – one then has no ground for attributing one type of emotion rather than another. Distinguishing a person's beliefs provides us with the interpretive grounds for recognizing his emotions. But in order to be angry there is no particular feeling or sensation I need have; indeed, if I happen to have a particular sensation (e.g. my stomach churns) it is relevant to my anger only if I believe (something like) it is due to someone's causing me harm. Detached from my beliefs, a stomach ache does not amount to anger or to any other emotion. We will be pursuing these points and looking at how understanding the ways in which we discriminate and identify emotions may help us in understanding how we may (in some ways) change them.

Different views on the roles of thought and feeling in the nature of emotions have further implications. For example, the Humean and Spinozist theories yield very different perspectives on the power of poetry. For the Humean, the poet can at best provide a new label for an old feeling. Where emotions are essentially affects, mental feelings or sensations or (as in the James-Lange theory) the perception of physiological changes, there is no reason in the nature of things why all people (and even all animals, i.e. non-language users) should not be open (without special training or contexts) to all emotions. Gaps in feeling would be rather like gaps in sensation, requiring either wider experience or (like colour-blindness) medical treatment. The poet would have nothing special to offer.

The situation is rather different on a Spinozist view. The poet, in giving one a new way of describing the world, could also be giving one a new way of conceiving and so perceiving and experiencing the world: he could extend one's emotional life. 'We say a dog is afraid his master will beat him; but not, he is afraid his master will beat him tomorrow. Why not?' (Wittgenstein, 1953, section 650). Conceptions of time depend on language, and so a creature without language will lack an emotional life extended in time. Where emotion is essentially characterized through thought, a new way of thinking can also be a new way of feeling (now taken in a broad sense). A person who was closed to certain sorts of understanding and perception, would also be closed to certain emotions. The poet might provide valuable therapy for such limitations (as Wordsworth did for Mill).

Here, however, I will be concerned with the implications of Spinozist theory in another area. I think that it can contribute to showing that Freudian or, more generally, analytic therapies make philosophic sense. That is, we can begin to understand how people's emotional lives might be transformed by consideration and interpretation of their memories, beliefs, fantasies, and so on; how knowledge might help make one free. If thoughts or beliefs are essential constituents of emotions, we can go some way towards understanding how psychoanalytic therapies (as opposed to 'non-rational' behaviourist manipulations) can alter emotional life by changing beliefs. This is not to argue that psychoanalysis works better than other therapies, or even that it works. It may well be that for some sorts of problems electrical shock, for example, is the most effective treatment available. But when shock works, its mechanism is opaque to us. When psychoanalysis works, we may find in Spinoza the beginning of an understanding of how it works.

Therapy through 'insight' depends importantly on the nature of unconscious thoughts and beliefs. Considering the role of thought in ordinary emotional contexts may help us to explain that importance. We may be able to extend our ordinary model of the emotions to include the cases dealt with by psychoanalysts. But before we can proceed to do so, we must determine the type of model to which our ordinary attitudes and emotions are amenable. The contrasting models I will explore are those delineated by Spinoza and Hume. I have said that Spinoza's view of the emotions is reflected in modern analytical therapies. I believe that Hume's view is similarly reflected in modern 'non-rational' psychological therapies. The theory that informs modern behaviour therapies apparently rejects reference to introspectable inner states (those states which Hume termed 'impressions' and 'ideas'). But more significant, I think, is the fact that both Hume and the behaviourists neglect the importance of thoughts. They do this in different ways, but the underlying theories of emotion and mind here come together. Hume neglected the significance of thoughts and beliefs, assimilating them (not to behaviour) but to feeling. The behaviourists, in their turn, assimilate both thought and feeling to their manifestations in behaviour. But thoughts cannot be simply read off from behaviour and mechanisms of association are inadequate for accounting for the relations of thoughts. In any case, the role of thoughts in discriminating mental states is not sufficiently appreciated. In this, and in their model and mechanisms of the mind, the behaviour therapists are among the modern representatives of the Humean tradition of argument about the emotions.

Our discussion here will begin with a detailed analysis of the theories formulated by Hume and Spinoza and move on to a survey of psychological therapies and the roles they assign to thoughts. We will find that there is a spectrum of philosophical theories of emotion and a spectrum of psychological theories of therapy, and that behind both lie differences on the nature and importance of thought-dependence. A Spinozist understanding of how thoughts are built into emotions can, I think, help us to understand Freudian and other analytic theories and therapies. That is, it can help us to see how reason can be more than merely the slave of the passions.

1
Ḧume

Hume treats emotions as discrete simple experiences: to each namable emotion there corresponds a specific and particular feeling. In his *Treatise of Human Nature* (*THN*), Book II: 'Of the Passions', he is not, despite appearances, a taxonomist compiling a vast Baconian catalogue of mental flora and fauna and their nice distinctions. His enterprise is closer to natural philosophy in the Newtonian tradition than natural history, only taking human nature as its sphere. Hume is to be regarded, as he regards himself, as a physicist of the emotions. A careful observer of the phenomena, he seeks general hypotheses (what Newton would insist on calling experimental laws or principles) to explain their interconnections and motions. His observations and hypotheses are, of course, informed by his general empiricist position. It is our own minds, our impressions and our ideas that we know most directly and most certainly and so these must be the terms at the ends of the emotional equations. His theory of knowledge also determines the form these connections may take: the principle of association of ideas is his universal law of gravitation. Does his general philosophy cause him to misperceive and misrepresent the world of emotions and so render him incapable of answering the sorts of questions a philosophical theory of the emotions should? For example, what sorts of possibilities exist for changing emotions?

1
Impressions of Reflexion

The contents of the mind are considered by Hume one and all perceptions. As passions are, undoubtedly, in the mind they must, for Hume,
be perceptions, i.e. impressions ('our sensations, passions and emotions,
as they make their first appearance in the soul') or ideas ('the faint
images of these in thinking and reasoning' – *THN*, I, p. 1). There
is in general little distinguishing these two kinds of perceptions (though
Hume does sometimes contrast them in ways which can perhaps be
traced to a lingering Hutchesonian position – see Kemp Smith, 1941,
p. 49, n. 1): ideas are simply less vivid versions of the impressions from
which they derive. Within Hume's philosophy there is also, apparently,
little to distinguish these two types of perception from 'belief', which
in Hume's account seems to be defined as very vivid perception (though
sometimes, following Hutcheson, it is treated as a state of mind in the
observing self – a creature giving Hume no end of difficulty – rather
than a quality of each perception – again, see Kemp Smith, pp. 74ff.).
Impressions and ideas plus mechanical principles of association seem
rather meagre equipment for reconstructing the whole of our mental
and moral life. Hume has more: a doctrine of reflexion. Passions are
not simply impressions or ideas, rather they are thought of as 'impressions of reflexion'.

Impressions of reflexion, when first introduced, are explained as follows:

> [Impressions of Reflexion are] derived in a great measure from our
> ideas, and that in the following order. An impression first strikes
> upon the senses, and makes us perceive heat or cold, thirst or
> hunger, pleasure or pain of some kind or other. Of this impression
> there is a copy taken by the mind, which remains after the
> impression ceases; and this we call an idea. This idea of pleasure
> or pain, when it returns upon the soul, produces the new
> impressions of desire and aversion, hope and fear, which may
> properly be called impressions of reflexion, because derived from
> it. These again are copied by the memory and imagination, and
> become ideas; which perhaps in their turn give rise to other
> impressions and ideas. So that the impressions of reflexion are only
> antecedent to their correspondent ideas; but posterior to those of
> sensation, and deriv'd from them . . . the impressions of reflexion,
> *viz*. passions, desires, and emotions, which principally deserve
> our attention, arise mostly from ideas (*THN*, I, pp. 7–8).

This is a genealogy. Causal ancestry is what distinguishes impressions of reflexion from impressions of sensation ('all the impressions of the senses, and all bodily pains and pleasures' – *THN*, II, p. 275); the latter, by way of contrast, arise 'in the soul originally, from unknown causes' (*THN*, I, p. 7). (Hume sometimes, e.g. *THN*, II, p. 275, describes the contrast as one between 'secondary' and 'original' impressions.) Taken in themselves, as impressions (which itself is a much broadened technical term in Hume), one would expect to perceive no difference between impressions of reflexion and of sensation – unless they show their pedigrees on their faces.

But genealogical metaphor will not do enough. The relation between impressions of reflexion and the ideas and impressions from which they derive must, in Hume's system, be causal. His problem then is to get the causal story right in accounting for the origin of each emotion. We, however, must enquire whether emotions viewed as impressions with a peculiar causal history will do justice to the phenomena at all. And, given Hume's account of the nature of causality, whether it makes sense to view them this way, even within his system.

2
Pride and Double Association

Hume divides passions into direct and indirect according to whether or not they involve other qualities in order to be derived from pleasure and pain (themselves viewed as impressions of sensation). An example and model of Hume's analysis can be found in his discussion of the four indirect passions: pride, humility, love, and hate. These four indirect passions are central and Hume devotes considerable space to discussing them both because they have connections with the passions of approval and disapproval so central to his moral theory and because they give full display to his principles of association.

Pride, one of the four indirect passions, is (like all passions) a 'simple and uniform impression' (*THN*, II, p. 277). It cannot be defined or analysed into parts, it is a simple specific feeling which we recognize immediately and which cannot be other than as we perceive it. One can, however, specify 'such circumstances as attend' it: causal conditions and consequences, and other externally related circumstances. The *object* of pride, Hume tells us, is always self. Of course it is we who experience our pride, but this is not what is meant. In that sense we could be said to be the *bearer* of the passion, but all passions would be alike in that respect. (All my feelings are had by me.) What is meant by saying I am the object of pride, is that the feeling of pride is always and everywhere *followed* by the idea of myself. When we are proud, we think of ourselves.

Kenny mistakenly treats Hume's statement that the idea of self is the object of pride as an odd way of putting the claim that 'whatever expression completes the sense of the verb ". . . is proud of . . ." must begin with "his own . . .", even if what a man is proud of is only his brother-in-law's acquaintance with the second cousin of a Duke' (Kenny, 1963, p. 23). This is actually a misstatement. The phrase 'his own . . .' is not in fact necessary – a proper noun, for example, could quite correctly be all that follows 'is proud of . . .' – but it is required that that noun name someone or something closely related to the individual. Kenny's grammatical language misstates the fact, which is not really a fact of grammar at all (except perhaps 'logical grammar'). This fact (concerning what might be called the 'prepositional object' of pride) is recognized by Hume in another form, and as a fact of a different sort than Kenny's 'must' might suggest; it is related to what Hume considers the *cause* of pride. The difference between cause and object of passions is the difference 'betwixt that idea, which excites them, and that to which they direct their view, when excited' (*THN*, II, p. 278).

The exciting causes of pride are many and various. They have in common, however, first that it is always in virtue of some quality or characteristic which is in itself pleasant that the passion is excited, and second that the quality always inheres in a person or thing ('subject') somehow related to us: 'Beauty, consider'd merely as such, unless plac'd upon something related to us, never produces any pride or vanity; and the strongest relation alone, without beauty, or something else in its place, has as little influence on that passion' (*THN*, II, p. 279). Their joint presence is a necessary condition of pride. Hume envisages his compound cause as operating through a complex process of double association between impressions and ideas. The qualities which excite pride produce a separate pleasure, which by its resemblance to the agreeable sensation of pride itself leads to that feeling. The subjects in which the exciting qualities of pride inhere are 'either parts of ourselves, or something nearly related to us' (*THN*, II, p. 285), i.e. involve the idea of self which is the object of pride.

> That cause, which excites the passion, is related to the object, which nature has attributed to the passion; the sensation, which the cause separately produces, is related to the sensation of the passion: From this double relation of ideas and impressions, the passion is deriv'd. The one idea is easily converted into its cor-relative; and the one impression into that, which resembles and corresponds to it: With how much greater facility must this transition be made, where these movements mutually assist each other, and the mind receives a double impulse from the relations both of its impressions and ideas? (*THN*, II, pp. 286-7).

Probably the most plausible way of interpreting this mechanism is to suppose that the initial pleasant impression calls forth all pleasant passions indiscriminately, but that the presence of an additional association leads to pride's (in this case) being favoured above its fellows (Kemp Smith, p. 185, n. 3; cf. *THN*, II, pp. 305–6). In any case, the *object* emerges directly from the passion (mysteriously) and not via the

```
CAUSE ─────────────────→ PASSION ────→ OBJECT

quality (inhering - - - - -►pleasure - - - - -►pleasant
in subject related                        sensation
     to) self - - - - - - - - - - - - - - - - - - - - - - - - - - - - - -►idea of
                                                                      self
```

association of ideas, whose role seems to end with bringing about the passion itself (*THN*, II, p. 280). 'Here then is a passion plac'd betwixt two ideas, of which the one produces it, and the other is produc'd by it' (*THN*, II, p. 278). So we have

> on the one hand, an association between the pleasure we take in
> (say) the beauty of our house and the agreeable sensation of
> pride itself; on the other, an association between the idea of what
> belongs to us (the house) and the idea of ourself (as the 'natural'
> object of all pride) (Gardiner, 1963, pp. 37–8).

Thus 'any thing, that gives a pleasant sensation, and is related to self, excites the passion of pride, which is also agreeable, and has self for its object' (*THN*, II, p. 288).

Many of the possible objections to this picture are irrelevant to our purposes. A group of objections might be based on the conjecture that pride in the eighteenth century may not have been what it is today. If this is a matter of different qualities producing pleasure, and so pride, it does not concern us. If this is meant to suggest that the raw felt quality of pride has altered, it seems untestable and perhaps undiscussable. Finally a claim that pride may have been simply a feeling then but is something else or something more today, must give way to the prior question of whether it could ever have been a simple impression (even of reflexion). Other objections possible concern the many different uses of 'pride' and 'proud', some of which may seem very mysterious if we take Hume's analysis of the primary use (when describing an occurrent state of mind, immediately experienced) as correct (Árdal, 1966, pp. 19–22). However, a discussion of some of the problems within Hume's particular analysis may point to more fundamental difficulties in his whole approach, and so be the most fruitful procedure.

3
'Limitations'

Hume himself introduces some modifications or 'limitations' into the general scheme 'that all agreeable objects, related to ourselves, by an association of ideas and of impressions, produce pride, and disagreeable ones, humility' (*THN*, II, pp. 290ff.). The modifications include that the agreeable object must be *closely* related to ourselves (otherwise only 'joy' and not pride is produced) and only to ourselves or at most to ourselves and a few others. One could add that the condition of closeness varies inversely with the extraordinariness of the causal quality (Árdal, 1966, p. 30). The pleasant object must also be obvious to others, and durable. It can, however, be efficacious in producing pride even if (because of 'peculiarities of the health or temper') we derive no pleasure from it, providing there is a general rule that such objects are a sign of rank. Certainly these complications do not amount to the special propensities Hume appeals to elsewhere to bolster his associationist accounts. Whether or not the four 'limitations' and one 'enlargement' are deviations from Hume's programme, they can be allowed by us. They can be viewed as more careful and precise specifications of the triggers to association. There are deeper flaws in Hume's associationist psychology of the passions.

4
Association: Resemblance and Simplicity

At the heart of Hume's analysis are his principles of association: 'however changeable our thoughts may be, they are not entirely without rule and method in their changes. The rule, by which they proceed, is to pass from one object to what is resembling, contiguous to, or produc'd by it' (*THN*, II, p. 293). According to his theory, 'ideas are associated by resemblance, contiguity, and causation; and impressions only by resemblance' (*THN*, II, p. 283). The principle of succession by resemblance for *impressions* is first introduced in the second book of the *Treatise*, where the problem is one of accounting for the appearance of passions, i.e. impressions of reflexion. It plays no role in Book I, 'Of the Understanding', where *ideas* are discussed.

Hume provides an example of the orderly displacement of emotions: 'All resembling impressions are connected together, and no sooner one arises than the rest immediately follow. Grief and disappointment give rise to anger, anger to envy, envy to malice, and malice to grief again, till the whole circle be compleated' (*THN*, II, p. 283). We have in fact already seen the principle of association of impressions invoked in the account of the internal mechanism of pride: a pleasant quality inhering in a subject related to ourselves is supposed to lead to the (resembling) pleasant sensation of pride. But it is difficult to see how *simple* impressions (or ideas for that matter) could be capable of relations of resemblance and so of association through resemblance: the question of the intelligibility of Hume's theory precedes the question of its truth.

The two impressions involved in pride are both species of pleasure.

But then there must be *differentiae* between them, and these *differentiae* must constitute discriminable aspects of the two pleasant impressions themselves. And is not this complexity just the sort of thing Hume meant to exclude by the alleged simplicity of the elements of the system? The similarity of two perceptions seems inconsistent with the simplicity of each of them.[1] Similarity or resemblance is an incomplete predicate. Resemblance is always resemblance in a certain respect: A is more like B with respect to F than A is like C with respect to F. Two objects can be said to be similar only in a certain respect or from a certain point of view, and so, since they are similar but not identical, there must be a further respect in which they are *not* similar and in virtue of which they are different; and they cannot, therefore, be simple. A partial purpose of Hume's concept of association by resemblance (and association in general) is to explain the emergence of complexity out of simples. Mere numerical difference (i.e. impressions which are in every respect similar except for occurring at different times) will not serve Hume's purposes because two simple impressions, each qualitatively identical, would not together constitute either a new simple impression or a new complex impression (Passmore, 1968, p. 110).

Hume insists (as he must) that one *can* characterize simple perceptions as similar or dissimilar, that there need be no further aspect (and its resulting complexity) in order to establish a respect of comparison on which to base difference. He argues (in a note in connection with abstract ideas):

> 'Tis evident, that even different simple ideas may have a similarity or resemblance to each other; nor is it necessary, that the point or circumstance of resemblance shou'd be distinct or separable from that in which they differ. *Blue* and *green* are different simple ideas, but are more resembling than *blue* and *scarlet*; tho' their perfect simplicity excludes all possibility of separation or distinction. 'Tis the same case with particular sounds, and tastes and smells. These admit of infinite resemblances upon the general appearance and comparison, without having any common circumstance the same. And of this we may be certain, even from the very abstract terms *simple idea*. They comprehend all simple ideas under them. These resemble each other in their simplicity. And yet from their very nature, which excludes all composition, this circumstance, in which they resemble, is not distinguishable nor separable from the rest. 'Tis the same case with all the degrees in any quality. They are all resembling, and yet the quality, in any individual, is not distinct from the degree (*THN*, Appendix, p. 637).

Passmore responds:

> Hume's argument is a very curious one: it amounts to saying that
> simple ideas must at least resemble one another in being simple,
> so that resemblance is compatible with simplicity. But, of course,
> if simplicity were genuinely a point of resemblance, the conclusion
> would rather be that there are no simple ideas: the least which can
> possibly confront us would be something simple, vivid (or faint) and,
> for example, blue, i.e., a complex idea (Passmore, 1968, p. 109).

I think this criticism sound, at least if one starts, as Hume appears to,
with the notion of a 'simple idea' ('X idea') rather than an 'idea of a
simple' ('idea of X', where X is in turn simple). In the former case one
seems to consider simplicity as a possible point of comparison, as itself
a 'part' (of the idea), and then the quality of simplicity seems clearly
incompatible with resemblance in any further respect. But Hume's
position (in connection with emotions, at any rate) may require only a
weaker concept. That is, his saying 'X is simple' may be merely a misleading way of saying that X cannot be characterized except as X
(Passmore, 1968, p. 110); or his 'X is a simple idea' may mean merely
that it cannot be taken to pieces by definition and so cannot be acquired
by acquiring the ideas of each of its pieces (Pears, private communication). We shall return to these naming and learning notions of
simplicity in a moment.

Árdal tries to defend Hume against Passmore's attack. Part of his
defence is the repetition of Hume's point about colours (Árdal, 1966,
p. 14). But here my intuitions are different: it does not make 'perfect
sense' to me to say that blue is more (or less) similar to green than
scarlet, where these are taken as simple impressions. My difficulty is
that if similarity is analysed in terms of partial identity it requires at
least two parts in one of the items. One can then make sense of the
comparison only by viewing green as a mixture (of blue and yellow),
and therefore as not simple. We can see that we make the comparison
in this way if we try to compare the primary colours (red, yellow, and
blue) and establish relative similarities among them. No pair is 'more
like' than any other. I suspect that if we did not know that green is
produced by combining blue and yellow, we would not be tempted to
say that blue is more like green than red. If we were still so tempted,
it might have to do with other extraneous features of colours, such as
associations with warmth and cold. There is, however, another way one
could make sense of comparison of simples, but it too seems to me to
leave the compatibility of simplicity and resemblance in question.

One might appeal to a spectrum or scale of degree. Thus, one could
achieve plausibility for a comparison of colours (as simples) by ranging
them in a series on a scale and then judging in terms of distances on
that scale. First, we should note that conclusions from the case of colours
are, in any case, dangerous. Far from being typical, that case is most

peculiar, as Hume himself recognizes in connection with the underived idea of blue in the very first section of the *Treatise* (*THN*, I, p. 6). Second, the scale would indicate degree, but degree of what? For colours, we can imagine it would be a spectrum in accordance with a measure of wavelength. Is there a natural analogue in the form of a spectrum of emotions? Hume's circle of associated impressions (grief-disappointment-anger-envy-malice-grief) assumes that there is. I would agree, but I doubt that it is based on similarities of feeling (except at the grossest level, e.g. as in a contrast between pleasant and painful emotions). I would argue (ultimately) that such a spectrum depends on the characteristic thoughts involved. (Thus regret, as involving a thought of loss, might be similar to remorse, as involving a thought of loss plus culpability. But the whole matter is enormously complex, and involves other factors in addition to thought.)

Still, the notion of 'scale' brings us somewhat nearer to the most interesting point in Árdal's defence, the meaning of 'simple'. Is possession of a degree on a scale of magnitude incompatible with simplicity of an object? In a sense, obviously not; the scale is a framework *outside* the object, in which the object has a place. However, the object has that place because of the degree it possesses. The degree is in the object. Hume's claim is that the degree is not distinct or separable from the simple quality that constitutes the object. It is not clear that this is true.

Certainly the degree is not distinguishable (perhaps not even discernible) on a single view comprising only the object. But a view of several objects on the scale in which they are compared would show that they differ in degree; and would perhaps reveal the specific degree of the particular object. That the degree requires comparison amongst objects in order to be discovered (seen) does not imply that it is not a distinguishable characteristic of the supposedly simple object, despite the fact that Humean doctrine would suggest that all characteristics should be directly discernible (and imaginable in isolation). The distinguishing in some cases may just require several steps and more encompassing views.

However, it seems that Hume would continue to consider such characteristics (as degree) compatible with the simplicity of an object. In the following passage, he seems to argue that 'distinctions of reason' leave ideas simple, because they are not really distinguished into parts which one can contemplate separately (i.e. imagine in isolation):

> 'Tis certain that the mind wou'd never have dream'd of
> distinguishing a figure from the body figur'd, as being in reality
> neither distinguishable, nor different, nor separable; did it not
> observe, that even in this simplicity there might be contain'd many
> different resemblances and relations. Thus when a globe of white
> marble is presented, we receive only the impression of a white

colour dispos'd in a certain form, nor are we able to separate and distinguish the colour from the form. But observing afterwards a globe of black marble and a cube of white, and comparing them with our former object, we find two separate resemblances, in what formerly seem'd, and really is, perfectly inseparable. After a little more practice of this kind, we begin to distinguish the figure from the colour by a *distinction of reason*; that is, we consider the figure and colour together, since they are in effect the same and undistinguishable; but still view them in different aspects, according to the resemblances, of which they are susceptible. When we wou'd consider only the figure of the globe of white marble, we form in reality an idea both of the figure and colour, but tacitly carry our eye to its resemblance with the globe of black marble: And in the same manner, when we wou'd consider its colour only, we turn our view to its resemblance with the cube of white marble. By this means we accompany our ideas with a kind of reflexion, of which custom renders us, in a great measure, insensible. A person, who desires us to consider the figure of a globe of white marble without thinking on its colour, desires an impossibility; but his meaning is, that we shou'd consider the colour and figure together, but still keep in our eye the resemblance to the globe of black marble, or that to any other globe of whatever colour or substance (*THN*, I, p. 25).

This passage would seem to support Árdal's view. As opposed to Passmore, who treats a simple idea as one which can only be named and not further described, Árdal takes the relevant sense of 'simple' to be: without parts, excluding all composition (Árdal, 1966, pp. 12–15). His argument is that the idea of a particular shade of blue is not 'composed' of vividness, blueness, and simplicity. In explicating 'composed', he cites Moore as viewing the analysis of a complex idea as analysis into the ideas of its various parts in certain relations: so the idea of a horse would be composed of the ideas of its 'parts', namely, legs, head, heart, etc. (Árdal, 1966, pp. 7, 13–14). Surely indeed, a particular shade of blue is not 'composed' of vividness, blueness, simplicity, etc. These are not equivalent 'parts' (as the legs, head, etc., of a horse might be). But is this the sort of composition that Hume means to exclude when he claims simplicity? All of his talk of 'parts' may be merely metaphorical; or at least one must ask for a criterion for what is to count as a 'part', and the criterion will ultimately, I think, have to do with learning.

Passmore's argument (1968, p. 109), as mentioned above, shows that one must start with an 'idea of X', and then establish whether X is simple. If one starts with 'X idea', the idea naturally is an entity which has other properties, such as vividness or simplicity, and (whether or not these constitute 'parts') the concept X cannot be acquired through these other properties. And Hume's concern, in the globe of white marble passage, and throughout, is really with the acquisition of concepts. His concept of simplicity is based on learning. (Hence the difficulty of the famous counter-example, the missing shade of blue.) Therefore the idea of the white globe is simple (despite what would seem obvious 'parts') because one could not construct it from separate impressions of roundness and white underived from conglomerate impressions or ideas. One acquires distinct ideas of shape and colour only after seeing or imagining them together and then (in reflexion) making a 'distinction of reason'. Similarly, the intensity of a colour and the colour itself are not imaginable separately from each other, and the place of a colour on a spectrum or scale of colours is not ascertainable independently of a view (or views) of that colour. So these characteristics of a simple idea do not conflict with its simplicity (in Hume's view), because they are not separately imaginable and so could not be used to teach the idea to someone who did not already have it. A simple idea is one that cannot be taken to pieces by definition (and so cannot be acquired by acquiring the ideas of each of its pieces). Characteristics of an idea, such as simplicity and degree, even if they are in some sense 'parts' of an idea, do not constitute 'pieces' of the *thing* of which it is an idea; and so they cannot be used (by themselves at any rate) in acquiring or teaching the concept of that thing. It is the simplicity of the thing and not of the idea of the thing that really matters. The problem when we turn to emotions is that the thing itself is in the mind, so the distinction that allows one to preserve simplicity while making comparisons necessary for association collapses.

If we accept Hume's concept of simplicity as based on learning, could emotions be 'simple' impressions? Could we make the classifications, discriminations, and identifications we do, and make them on the basis simply of the impressions, if emotions really were 'simple' impressions? More immediately, could emotions be produced by mechanisms involving association by resemblance of 'simples'? And, most immediately, could emotions (as simple impressions) be associated with each other (as in Hume's circle of passions) through resemblance?

5

Association: Simplicity and the Essential

Let us suppose that emotions are impressions (of reflexion), and that they have no constituent parts – or (more weakly) that they are indefinable or simple in the sense that there are no distinguishable constituents essential to their recognition or the acquisition of their corresponding ideas. If we say this, it follows that if two impressions resemble each other, they must do so in a respect that lies outside their simple essence; they will never be similar as impressions *simpliciter*. For one must be able to specify the respect in which similarity is claimed, and to specify would be to distinguish, and whatever is distinguishable is distinct (even if the distinction is only a 'distinction of reason'). ('Whatever is distinct, is distinguishable; and whatever is distinguishable, is separable by the thought or imagination' – *THN*, Appendix, p. 634; cf. *THN*, I, p. 18.) Shared determinables, such as 'colour' for red and blue, and 'flavour' for vanilla and chocolate, are not here in question. But the length of a line, the shape of a red idea (or an idea of red), and the intensity of an emotion would all have to stand distinct from the essence of the simple being considered. Though these qualities or degrees are not strictly 'separable' in that they cannot be imagined in isolation, they can be distinguished (or abstracted) by reflexion. Determination of degree is not in general essential to acquisition of a concept (it is not part of a definition of a quantity or quality even if some determinate degree is always present in any given quantity or quality). So we need not say that 'if simplicity were genuinely a point of resemblance . . . there are no simple ideas'; just that if simplicity were genuinely a point of resemblance, then simplicity would be extraneous to the essence of the simple ideas it characterizes. (This is a strategy which, I suspect, quickly leads to bare particulars.)

Árdal says,

> It seems to me clear that it is not absurd to suggest that simplicity may be consistent with similarity, unless you want to define a simple idea as that which can only be named and not described in any sense of 'describe'. Hume does not use the term 'simple' in this way, and I see no very obvious reason for claiming that he ought to have done this (Árdal, 1966, p. 15).

I have been arguing that on Árdal's interpretation of 'simple' (as denial of component parts) simplicity is incompatible with resemblance in a certain respect (except where the respect refers to features external to the simple entity). I have been arguing further that Hume's notion of simplicity does exclude some (though not all) forms of description, in particular it excludes those forms that would allow for resemblance (again, they become external features). And Hume takes this line on simplicity because of his concern with problems of learning, understanding, and meaning of ideas.

Now Árdal may be right that 'a simple perception is not just something that can only be pointed to and given a name' (Árdal, 1966, pp. 12, 15). He is right if the naming is meant to exclude *all* further description, of causal circumstances or consequences or whatever. (This is how I think Árdal reads Passmore.) But Árdal is wrong if the naming excludes *only* additional conditions on, or other ways of learning to distinguish and recognize, the thing named – which conditions may well include causal circumstances and consequences and so on. On this account, causal circumstances, etc., get excluded from further description of a simple perception only in so far as they are claimed to be *essential* to or sufficient for learning or acquiring the concept of the thing perceived. The simple impression by itself is supposed to be necessary and sufficient for that.

And this account is how I think Hume is to be understood. He goes to considerable trouble to give 'such circumstances as attend' the passions, and passions can be compared and contrasted in strength, violence, vividness, etc. But the pleasant sensation of the exciting cause of pride is not similar to the pleasant sensation of pride itself in degree of intensity or nature of attending circumstances; they are supposed to be *associated* because of the similarity of the pleasures viewed in themselves. And it is not clear what this means. Taken *in themselves*, it would appear that 'X is simple' *is* merely 'a misleading way of saying that X cannot be characterized except as X' (Passmore, 1968, p. 110), where this in turn is a way of saying that the concept of X can be acquired only by direct acquaintance *and* such acquaintance is all that is needed for acquisition and understanding.

In accounting for the emergence of pride, Hume takes certain 'facts' about the sources of pride and 'facts' about the object of pride and pride itself and relates them, then claims that it is those relations operating through the principles of association that account for the emergence of pride. Our argument about the incompatibility of similarity and simplicity suggests that if pride resembles its exciting quality in pleasantness, then its pleasantness will be a distinguishable characteristic (if only by a 'distinction of reason'), and so pleasantness cannot be its distinctive essence. But this, of course, is precisely what Hume claims: the peculiar and distinctive pleasure and pain of pride and humility 'constitute their very being and essence. Thus, pride is a pleasant sensation, and humility a painful; and upon the removal of the pleasure and pain, there is in reality no pride nor humility. Of this our very feeling convinces us; and beyond our feeling, 'tis here in vain to reason or dispute' (*THN*, II, p. 286). The feeling is all there is to the emotion. Now there is a sense, of course, in which it is perfectly possible to say that the sensation of pride and the sensation of its cause resemble in being pleasant (while the pride remains 'simple'). They can both be pleasant sensations in the same way that blue and green are both colours. They share a common determinable. But what is required is that they resemble (be more or less alike than other members of the category) in respect of pleasantness (in felt quality), not merely as being pleasant; just as Hume claims blue and green resemble in respect of colour (as determinates of a shared determinable), not simply as being colours (as sharing a determinable). Otherwise (among other problems) why should a pleasant impression lead to any one other pleasant impression rather than another? The causes of pride are very various, involving many different sorts of pleasure, so they would presumably resemble, and thus lead to, different impressions of reflexion. It would seem, therefore, that on this interpretation, each different cause of pride would be associated with a different impression of pride, that the pleasure of pride would vary with its causes. But this cannot be Hume's view. He emphatically insists that the pleasure of pride, as of each emotion, is a simple, distinctive, and *uniform* impression. One way round this difficulty would be to interpret the mechanism in the way suggested in section 2, so that it is the double association of impressions and ideas (and not merely association of resembling impressions) that accounts for one pleasant impression rather than another being called up. The initial pleasant impression calls forth all pleasant passions indiscriminately, but the presence of an additional association (of ideas) leads to pride's (in certain cases) being favoured above its fellows. This must surely be the correct interpretation of the mechanism, and it might leave the pleasure of pride a simple and uniform impression, but it still would not account for Hume's circle of emotions. And, in any case, could we acquire the concept, could we recognize and identify pride (distinguish it from other emotions) if it were such a simple impression? In fact, I think there is not enough discernible variation in our feelings (in the narrow sense – sensations) to match and account for the subtlety in our distinctions and discriminations of feelings (in the broad sense – emotions).[2]

Hume seems caught in a dilemma: Either simplicity is a matter of 'parts', in which case the sorts of resemblance it allows will not account for the learning of emotion concepts or the discrimination of particular emotion states. Or alternatively, simplicity is a matter of 'learning', in which case there must be more elements in an emotion than a simple impression would allow, if we are to be able to identify and discriminate that emotion from others – i.e. if we are to acquire the concept of that emotion. Chocolate and vanilla may be 'simple' flavours, but they do not 'resemble' each other more than (say) chocolate and strawberry. Regret and remorse may resemble, but they are not simple like vanilla and chocolate, or even complex in the (simple) way of vanilla fudge.

Even if Hume's mechanism for producing pride requires resemblance of impressions only in the way that blue and green resemble by both being colours (i.e. in sharing a determinable), a metaphysical problem with simplicity might return if we pressed our earlier argument and used 'distinctions of reason' to split off characteristics until we reached bare particulars. But it is not clear how much of a loss Hume's theory would suffer if pleasantness, the relevant determinable, were external rather than internal (provided that everything else was as well). In any case, the substantive difficulty does not disappear quite so readily. The double association interpretation has to survive difficulties in Hume's doctrine of the association of *ideas* (some similar to those concerning the association of impressions). We shall be discussing these difficulties, and the resulting interpretation may well rely on an impossible resemblance in respect of pleasantness *simpliciter* between simples. In any case, this resemblance is certainly required by the Humean account of a chain of emotions, such as the grief-disappointment-anger-envy-malice-grief circle he cited when introducing the notion of association of impressions.

6

Impressions of Pleasure and Pleasant Impressions

For the mechanism of association of impressions to be at all plausible, there must be impressions available at both ends of the machinery. The passion itself is, of course, thought by Hume to be an impression (of reflexion), but there must also be an initial impression which, through association by resemblance, yields the secondary impression. Hence Hume argues at length (*THN*, II, i, sections 7 to 11) for a separate impression of pleasure with every subject of pride. In typical fashion, the argument moves from the impossibility of definition to the awareness of an impression. The 'power of producing pain and pleasure' is thus the 'essence of beauty and deformity' (*THN*, II, p. 299) as also of 'wit' (*THN*, II, p. 297). Because beauty and pleasure cannot be defined the first must produce and the other must be an impression. However, while it may be true that impressions cannot be defined, it does not therefore follow that whatever cannot be defined must be an impression. Even if pleasure is somehow involved in every experience of beauty, it need not always be an 'impression of pleasure'; indeed, it is doubtful, as will be discussed, that it could ever be an *impression* of pleasure. Given Hume's theory of meaning, however, it could be nothing else. Every meaningful expression (such as 'pleasure') has to be traced to its origin in a corresponding perception. All words (and perhaps propositions) are names acquiring their meaning, either directly or indirectly, by standing for impressions. This is not the place for a general critique of Hume's theory of meaning, but we can say something about how it affects his account of pleasure: it makes it inadequate.

What manner of impression is pleasure supposed to be? It is an original sensation, not an impression of reflexion. Though passions, direct and indirect, are derived from pleasure, it is not itself a passion. At least this is true for *bodily* pleasures: 'Bodily pains and pleasures are the source of many passions, both when felt and considr'd by the mind; but arise originally in the soul, or in the body, whichever you please to call it, without any preceding thought or perception' (*THN*, II, p. 276). Certainly those pleasures which consist of sensations are sensations, but can all pleasures plausibly be viewed as consisting of sensations, as bodily? What sense can this help us make of the relation between pleasure and the things we take pleasure in, between enjoyment and the things we enjoy? To say that *all* pleasures are unconnected with 'any preceding thought or perception' would be simply false. To call the relation of pleasure and its objects 'original' would be simply to deny that the relation can be explained. To shift to the position that pleasure is an impression of reflexion would still leave the question whether it can (in all cases if in any) be an impression of any kind.

Hume seems to acknowledge that the objects of pleasure are very various, but pleasure itself he considers to vary only in felt quality:

> 'tis evident, that under the term *pleasure*, we comprehend
> sensations, which are very different from each other, and which
> have only such a distant resemblance, as is requisite to make them
> be express'd by the same abstract term. A good composition of
> music and a bottle of good wine equally produce pleasure; and
> what is more, their goodness is determin'd merely by the pleasure.
> But shall we say upon that account, that the wine is harmonious,
> or the music of a good flavour (*THN*, III, p. 472)?

Particular emotions, such as pride, are simple and uniform impressions of pleasure, but pleasure itself is various. Its varieties together constitute the set of pleasant emotions. Now to call anything, including an emotion, 'pleasant' should signify its accompaniment by one of the (various but resembling) impressions of pleasure. We can perhaps understand the word 'pleasant' in the phrase 'pleasant emotions' to refer to the pleasure in or constituting the emotion itself. But in general, a 'pleasant impression' (of a country scene, etc.) would be one accompanied by an additional, separate and distinct impression of pleasure. I do not see how Hume can avoid regarding this accompanying impression as an impression of reflexion – though he might, regarding the pleasure in that way, give it the name of a passion: joy, or pride, or love, and so forth. But even those impressions of reflexion which are direct passions ('desire, aversion, grief, joy, hope, fear, despair and security' – *THN*, II, p. 277) are *derived* from or reactions to pleasure or pain. 'Directness' here indicates only that these passions require no further associations (of ideas of cause and object, of 'self' in the case of pride) in order to be derived. Direct passions do not involve double association, but they still require an initial, separate and distinct pleasure (or pain). It would appear that the impression of pleasure would, in each case, have to arise 'originally', and not by 'reflexion', from the pleasant object it accompanies. Perhaps 'original' connections here need be no more mysterious than connections of 'reflexion', perhaps impressions of pleasure arise based on their resemblance to the impressions they accompany, despite the fact that these impressions themselves (e.g. music and wine) do not much resemble each other. (But then original connections are obviously no less mysterious.) Perhaps we should assume that Hume regards pleasure, in these sorts of cases, as an impression of reflexion, despite the fact that his system seems to leave no room for any such (pleasure being always either original and bodily or itself a passion), but we should recognize that it may not give much gain in clarity over the notion of an 'original' connection. And, in any case, pleasure as an accompanying impression, whether of reflexion or not, will not give an adequate account of our concept.

First, pleasure, unlike bodily sensations, is not always located either specifically or as a pervasive feeling throughout the body. Since pain is generally localized, this comparison should be enough to show that pleasure and pain cannot be understood as simple opposites, or extremes on a common scale. The point is not that pain is always localized. The point is, rather, that the matter is a complex one, and an analysis that allows only simple sensations and their felt differences is unlikely to do justice to that complexity. (See Ryle, 1954a; Penelhum, 1956–7, pp. 232–4; Trigg, 1970.)

Second, where pleasure is not simply a bodily sensation, it is probably a reaction or response to something; but it does not then take the form of a localized sensation associated with that 'something'. That is, where pleasure is not simply a localized sensation, it is also not simply added on to something else (which may or may not be a localized sensation itself) as a localized sensation, so that the two together constitute the pleasure. For example, the difference between taking a walk which one enjoys and taking a walk to which one is indifferent, is a difference different from that between walking with a headache and walking without one (Ryle, 1954b). If pleasure is not a bodily sensation, neither is it a non-bodily or non-localized sensation or impression – at least if we give these terms any reasonable force. I do not propose to give a comprehensive argument or analysis of pleasure here, so I will confine myself to a few points that bring us close to central difficulties in Hume.

Third, if pleasure in a thing consisted of an independent impression of pleasure, one would expect that the enjoyment could be produced independently of the thing enjoyed. But one cannot get the pleasure of watching a play or of playing tennis by swallowing a pill (Ryle, 1949, p. 132). This inability is not merely a technological problem. Whatever happened, whatever sensations or even 'pleasure' occurred, it would not be the pleasure *of* watching a play unless one believed that the pleasure derived from watching a play. One cannot have the pleasures of an activity without the activity, or at least a *pseudo* or notional activity. Whatever the mechanism of the pill, it would not be enough for it to produce a sensation (however titillating), it would have also to produce some sort of belief connecting the feeling with a play. To believe, even mistakenly, that one is enjoying something, there must be some description under which one believes (even though mistakenly) that one is enjoying *it*. (See Williams, 1959, esp. p. 237, on types of belief and types of mistake.) The precise character of the belief need not be of concern here. The important point is that, whatever the normal mechanism of pleasure, there are conceptual constraints on how we can regard its products. Whether or not Hume brings out the mechanisms, it is certain that his language of impressions (even impressions of reflexion) cannot bring out the conceptual constraints on those mechanisms.

Fourth, it is at least odd, if pleasure is an independent impression (however it might be produced by or associated with other impressions), that it cannot outlast its objects. The enjoyment of an activity is coterminous with that activity. One cannot enjoy a walk after it is over (though one might be pleased at 'having walked') (Ryle, 1954b, p. 198). And the force of the 'cannot' is again conceptual. Whatever happened, whatever independent impressions occurred, they would not constitute enjoyment of the past activity – even if they were a product of or reaction to it. The more one considers points like these, the more certain it seems that to clarify the concept of pleasure in Hume's terms, it must be considered as an aspect of impressions, rather than as itself an independent impression.

Fifth, even where pleasure is very clearly a sensation, what constitutes the pleasantness of the sensation? Is an impression of pleasure always pleasant? We have seen some of the problems raised within Hume's system by the converse question, 'Is a pleasant impression always an impression of pleasure?' The present question extends those difficulties in at least two directions. First, consider the parallel question, 'Is an impression of blue always blue?' This direction clearly leads us to question the nature of impressions. Just what are they? Are they the sorts of things that could be either blue or pleasant? Are they things? Leaving these depths of difficulty aside, the second direction takes us back to the converse question. Is the pleasantness of a pleasant impression an additional impression? An additional pleasant impression? Here lies infinite regress. An additional impression of reflexion, e.g. desire? Could desire or other attitudes themselves be impressions (even of reflexion)? If the pleasantness of an impression is ever an attitude (e.g. of desire) towards an impression, is it always?[3]

Sixth and finally, one could adduce other arguments to show the inadequacy of viewing pleasure as an impression (even of reflexion), but the most interesting from our point of view are those supporting the claim that pleasure is a form of effortless attention (enjoying is a form of attending). I will not rehearse the arguments here;[4] but I think the claim is very plausible. In relation to Hume, the important point to add is that it is unlikely that one can account for attention in terms of impressions and ideas. Attention is rather an attitude *towards* impressions and ideas. Could one impression perceive or pay attention to another? Here one encounters Hume's problems with a perceiving self. Within his system, that self tends to collapse into the perceptions themselves – there is little (nothing) else around to constitute the perceiver (*THN*, Appendix, pp. 633–6; Hampshire, 1959, ch. I). Bating those problems, it seems difficult to see what more paying attention to an impression could mean within Hume's system than merely *having* it. Even vividness is not available to do duty for attention; it already has too heavy a burden in accounting for belief. Though even if vividness were available, whenever one was attending to an idea the added intensity would put the idea in danger of becoming an impression. (We do not hallucinate every time we concentrate.) So if pleasure is a form of attention, and attention is an attitude towards impressions rather than itself an impression, it is unlikely that pleasure (in general) can be accounted an impression (even of reflexion) within Hume's system.

The narrowness of the system produces other, but not unrelated, problems. For example, when Hume claims that the 'anticipation of pleasure is, in itself, a very considerable pleasure' (*THN*, II, p. 315 – in connection with the pride derived from property and riches), it does not seem that he can treat this anticipation of pleasure as itself an impression of pleasure: for how could an impression contain the needed reference to the future?[5]

In the cases of 'beauty' and 'wit', and the other occasions of pride, I want to say Hume makes a mistake. Not simply the mistake (which he may also make) of failing to distinguish the conditions under which we call something 'beautiful' or someone 'witty' and what we mean when we call it that (what would be the naturalistic fallacy in relation to 'good'), but a mistake in thinking those conditions include a sensation of pleasure. Even if finding a picture beautiful is to contemplate it with pleasure, is the pleasure a feeling or sensation or impression? It seems more likely that it is a form of attention, and so precisely not an impression, but at best an attitude towards or an aspect of impressions. And, as we have seen, Hume's mechanisms for explaining emotions require separate, distinct, and independent impressions of pleasure.

7
Self and the Idea of Self

Hume's mechanism of double association to produce pride and the other indirect passions brings into play the association of ideas as well as of impressions. The association of ideas introduces the principles of association by contiguity and causality (in addition to the principle of association by resemblance allowed by impressions). It also brings additional difficulties of interpretation.

As we continue to examine the case of pride, we see that the idea of self is introduced as its object. That the idea of myself is the object of pride is, for Hume, a fact of natural history (*THN*, II, p. 280). It should, for him, be an awkward fact: for he elsewhere denies, in connection with personal identity, that any such idea of self can be found (*THN*, I, p. 252; Appendix, pp. 633–6). Yet, in contradiction, he asserts its existence again in connection with the doctrine of sympathy, where, needing a source of vivacity, he refers to 'the idea, or rather impression of ourselves' (*THN*, II, p. 317). When speaking of the object of pride, Hume sometimes expands 'the idea of ourselves' into 'self, or that succession of related ideas and impressions, of which we have an intimate memory and consciousness' (*THN*, II, p. 277) and 'self, or that individual person, of whose actions and sentiments each of us is intimately conscious' (*THN*, II, p. 286). But these expansions do not help.

And certainly such expansions are no help in relation to the problem of personal identity. Hume takes that problem to be one of finding a numerically and qualitatively constant impression in order to explain the continuity of identity through time. For that purpose, a complex set of impressions would be useless. Even if such a set could constitute our self at a particular time, its membership would be constantly shifting, and so would be no better than ever-changing single impressions for continuity of self. In any case, Hume misconceives his problem. Constancy (whether real, imagined, or 'fictional') of impressions cannot serve as an analysis of numerical identity (Penelhum, 1955). Identity as a particular is always identity under a concept, and the notion of identity under a concept (the same tree, the same house, the same person) allows for change, the limits of change being defined by the concept (the child becomes a man, but both may still be the same person).

In fact, Hume's entire project of treating persons as disembodied collections of experiences is misconceived. No set of impressions (however complex) is sufficient to distinguish one person from another (see, e.g. Williams, 1973); though an egocentric statement of the problem of personal identity might help one think that it could be (Pears, 1963). Hume, I think, came to see that if self is to serve (among other things) as perceiver of one's impressions, it cannot itself be yet another impression or collection of them. Árdal suggests that such a collection could at least serve as object of pride at a given moment (Árdal, 1966, pp. 44–5). Though this suggestion might partially correct Hume's inconsistent use of an 'idea of self', I think the failure is rather one of principle; and such an amendment would not obviate these difficulties. Indeed, it might create additional ones. The substitution of a set of impressions for a simple idea would not leave Hume's claims quite unchanged. To say that an idea of self is the object of pride is to claim that there exists a constant conjunction between pride and its object (the idea of self) and that the first precedes the second as its sufficient condition. Just how the second conjunct is specified is crucial to any empirical confirmation of the claim. And it appears quite simply false that whenever I am proud there occurs to me whatever complex set of impressions constitutes myself at that particular time, unless, of course, this means merely that I have whatever experiences I have at that time. But in that sense the idea of self is always present and it would be the object of every passion if it were the object of any.

Hume's doctrine of sympathy, in fact, requires 'that the idea, or rather impression of ourselves is always intimately present with us' (*THN*, II, pp. 317, 320, 340). However there is a difference between being ourselves and thinking of ourselves. The former we cannot avoid, the latter most of us can. Hume's analysis of mind as a set of impressions and ideas helps him assimilate identity to an idea of self (being ourselves to thinking of ourselves). It is this special idea of self which is supposed to emerge as the object of pride. How is it supposed to emerge? Certain problems about self may be peculiar to the objects of pride and humility, but the sense in which it is the *object* of an emotion (pride) is a problem for all emotions. I shall argue that if not omnipresent, the idea of self is present at least on all occasions of pride, and so Hume's account of its 'emergence' cannot be accepted. And with that account goes much else.

8

Emotion and Object

I have above described the emotion-object relation in causal terms: the object is the effect of the emotion. In fact, Hume leaves the precise nature of the relation unclear. For, in addition to being natural, the relation is said to be original, that is, unexplainable, mysterious.

It is an empirical, but not further explicable, fact that self is the object of pride (*THN*, II, pp. 280, 286). Invariably, the object follows on the occurrence of the emotion. The idea which is the object succeeds the impression which is the emotion. But why and how? And, more immediately, does it? Hume leaves unclear not only the mechanism of this succession, but also its meaning. Passmore gives a good description of the confusion:

> A particularly important problem arises out of his description of the passions – which, after all, are only 'impressions' – as having 'objects'. The fact is that Hume never really thinks out the relation between his epistemology and his theory of passions; sometimes 'the view' (whatever this is) 'fixes on ourselves', when pride 'actuates us' (T, 277); sometimes pride 'produces' the idea of the self (T, 287); sometimes pride is described as something which can never 'look beyond self' (T, 286). If what really happens is that pride 'produces' the idea of self, that idea will be its effect, not its object; if, on the other hand, pride *itself* views the self,

this will involve a complete revision of Hume's epistemology. The consequences will be no less far-reaching if pride somehow provokes the mind to have an idea of itself; and in this case, too, that idea is in no sense the 'object' of pride, but only an idea which regularly occurs *later than* pride (Passmore, 1968, pp. 126–7).

So far as one can extract a considered and coherent notion of object from Hume, the notion of the mind being provoked to have an idea seems to come closest. At least it is his most frequent picture. It is not quite that the emotion of pride produces or provokes the mind to produce an idea of itself; rather, that idea 'is always intimately present with us' (*THN*, II, p. 317 – never minding problems of unperceived perceptions) and the passion 'turns our view to ourselves' (*THN*, II, p. 287) where it 'fixes' (*THN*, II, p. 277) and 'rests' (*THN*, II, p. 286). 'Pride and humility, being once rais'd, immediately turn our attention to ourself, and regard that as their ultimate and final object' (*THN*, II, p. 278). Self is the object of attention.

As we have seen, however, a Humean analysis of attending to an object would seem to allow for little more than merely having the impression or idea of it. So if I am angry at my uncle, this means merely that the idea of my uncle accompanies my anger. But let us imagine that the wrong idea occurs, the wrong image pops into mind. On this account, it would still (necessarily) be the image of the object of my emotion (cf. Pitcher, 1965, p. 328). There is no room for mistake. Whatever idea strays into view, if it is the object of my attention, it will be the object of my anger. The ordinary (and psychoanalytic) notion of displacement, the notions of mistake and recognition of mistake, become unintelligible. There is no *real* object other than whatever happens to draw my attention while (or after) in the grip of the emotion.

Even in the case of pride, which always has the same object, attention (on a Humean analysis) provides an inadequate understanding of the notion of object. When a man is proud of his son, he need not think of himself. Indeed, he is most likely to think of his son and concentrate on his outstanding qualities. So whatever point Hume is making by claiming that self is the invariable object of pride, it cannot be that thoughts of self always follow on the feeling – at least in so far as his point is a true one.

And Hume does have a valid point to make. He has noticed a genuine feature of pride: it arises from reflexion on the valuable qualities of things closely associated with ourselves. But on such occasions our attention is *already* directed to ourselves. Hume never states how the idea of self is *involved* in the idea of a 'subject' related to us or how (by resemblance, contiguity, or causation)[6] it is supposed to be associated with that idea of self (which he calls its 'cor-relative' – *THN*, II, p. 286) which is the object of pride. This involvement clearly exists. According to Hume, a cause of pride requires a pleasing quality inhering in a subject related to self. The existence of the thing is not enough, one must be aware of it and aware of it as related to self. One must have the idea of self in contemplating the thing and its pleasant quality if one is to experience pride (rather than mere joy), so the idea of self is involved in the very idea of the subject or cause of pride. But if it is involved it is present, and if it is present it need not *arise* (through a sensation of pride or by any other means). No new idea of self emerges as object. If the idea of self is still said to be the object of pride, the relation may still be said to be causal, but now the relation is seen to be reversed: the 'object' must be seen as a part of the cause of the pleasant sensation which is pride, and not its effect.

Hume would, I think, find this emendation to his notion of object devastating to his theory. He explicitly insists that the object of pride could not be its cause (*THN*, II, pp. 277–8). We shall return to this point, but I wish first to explore what I think is devastating about the emendation. I have shown that one is forced (on pain of more immediate incoherencies) to understand Hume's notion of object in such a way that the object is not an effect either of the emotion itself or of the cause of the emotion, but rather is a cause of the emotion. That is, within Hume's system, the object collapses into the cause. And this is devastating to the whole system (most importantly), because without an idea of an object distinct from the idea of the cause the association of ideas is lost and so the whole mechanism of double association collapses. And with that collapse, one is forced back to an interpretation which relies on association of impressions alone, which in turn allows for association only by resemblance. So one ends up with (an impossible) association by resemblance of simples as simples, which is in any case (even were it possible) inadequate to produce emotions which do not vary with their objects. So pride would have many meanings, as many as it has possible causes and objects, instead of the single meaning Hume undertook to explain. (Pleasure is supposed to be a peculiar and varied impression, but pride – like many other emotions – is supposed to be a peculiar and *uniform* pleasure.)

9
Object and Effect

If the object of an emotion were simply an effect, it would have to be the effect of the emotion itself and not of the cause of the emotion. Hume says directly and in a variety of ways that the idea which is the object of pride emerges (mysteriously) out of the impression of reflexion which constitutes the emotion. The alternative, within Hume's system, would be that the idea which is the object emerges through association with the idea of (the 'subject' part of) the cause. But this process would leave the importance of the impression itself, the supposed essence, unclear. Perhaps it would still provide an essential emotional turbulence. But is 'turbulence' essential to emotion? We shall consider this issue when we come to discuss what Hume calls the 'calm passions'. It looks as though the impression would, in any case, no longer be essential to the appearance of the object. Perhaps it could be argued that without the impression, the object would not be an 'object of emotion'; that is, the impression is essential to the idea's being an object. But that would call for explication of the notion of object, and that explication would necessarily be more demanding than a Humean account of an object of attention. So, we would no longer be considering Hume's notion of object.

By what principles of association could the idea of an object arise from the idea of a cause (assuming it did not arise from the emotional impression directly and that it was not already involved in the very idea of the cause)? Since the association would be one between ideas, the full arsenal of resemblance, contiguity, and causality would seem to be available. But here we must note a central ambiguity in Hume's language. In his discussion of association of ideas, there is constant slippage between resemblance, contiguity, and causality among the *ideas* themselves and resemblance, contiguity, and causality among the *things* they are ideas of. Ideas should succeed each other, in accordance with the principles of association, in virtue of properties of the things they are ideas of. But these properties can have no effect unless we are aware of them. And Hume's notion of awareness in terms of ideas understood as images tends to confuse ideas with the things they represent. The represented properties seem to become properties of the representation, the idea. (The 'object' of an idea gets assimilated to the idea.) So association in virtue of resemblance, contiguity, and causality of the things represented, tends to become resemblance, contiguity, and causality of the ideas themselves. Where one's interest is in the ideas as such (and it would seem that it is the idea of self, whether or not there is a self, that is the object of pride), these difficulties begin to make themselves disturbingly felt. Now we should say a bit more about these difficulties, and a bit more about whether one's interest in 'objects' of emotion is an interest in ideas as such.

Even if the idea of the object (or the idea which is the object) could be the effect of the idea which causes (along with an impression of pleasure) the emotion itself, it could not arise through association by causation. Indeed, association by causation would preclude the object of the emotion's being the effect of the cause of the emotion. To clarify this, consider association by contiguity. Spatial contiguity requires that ideas have spatial location. But if they are extended in space they then have (spatial) parts, and are not simple. But if they were not extended, how could they combine to make up space? 'Two points can never lie contiguous to one another, because to be contiguous they would have to touch only at a certain point; and a point cannot itself touch at a point except by being that point' (Passmore, 1968, p. 112). Association by contiguity would require that ideas be near without appearing near – otherwise the *emergence* of the associated idea would not be explained, for it would be already present. And how can ideas have unperceived properties or relations?

Whatever Hume's ultimate doctrine on space, we can see that these difficulties extend to explaining the emergence of the idea of the object by association (through resemblance or causality, also) with the idea of the subject. Causality, as a means of association, is, in fact, much the same as regular temporal contiguity of ideas. This does not preclude a causal analysis of the notion of object, but it does preclude a causal analysis in which the object appears as *effect* of an initial idea. In talking of objects, we must be clear whether we are referring to the perishing immediate objects of perception or to the independent existences of an external world. If we are talking of the object of an emotion as an idea which emerges, then we cannot explain the occurrence of that idea in succession to another idea by that rule according to which ideas 'pass from one object to what is . . . produc'd by it'. That is, one cannot explain why an idea (B) follows another idea (A) by saying that the first idea (A) 'produces' the idea which follows it (B). The claim that A produces B is based on the observation that B follows it.

In the present case the second idea is not just a causal expectation, but also a causal product. When one perceives an object A and then its effect B, the first *perception* does not cause the second perception, though each may be caused by the event (A or B) perceived. One can step back into the mind to explain our belief in external causal relations, but there is no further place to step back to if one wishes to claim that external causal relations are explained by internal causal relations. When explaining the idea of expectation involved in causal belief, Hume uses the objective conjunction of two external events to explain the emergence of expectation after an impression of the first event. Where the second event is the appearance of the idea, the conjunction would thus be called upon to explain itself. This does not mean that thoughts cannot have causal relations, but one must be careful about what is supposed to be explaining what. What can it mean to say that the occurrence of an idea leads by a principle of association to another idea which is causally connected with the first? Where the initial object is itself an idea, the association reduces to a restatement of that causal relation from which it is supposed to stem. In any case, in the end the object of the emotion collapses into the cause of the emotion, and so those 'two' items (at any rate) could not be causally related: an effect must be distinguishable from its cause.

Hume's notion of object is a technical one, and we shall be returning to some of its peculiarities, but I think one ambiguity can be resolved. If the notion is to have any connection with ordinary notions, it should be taken to refer to things in the world. When I am angry, I am generally angry at a person (or by extending my views of agency) a thing, or event. The notion of object reaches out from my mental state to attach it to things in the world. What exactly we should say when the world fails to contain any appropriate thing may be a very complex issue (see Wilson, 1972, chs XVI to XVIII); but we should be able to mark a distinction at least between being angry at a thing and being angry at an idea. The latter is also possible. The very thought of so-and-so may make me angry, and in certain cases it may be only the thought which does so. We should not collapse being angry at a thing into being angry at the idea of that thing. The objects of our attention are generally things, not the ideas of things – even if our interest must be mediated through thoughts (and, presumably, physiological mechanisms), it should not be confused with an interest *in* thoughts (or in physiological mechanisms). When Hume speaks of an idea as object, he should, in general, be understood to mean the idea of the object (which is itself a thing). (Spinoza's language allows one very neatly to refer to ideas when they are in fact themselves objects through the notion of 'ideas of ideas'.) With this understanding, we can then go on to clarify the role of thought and thoughts in emotion.

If one insisted on assimilating all objects to ideas, a sort of disaster would follow. If particular ideas, and for Hume ideas are particulars, cannot be had by more than one person how could both John and Paul be angry at the same person, say Judas? How could any two persons experience a passion with the same object? The reply, of course, is that they are not angry at the *idea*. If one loves the idea 'Lola' one is in a very different state of mind than one who loves Lola, and both differ from one who loves 'the idea of Lola'. Focusing on the phenomenological embodiments of objects in ideas when our interest is in objects may be as misleading as focusing on the physiological or anatomical embodiments of ideas (an enquiry which Descartes takes up, but Hume – rightly – eschews as the province of 'the sciences of anatomy and natural philosophy', *THN*, II, pp. 275–6). Our interest in objects is not an interest in ideas as such.

With this in mind, we can begin to see some of the ways in which association by causation might find a better place in a Humean account of the passions. We would look through the idea of the object to the object. Hence, for example, one might be able to explain the idea of a son as object of my anger by association through causation with the idea of the father (father being cause of son). Here the concrete objects give the principle a place to catch hold.

10
Object and Cause

I have mentioned Hume's insistence that the cause and the object of an emotion are distinct. If the object could be the cause, or part of the cause, of the emotion, his whole complex machinery of double association would collapse. I have argued that within his system, however, object does collapse into cause and the machinery does collapse with it. Hume offers an argument to show that cause and object must be distinct. It is a bad argument, based on a faulty analysis of the nature of emotional conflict.

On his account, both pride and humility have 'self' as object, and 'as these passions are directly contrary, and have the same object in common; were their object also their cause; it cou'd never produce any degree of the one passion, but at the same time it must excite an equal degree of the other; which opposition and contrariety must destroy both' (*THN*, II, p. 278). This might be an effective argument against the object's being *the* cause, but Hume himself insists that pride has a

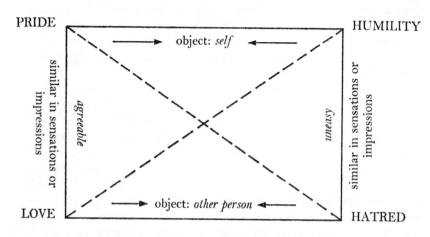

Hume's Square (*THN*, II, p. 333)

compound cause. The above passage offers no argument against the object's (like the subject's) being *part of* the cause of pride. Self by itself would in that case produce neither pride nor humility. But there is also a deeper mistake. Hume's mechanical model of the mind leads him to view the passions as vectors which can cancel each other out:

'Tis impossible a man can at the same time be both proud and humble; and where he has different reasons for these passions, as frequently happens, the passions either take place alternately; or if they encounter, the one annihilates the other, as far as its strength goes, and the remainder only of that, which is superior, continues to operate upon the mind. . . . To excite any passion, and at the same time raise an equal share of its antagonist, is immediately to undo what was done, and must leave the mind at last perfectly calm and indifferent (*THN*, II, p. 278).

The implausibility of this argument becomes plainer when it is repeated for the case of love and hatred, where the object of both is said to be the same (some other person) and it is argued that it cannot, therefore, be the cause of either (*THN*, II, p. 330).

This picture of conflict of passions is untrue to our experience. There are more possibilities than those of alternation of 'contrary' passions and perfect calm: We are often subject to turbulence. Precise description of this turbulence arising from conflict may be difficult, but there is reason to believe that simultaneous love and hate of the same object is, far from being inconceivable, in fact a familiar state.[7] A theory which yields so unrealistic a model of conflict of passions, one which sees no difference between the presence of two 'contrary' passions and no passion at all, is seriously defective.

Hume's theory is presented in terms of impressions or feelings, making his position even less plausible. For the elements of Hume's analysis are not the sorts of things which could serve as vectors to be mechanically summed. If passions are, in essence, feelings or sensations, how can they be said to have a direction, to be 'directly contrary in their sensation' (*THN*, II, p. 330)? Surely they can *differ* in sensation. Some are pleasant and some are painful. But pain and pleasure, as we have seen, are not to be simplistically contrasted as straightforward opposites. And even where we are careful in contrasting them, confining ourselves to where they appear on the same plane, e.g. where they can both be regarded as localized sensations, how is the difference to be interpreted as one of direction, in the way required? Certainly pleasures and pains can be weighed (where would utilitarianism be if this were not possible?), but they do not 'cancel' each other. We may feel both pleasure and pain, and where we feel more of one than the other it does not follow that we do not feel the lesser at all. Our mental life is not so neat.

We should perhaps note that Hume does later advance, at least for a narrow range of emotions, to a more plausible picture of conflict. When accounting for the origins of fear and hope he turns to a chemical analogy – the mixing of 'oil and vinegar' as opposed to the neutralizing properties of alkali and acid (*THN*, II, p. 443). He allows that, where dealing with probabilities, contrary passions instead of either alternating, or producing calm, or one predominating can 'both of them remain united in the mind' (*THN*, II, p. 441). 'The contrary passions will both of them . . . produce a third impression' (*THN*, II, p. 442) and thus hope and fear will emerge from different proportions of grief and joy. (See also *THN*, II, p. 421, where it is claimed that conflict of passions can actually result in increasing the force of one of the passions.)

Conflict of passions is thus no impediment to collapsing object into cause. But, as I have mentioned, object and cause are meant to be distinct within Hume's system. That distinction is essential to his system because it introduces the possibility of the influence of association of ideas – between an aspect of the cause (the subject) and the object. Without that added association, Hume's mechanism must rely on association of impressions alone, and thus on (an impossible) resemblance between simple impressions. And, in the case of pride, for example, the mechanism relying on association of impressions alone would produce a different impression of pride for each cause. So the only mechanism that is available would produce results contrary to the theory. But if we do not insist on providing an added association, we may still be able to allow Hume a contrast 'betwixt the cause and the object of these passions; betwixt that idea, which excites them, and that to which they direct their view, when excited' (*THN*, II, p. 278). We have rejected Hume's view of the idea of self as the effect of pride. There are defects in the particular idea, but more importantly it seems empirically false that any such idea does regularly arise on occasions of pride or could be explained to arise (if it did) on Hume's associative model. But we have seen that some such idea is already present in what Hume takes to be the cause of pride. The argument from conflict discussed above is aimed mainly at the view that the object could be *the* cause, 'or be sufficient alone to excite'. The object on our present view is only a *part* of the cause, there must also be a separate pleasure or pain in order to produce pride or humility. We still have a causally related object of attention, but no longer following after the passionate sensation. And there is still some contrast between cause and object (which is only part of the cause). So the emendation is not by itself a total rejection of Hume's theory.

But the emendation calls for further qualifications to Hume's approach: the loss of the added association is a real loss. Having incorporated the object of pride in its cause, we can no longer make sense of Hume's mechanism of double association. We may still allow that the separate pleasure produced by the quality occasioning pride 'calls up all other pleasant passions indiscriminately' (Kemp Smith, 1949, p. 185, n. 3), but there is no room for an additional principle of association to favour the pleasant passion of pride. So whence the peculiar feeling of pride? We are left without the second principle of association (between idea of subject and idea of object) because the object is already present in the very idea of the causal subject (in which the valuable quality inheres). That leaves us with association of impressions, degrees of resemblance among simples, and non-uniform impressions of reflexion. Alternatively, we could regard the simple presence of the object in the idea of the subject (without any further association) as sufficient to call forth the peculiar pleasure of pride from among its fellows. But this leaves the mechanism at this point as mysterious as the alleged emergence of the object out of pride itself (when it in its turn was supposed to come out of the double association between impressions and between subject and object). There is, I think, room for mystery in philosophy, but it is not necessary here.

What sort of feature of the cause is its (what Hume calls the 'subject's') relation to self? If I am to be made proud by a chair, it is not enough that I regard it as simply a 'chair', however fine. I must think of it as 'my chair' or 'chair produced by me' or in some other way intimately related to myself (even if I cannot claim responsibility for its particular virtuous quality – it may be taken to reflect on my worth in very devious ways). The chair appreciated simply as a chair can be a source of pleasure, and so perhaps joy, but the word 'pride' would then be out of place. This is not what Hume would call an 'original' property. It is not a limitation on what we can feel, but on what we can say. That it is a conceptual point does not make it a negligible one. It reveals something about our resources for description and discrimination of states of mind and so something about the nature of those states. If it were merely a verbal agreement narrowing the class of pleasurable sensations classed as 'pride' to those with a certain sort of cause, it might be a not very revealing point. This is not to say it would have to be an arbitrary agreement; it might be a very reasonable limitation, there might not be any such peculiar sensations without such causes. The regularity in our verbal designations might reflect a regularity in our experience. But pride (at least) is not (at least not always) simply a simple and peculiar pleasurable sensation. We are proud only when self is involved in the cause of our feeling, i.e. the feeling is identified as one of pride only in a particular causal context. The feeling of pride cannot occur outside this context because outside this context it could not be classified as pride: outside this context it is not a feeling of pride. Whatever feeling occurs, if I am to believe it is pride, I must believe it to have a certain sort of cause. The restrictions on the cause amount to a requirement of an *appropriate* object.

Perhaps there is no particular feeling constantly associated with pride at all, but that is not the point here. If someone says he is proud, but insists that he is simply proud without being proud of anything in particular (or only proud of himself and unable to say why), we will ask him to think again. Our demand would not be that he take a closer look at his feeling, but that he think whether he is using the word 'pride' as the rest of our language community uses it. If he persists in his deviant usage, we would have to conclude either that he does not know what 'pride' means, or (if he applies the word properly to others and himself on other occasions, so that we have grounds for believing he does know what the word means) that he has no reason for regarding his state of mind as 'pride' rather than a dozen other things in this particular case. And it is precisely his having certain sorts of reasons that makes his state what it is. My beliefs about the causes of my state of mind are built into my state of mind itself. In a sense, the effect (if it is an 'effect') depends on the recognition of the cause as the cause.

By emending Hume's notion of 'object' (as described above, that is by leaving out his second principle of association and so obviating his whole double-association mechanism) and recognizing the essential role of the 'object' – or, more generally, the believed context – in identifying the emotion and so making the feeling the particular emotional feeling that it is, we have in effect abandoned Hume's theory. Our main interest in Hume's theory is as the most articulated version of Humean theory, that is, as a thoroughly worked out example of a type of theory that emphasizes causal connections, associative mechanisms, and felt affects, while neglecting the role of thought and thoughts in the emotions. The particular defects in Hume's presentation do not necessarily condemn all versions of such theories, but the neglect of the importance of thoughts in emotions raises difficulties which are quite general and which cannot be made up for by associative mechanisms. I will now explore further the place of thought in the analysis of emotion and object, and then go on to consider some of the limitations in associationist approaches to the connection between emotion and behaviour and expression.

11
Thought-Dependence

I should first note that I use the word 'thought' very broadly. In some contexts, perception, awareness, judgment, appraisal, suspicion, etc. might be the more natural expression. Indeed, I usually use 'belief' interchangeably with 'thought', although there are many propositions or passing fancies constituting thoughts which we entertain or have but do not believe. I use the word 'thought' as a blanket term to cover the cognitive element in emotions. 'Cognitive' does not preclude unconscious. Indeed, as will become evident, I believe that it is the requirement of an appropriate thought that leads psychoanalysts to postulate that an unconscious thought, or unconscious belief, or unconscious fantasy exists, wherever behaviour and other grounds lead them to postulate an emotion in the (apparent) absence of the (normally) required thought. Some purposes might require greater care and finer distinctions than my usage of 'thought' allows, but it is adequate for this purpose of clarifying the role and importance of a cognitive element in the recognition, classification, discrimination, and, therefore, change, of emotions. Now back to Hume.

Hume's notion of an object, taken as 'object of attention' (Árdal, 1966, pp. 18–19) or 'object of concern' (Gosling, 1965, p. 499), is meant to capture one of the consequences of experiencing an emotion. The object is one among 'such circumstances as attend' it, in its train. If it is such a circumstance, we have been arguing that it is more plausible to suppose that it is a condition on the emotion rather than a consequence that follows upon it. The sense in which it is a 'condition', of course, requires further explication. It is important to see that Hume's notion is not a simple intuitive or grammatical notion of object; else the object of pride would seem obviously to be whatever one was proud *of* (son, country, appearance, etc.) in a particular case, rather than what Hume says it invariably is, self. Kenny, we said earlier, misstates Hume's point. We should now see that his misstatement comes close to what Hume's point *should* be: that belief in a relation to self is required if a thing or quality is to serve as a ground or source of pride.

Pride is a form of self-evaluation: 'According as our idea of ourself is more or less advantageous, we feel either of those opposite affections, and are elated by pride, or dejected with humility' (*THN*, II, p. 277). If all self-ascriptions of pride were recast in the form, 'I am proud of myself because . . .', the justifying clause would always refer to some quality or object related to self. It may be precisely because this relation is always present (i.e. because self is always the object of pride or because we are always proud of ourselves) that the other element in the compound cause, the valuable quality, can sometimes stand alone as the prepositional object. (As one commonly says, 'I am proud of the school', for instance, without reference to the 'myself' – which would in any case be an idea occurring before, not after, the feeling of pride.) The issue of relation to self is conceptual rather than causal. Hume misconstrues the nature of the constraint that an object places on an emotion. In his mistaken causal account, lacking the object one would lack the double association needed to produce pride. Rather, I would say, lacking the object, whatever was produced would not be considered pride. The nature of this constraint can be understood in terms of 'appropriateness', 'reasons', and the role of 'thought'.

Kenny presents a formula meant to provide a criterion for the 'object' of an emotion, such that emotions could be distinguished from sensations through the possession of 'objects'.

> The distinction between the cause and the object of an emotion
> is . . . most easily made out by reference to the knowledge or
> beliefs of the subject. Faced with any sentence describing the
> occurrence of an emotion, of the form 'A φd because *p*', we must

ask whether it is a necessary condition of the truth of this
sentence that A should know or believe that *p*. If so, then the
sentence contains an allusion to the object of the emotion; if not,
to its cause (Kenny, 1963, p. 75).

This formula has been much criticized. It does not apply in all cases
(Gosling, 1965, pp. 492ff.). Where it does apply, it will not always
distinguish emotion and sensation (emotions *can* have causes, and some
sensations it seems, e.g. hunger, *can* have objects). Indeed, the formula
seems to rely on a prior distinction between emotion and sensation, and
that distinction must be based on something other than the notion of
object (Gosling, 1965; Wilson, 1972, p. 99). It needs amendment
to deal with emotions which take agents as objects (e.g. anger –
Green, 1972, p. 29). And it is in many cases inconclusive (Green,
1972, p. 30). I would insist, however, that it does *try* to do something
that moves in the right direction: it tries to bring out the knowledge, or
belief, or (most generally) thought-conditions on emotions. One need
not argue, for our purposes, that the conditions brought out are non-
causal. Within Hume's system, they would have to be causal (though,
we have argued, a part of the cause rather than, as he presents it, the
effect). Within Kenny's argument they are assumed not to be causal.
Despite that argument (and others), and without reference to Hume's
system, I think that these conditions could be considered causal.
Without claiming that they *are* causal, I would argue (following Pears,
Wilson, and others) that they could be, that conceptual constraints do
not preclude causal connections. (See Appendix A for discussion of
this point.) But here what I wish to emphasize is that certain thoughts,
whether or not they are causal conditions on emotions, are indeed conditions; that without the thought one cannot have the emotion. To
attribute an emotion and deny the characteristic thought is to deny the
emotion. Emotions are thought-dependent.

My point here is stronger than that emotions are mediated by
thoughts, though that too is being claimed. The contents of the relevant
thoughts help determine what one's state of mind is. Kenny puts this
point in terms of his notion of 'formal object'. There are conceptual
restrictions on the type of object which each emotion could have
(Kenny, 1963, p. 191).

The formal object of φing is the object under that description
which *must* apply to it if it is to be possible to φ it. If only
what is P can be φd, then 'thing which is P' gives the formal
object of φing. Descriptions of formal objects can be formed
trivially simply by modalising the relevant verbs: only what is
edible can be eaten, only what is inflammable can be burnt, only
what is tangible can be touched. But there are other descriptions
of formal objects which are not trivial in this way. Only what is

dirty can be cleaned, only what is wet can be dried, only what
is coloured can be seen . . . (Kenny, 1963, p. 189).

This way of putting the point, however, may be a little misleading: it
obscures the role of thoughts and it tends to reverse the order of
dependence in so far as it does suggest a role. When the formal object
of an emotion is described in non-trivial fashion, where does that
description come from? If the formal object of fear is things that are
dangerous, this is not because we have noted that fear arises only in
dangerous circumstances. One may be afraid in circumstances which
are not dangerous, what matters is that one believes them to be
dangerous. So the formal object of fear would be things that are
believed to be dangerous. And it is not until one has determined the
content of the associated beliefs that one can be sure of the correct
description of the emotional state of mind. 'It is not so much that the
emotion restricts the object, or the beliefs about the object. Rather it is
that the object, or the beliefs about the object, restricts the emotion.
That is, what emotion I can feel towards an item in the world is
restricted by what I take to be true of that item' (Wilson, 1972, p. 101).

These points are of sufficient importance to warrant a closer look at
Kenny's presentation. He claims that 'Emotional attitudes, like other
mental attitudes, have formal objects . . . each of the emotions is appropriate – logically, and not just morally appropriate – only to certain
restricted objects. One cannot be afraid of just anything, nor happy
about anything whatsoever' (Kenny, 1963, pp. 191–2). In fact, one *can*
be afraid of anything or happy about anything; all that is required, as
revealed by the continuation of the quoted passage, is the appropriate
beliefs:

> If a man says that he is afraid of winning £10,000 in the pools,
> we want to ask him more: does he believe that money corrupts,
> or does he expect to lose his friends, or to be annoyed by begging
> letters, or what? If we can elicit from him only descriptions of the
> good aspects of the situation, then we cannot understand why he
> reports his emotion as fear and not as hope. Again, if a man says
> that he feels remorse for the actions of someone quite
> unconnected with him, or is envious of his own vices, we are at a
> loss to understand him (Kenny, 1963, p. 192).

The gap must be supplied by appropriate beliefs. And Kenny does
explicitly give place to them:

> It is not, of course, correct to say e.g., that the formal object of
> envy is another's good *tout court*: one must say that it is something
> *believed to* be good and *believed to* belong to another. . . . The
> description of the formal object of a mental attitude such as an
> emotion, unlike a description of the formal object of a

non-intensional action, must contain reference to belief. Only what is wet in fact can be dried; but something which is merely believed to be an insult may provoke anger (Kenny, 1963, pp. 193–4).

But one may still wonder how formal objects, however notional, are fixed. Why is anger related to insults and the like? Here I think it is helpful to consider that one cannot describe a state of mind as a certain emotion independently of the subject's beliefs about its explanation. The 'state of mind' to be explained and the relevant thoughts bear a very complex relationship, which is merely pointed to when one says that emotions are 'mediated' by thoughts.

Gosling distinguishes three points:

first, I cannot be grateful, but to no one for nothing; second, I cannot realize I feel grateful, but have no idea of to whom or for what; and third, if I feel grateful it must be for some reason, which it will be possible to give in a 'because clause,' and the reason cited be believed. All three seem to hold with gratitude. None seems necessary with depression. With love the first one holds: I cannot just be in love and with no one. Perhaps the second: can I realize that I am in love but have no idea with whom? The third seems not to hold at all (Gosling, 1965, p. 499).

We are not concerned with precisely delimiting the scope of the concept 'emotion'; and so the usefulness or lack of usefulness of the concept of 'object' to that end does not concern us. It does not matter that love and depression, or other mental states, may not seem to have objects in all the ways or with all the implications that gratitude seems to. Our concern is with certain mental states (typified by certain standard emotions) and the ways in which they are characterized or mediated or dependent upon thoughts. Gosling goes on to suggest an explanation for the applicability of Kenny's much-criticized formula (where it *does* apply):

The third applies where it does . . . because of a feature of those feelings. With fear, anger, jealousy, pity and some others it seems possible to give a list of characterizations of what is feared, raged at, envied, or pitied such that only what is so characterized is reasonably so reacted to. Thus, roughly, fear is a reaction to danger, anger to offense, jealousy to preference being given to others, pity to the misfortunes of others.

The point, however, concerns more than the reasonableness of an emotion. Even an unreasonable emotion cannot be the emotion it is unless the subject's relevant beliefs fall within the restrictions required by the formal object. If the beliefs are unreasonable, the emotion may be unreasonable also – but it will not be an unreasonable *fear* or *anger* or whatever, unless the beliefs are of the appropriate kind. An emotion must be had before it can be either reasonable or not; and in most cases in order to have the emotion at all one must have the correlative concepts. In order to explicate jealousy, and explicate it in a way that shows what distinguishes it from mere anger, one would have to fill in a conceptual background. One could not recognize any case of jealousy (reasonable or unreasonable), unless one were prepared to ascribe appropriate beliefs involving the relevant concepts. Where the emotion is unreasonable, the beliefs may be mistaken, but they are none the less essential to the characterization of the emotion.

Gosling suggests that certain emotions, such as love, cannot be judged in terms of reasonableness, and so, perhaps, do not have formal objects.

[For the concept fear] being normally able to refer to a supposed danger seems a requirement for the application of this concept. Further, 'that such and such is dangerous' is the 'reason for' a person's fear. If it turns out not to be dangerous, he was still afraid, but unreasonably so. There are many complexities to this situation, but it is this feature of these feelings which makes it normal that there should be a 'because p' available. Because danger is the reason for fear, offense for anger, and so on, normally it will be possible to say 'A ϕ's because p' where p gives something characterized by the partial correlative of the feeling and A believes that p. Now there is no similar partial correlative with love. It is impossible to find any manageable characterization to which loved ones must be liable, except such non-informative ones as lovableness. Love is never reasonable – though sometimes understandable – because it is neither reasonable nor unreasonable.

What makes Kenny's test work in some cases is that these are cases which have a partial correlative, and so usually 'have a reason.' The relevant 'because clause' leads us to what is supposed to be characterized by the partial correlative. It is an interesting fact about some emotions that they have this feature, but it is not a universal feature of emotions (Gosling, 1965, p. 500).

But even love may exhibit the sort of thought-dependence we have been talking about: i.e. there are conceptual restrictions on what can count as love, there are beliefs that a lover must have if his state is to count as love. And this is true despite the facts (if they are facts) that love can be neither reasonable nor unreasonable, and that its formal object is only trivially characterizable. First, it is notorious that 'love' is a word of many meanings. Without counting the ways in which one can love, it should be obvious that differences in meaning depend very often on the beliefs (particularly as they relate to the desires) of the lover.

In a romantic sense, for example, to offer certain explanations of an emotion necessarily disqualifies that emotion as love. Certain sorts of ulterior motives, certain sorts of characterizations of the loved object (such as extremely wealthy, etc.) are unacceptable in the explanation of a state which is to count as (romantic) love. Not all qualities are allowed to be significant. Second, without looking to special conceptions of love, one can see that love in general must meet certain conceptual restrictions. These conceptual restrictions, however, enter at a different point, particularly in connection with action and desire. Beliefs and reasons are connected with emotions from two directions. There are both the subject's beliefs about the explanation of his state (which may amount to reasons), and the subject's (or agent's) beliefs about how his state explains his actions. The proper characterization of both his state and his actions will in general depend upon these explanations; descriptions are correlated with explanations. Or, more strongly, what precisely one is explaining will in general depend on the available explanations. Both action and emotion depend on thought. Love is thought-dependent in the way we are considering, not because it would otherwise be unreasonable, but because it otherwise would not be love.

Gosling is right that there are many complexities here. We can sort out some of them. The three points about objects he distinguishes, suggesting that they all apply only where a non-trivial characterization of a formal object can be supplied, can be understood as different aspects of thought-dependence, which applies quite generally. In sum, thought-dependence here amounts to conceptual restrictions on what can count as a particular state of mind, i.e. certain thoughts or beliefs are required if one is to be properly described as in a certain state. As we have seen, his third point, concerning reasons, can be understood more broadly in terms of beliefs about explanations. Even love, though it may never be reasonable, places certain restrictions on explanations of the state itself or of actions (or dispositions to action) following from the state, if it is to be properly characterized as love. It is partly through these sorts of beliefs that we *discriminate* one state from another.

But these are requirements for *sorts* of beliefs. To *identify* a particular state may require more particular beliefs. Here we find an obvious ambiguity, indeed a double ambiguity. First, is one interested in the identification of a state as a state of a particular kind, or as a particular state? These different interests may require specifying different beliefs. And, the second ambiguity, is one interested in identification of a mental state from a third-party standpoint, or in its recognition by the subject himself? Gosling tells us that 'I cannot realize I feel grateful but have no idea of to whom or for what', and this may apply to love: 'can I realize that I am in love but have no idea with whom?' In no case will one have *fully* identified the particular state if one has not supplied its object. And it may be that in some cases one cannot say what sort of state one is in if one cannot fully identify it. But one need not always know the object of an emotion in order to recognize the emotion. Certainly one can be afraid and know one is afraid without being able to specify the object of one's fear. (It is salutary to remember here that though thought is important, it is not the only constituent of emotion or the only way to identify it. Certain primitive states, including basic fears, may be most strongly characterized by physiological upsets and inclinations to behaviour, without any but the most general thoughts.)

This aspect of identification holds even more widely when one thinks of it from a third-party point of view. Identifying an emotion, in the sense of telling what kind of emotion another person is having, does not require being able to specify the particular object, though one must be able to specify the kind of object. (This is perhaps redundant: in specifying the emotion as of a certain kind, one is restricting the range of appropriate objects.) I may know that someone else is angry or afraid without knowing, or being sure, what in particular he is angry at or afraid of (though, whatever it is, I know that he will, consciously or unconsciously, think it offensive or dangerous) (Wilson, 1972, pp. 47–50). In terms of thought-dependence, the interesting point about identification is the same as that about discrimination (or classification): even where one does not need to know the specific object in order to know the type of state, one does need to know the type of object. If one does not ascribe thoughts in the appropriate range, if the formal or conceptual limits on objects are not adhered to, one cannot ascribe an emotion of a particular type to oneself or others.

Hampshire elaborates *his* notion of thought-dependence in a passage about desire:

'Smith wants to buy the most expensive picture in the gallery.'
Suppose that I read, or hear, this statement, and want to know
whether it is true. It would be incorrect to say that the statement,
the truth of which I am inquiring into, is ambiguous; perhaps it
would not even be correct to say that it is, as quoted, indeterminate
in sense. But there are two or more distinct states of affairs, or
situations, which it might represent. It might be the case that
Smith had conceived the desire of buying whatever picture
happened to be the most expensive picture in the gallery. Or he
might have seen a picture, which he immediately liked and wanted,
and which happened to be the most expensive. In the second case,
his desire to buy the picture is unmediated by this, or by any
other, description of the picture: in the first case the desire to buy
the picture is mediated by the description, which is essential to
the desire, and specifies the exact nature of the desire. The two

> desires are entirely different and reveal very different characters;
> but the same form of words may truthfully represent both these
> situations. And of course this form of words might represent
> various other situations intermediate between these two
> (Hampshire, 1965, p. 46).

But it is misleading to think of this example as showing a contrast
between thought-dependent and non-thought-dependent desires. As
Wollheim argues, both desires may be regarded as thought-dependent,
but dependent upon different sorts of thoughts: 'in the one case, Smith
desired a picture of a particular kind, and, in the other case, he desired
a particular picture, and in each case the desire could be identified
through, or be mediated by, the corresponding kind of thought'
(Wollheim, 1967–8, p. 18). We should reserve the term thought-
dependent for this broad usage, and introduce a special expression, such
as description-dependent, for those states which are dependent on
thought of something as a thing of a particular kind. It is this latter
notion that Hampshire is interested in singling out, because he is concerned with that which is distinctively human, and the complications
introduced into mental life through the distinctively human capacity to
reflect on our own mental states. If we are prepared to ascribe certain
desires (as opposed to bare needs) to non-language-users (e.g. animals
and infants), we need not hesitate to ascribe certain thoughts to them
as well. But the range of thoughts, and so of desires, may well be
restricted. Where desires are formed desires, where they are deliber-
ative desires, where the subject's conception of the object is essential
to the characterization of the desire, there the subject has to be a
language-user: otherwise the ascription of the required sorts of thoughts
(and so desires) will not make sense. At least this may be so. Discriminating one description-dependent desire from another probably
requires more than is revealed by non-linguistic patterns of behaviour.

When a desire is description-dependent, the description would
appear in a complete statement of one's reason for desiring; and it is
only with the ability to reflect that the notion of having reasons for one's
desires can enter in. Hence Hampshire links his account of what it is to
have a reason with the capacity to reflect, and to the notions of becoming
doubtful and reconsidering. (Cf. Neu, 'Hampshire on Reasons, Causes,
and Counterfactuals'.) To have a desire may be to have a reason for
doing or pursuing whatever it is one desires, but not necessarily to have
a reason for the desire. And it is reasons for one's desire we are here
concerned with. One may have many reasons for doing or pursuing
things which are not reasons for wanting them (as opposed to wanting
that they be done or possessed). If description-dependent desires are
desires for something of a certain kind, it might seem that animals

could have them also, since animals do seem to have desires for things of a certain kind, e.g. grass (rather than particular tufts of grass – Watling, 1973, p. 20). But these cases may in fact terminate in their object. That is, the description does not give the animal's *reason* for its desire. The desire is not for a thing of a certain kind *because* it is of that kind; and that is the sort of description-dependence intended. (The desire for grass may be thought-dependent without being description-dependent.)

Alternatively, one could concede that animals have desires for things of a certain kind, but one would then have to concede that they have reasons (for desire) as well. Watling (1973, p. 21) seems misled because he does not see that a desire in which a particular thing is desired for a reason (e.g. the most expensive picture) is a desire for a thing of a certain kind, not merely a desire for a particular thing; it is a conditional desire, the reason gives the condition, and the condition picks out a kind. Whether the concern is for a particular or a kind cannot be determined by merely looking at the description one uses to specify the desire. The connection with reasons is what matters. What changes with what? If a horse's desire for grass is not belief-dependent (as Watling seems to think, 1973, p. 21), then it is not a desire for a thing of a certain kind, even if one specifies the desire in terms which seem to characterize a kind rather than a particular. (If someone says they want 'that', pointing to a picture, one does not know whether it is a desire for a particular or a thing of a certain kind (though the item pointed to is doubtless a particular), unless one knows what the desire depends on.) *Contra* Watling, if a desire is not belief-dependent, it is not a desire for something for a reason.

In any case, we can allow 'description-dependent' to serve for those special sorts of cases which Hampshire (usually) singles out as 'mediated by a description'. The main point is that emotions are, in general, thought-dependent. For each emotion, some characteristic thought or thoughts is essential so that one must ascribe the appropriate thought if the psychological state is to be correctly classified as a particular emotion. In some cases, of course, the thought may not reveal the reason for the state, and in those cases it is not description-dependent. In these cases a change in the description might leave the state unchanged; the person or thing which is the object may not be desired, or hated, or whatever, under any particular description. But in some cases the description may be essential to the specification of the state. This is especially clear in those cases where one is describing a conditional desire, or emotion; that is, a desire or emotion which has a condition built into it and is not simply conditional on thoughts in the general manner of thought-dependence. In discussing hypotheticals like 'I would not have gone to the opera last night, if Callas had not been singing' Hampshire claims:

the condition stated in the if-clause gives a reason which will serve as a partial explanation. At the same time the condition stated can be viewed as specifying more fully the intention, the desire, the fear, the belief, the state of mind. I may simply recall that my intention to go to the opera was in this way conditional (Hampshire, 1967, p. 9).

How do thoughts get built into emotions? Certainly more than simultaneous occurrence is required. Where the thought is a thought about the explanation of the state, or of the rest of the state (excluding the thought itself), matters are relatively clear. But thoughts may 'mediate' emotions in a variety of additional ways which I will not attempt to delineate here.

There is another dimension I shall consider briefly: thoughts can be active or passive. As we shall see when we come to Spinoza, the activity of a thought for him has to do with the thought's flowing from one's own nature, that is, being explainable in terms of previous states of the self rather than external circumstances. The model is rational, especially logical or mathematical, thought. In more ordinary contexts, we distinguish between thoughts which simply occur and thoughts which we have. In extremes, thoughts which occur may be felt to be intruders, alien invaders. Just how we can make such a distinction, how we can give these spatial metaphors force raises difficult and fascinating questions. (Wollheim, 1969, suggests that the matter is linked with unconscious fantasies of incorporation.) Where a state is itself passive, a passion, it may be enough that the thought by reference to which the particular mental state is identified merely passively occurs, without being actively thought (see Wollheim, 1967–8, pp. 23–4), so we may be able to avoid those questions for now.

How does a state, where it is thought-dependent, depend on thought? Partly, of course, as we have seen, there is a conceptual constraint. A state would not be the state one takes it to be if one did not have the appropriate beliefs. For example, regret is said by Hampshire to be thought-impregnated or belief-saturated in this way: a person who does not believe an action of his to have been mistaken does not regret that action. If the belief were to change, the state would change also, for the belief is an essential constituent.

12
Sympathy and Knowledge of Other Minds

Hume tends to assimilate belief to emotion and this seriously distorts his account of our knowledge of other minds. (A corresponding mistake would be to assimilate emotion to belief alone. See Appendix B.) There are differences between thinking of an emotion and having that emotion. Humean mechanisms, however, move inexorably from the idea to the impression; and, within the terms of his theory, having moved thus far one comes to an emotion.

Hume mentions belief in his discussion of one's expectation of an effect on presentation of the impression of a cause to consciousness. In that context, belief turns out to be a matter of vivid perceptions. He does not say much about belief elsewhere and it is perhaps unfair to generalize this into an account of belief in other contexts (see Price, 1969, pp. 164–7). But it does help make clearer what Hume takes to be the source and nature of our knowledge of 'other minds', and the prominence given to the mechanism of sympathy in that knowledge.

Belief, according to Hume, is in the eye of the beholder. Discussing ideas of memory as opposed to ideas of imagination, he tells us that belief is vivacity of perceptions – a vivacity present in the former and absent in the latter. 'To believe is in this case to feel an immediate impression of the sense, or a repetition of that impression in the memory' (*THN*, I, p. 86). To have an impression is to believe in it, and so (it would appear) to believe one is in a certain state is to be in it. (It would be interesting to know how Hume would hope to make sense of a person entertaining an idea precisely in order to *decide* whether he ought to believe it, since for Hume that would seem to amount to the same as his believing it. How could a person dissociate from a, perhaps obsessive, thought?) Hume presents a scale of liveliness of perceptions, with ideas at one end, impressions at the other, and beliefs in between. Kemp Smith argues that the difference between impressions and ideas should (at least often) be interpreted as a difference in kind, as great as 'the difference betwixt feeling and thinking' (Kemp Smith, 1941, pp. 109–10), and not as a difference merely in degree of force and liveliness. His argument is not wholly convincing, especially as there are explicit formulations to the contrary. For example, he claims that Hume thinks impressions can be 'confounded' with ideas and ideas 'mistaken' for impressions. And degrees of liveliness might not allow for such mistakes (Kemp Smith, 1941, p. 210). But the concepts of 'confounding' and 'mistaking' are Kemp Smith's, not Hume's. Hume thinks only that ideas and impressions are sometimes 'indistinguishable', and *that* requires only closeness of degree (as one would expect, scales have unclear borderlines) in some cases, not confusion of distinct kinds. Whether or not Hume's theory of belief is, in general, a straightforward feeling theory of belief, it is such a theory in the area that concerns us. In connection with the passions, Hume does treat belief as a feeling theory would suggest:

> two points had to be made good: (1) that ideas are *exact* copies of impressions, and (2) that the difference being in the *manner* of their apprehension, a process of *enlivening* is all that is needed to

47

induce the mind to adopt towards an idea the attitude which it instinctively adopts towards the corresponding impression. He is thus led to declare that belief itself consists in 'force and liveliness', and to interpret the phrase in a quite literal fashion. This, unquestionably, is how he himself interprets it in the course of his argument in Book II, in dealing with the passions (Kemp Smith, 1941, pp. 210–11).

In connection with Hume's account of causation, belief is defined as 'a lively idea related to or associated with a present impression' (*THN*, I, p. 96). Belief is, in degree of force and liveliness, almost an impression ("'tis only a strong and steady conception of any idea, and such as approaches in some measure to an immediate impression'). In the context of causality, belief in the imminent emergence of the effect is excited by the 'present impression' of the cause; it is 'produc'd by a relation to a present impression' (*THN*, I, p. 97), the impression of course being different in each case, for each belief. Belief itself is an effect, but the sense in which it is 'produced' (the mechanics of the objects of our internal universe) would take us into Hume's analysis of causation. In connection with the passions, I think we need note only that belief (as defined in *THN*, I, iii, section 7) is an (almost-) impression of reflexion.

Because of this reflexive element, differences in the content of beliefs need not be simply differences of feeling. But the essence of belief is feeling (here speaking of memory): 'to believe is in this case to feel an immediate impression of the senses, or a repetition of that impression in the memory' (*THN*, I, p. 86). If one believes, one infallibly knows one believes. If one is in an emotional state, one is infallibly aware that one is. For the belief and the state just are an awareness, a perception of impressions or almost-impressions.

> every impression, external and internal, passions, affections, sensations, pains and pleasures, are originally on the same footing; and that whatever other differences we may observe among them, they appear, all of them, in their true colours, as impressions or perceptions. . . . For since all actions and sensations of the mind are known to us by consciousness, they must necessarily appear in every particular what they are, and be what they appear. Every thing that enters the mind, being in *reality* perception, 'tis impossible any thing shou'd to *feeling* appear different. This were to suppose, that even where we are most intimately conscious, we might be mistaken (*THN*, I, p. 190).

This seems to imply a very odd view of our knowledge of our own mental states. The only errors open to us would seem to be those (if any) open to us in regard to simple sensations. But it is a familiar fact

that a person may well be the last to be aware of, or refuse to acknowledge, a state that others (lacking his preoccupations and prejudices)
may be able to ascribe without difficulty (e.g. jealousy). In these cases
his evidence may be no better, and in fact no different, from the evidence
available to and used by others. We, like others, can be deceived in the
nature of our emotional states, and if we cannot be deceived in 'the
nature of our impressions' perhaps this just goes to show that our
emotions are not (or are not simply) impressions. And this problem
arises independently of psychoanalytical claims; though of course,
those claims, in particular the doctrines of the unconscious and repression, make the difficulty even more acute: our unknowingness,
our self-deception, can be even deeper than feeling theory and ordinary
notions allow. Hume thinks that 'the perceptions of the mind are perfectly known' (*THN*, II, p. 366). If we take belief as simply a certain
specific degree of force and liveliness, Hume is committed to a doctrine
of privileged infallibleness in determining our emotional state and to
an extreme feeling theory of emotion; to have an impression is to
believe one has it, and to believe one is in a certain state is to be in
it.

Not only will certainty seem to arise with every emotion, but
emotions would seem to arise with every occasion to think about them.
The meaning of a word is not the image of a thing. But if one follows
Hume in thinking that it is, to understand a word, one would have to
have the corresponding image, and in having the image – where the
thing is an emotion – one would be having the thing itself. In thinking
of grief, someone else's or no one in particular's, one would be feeling a little grief (and it could easily deepen through attachment to
self).

Kemp Smith claims that Hume modified his doctrine of belief in
certain connections, in particular in relation to perceptual knowledge
of the external world (Kemp Smith, 1941, p. 222). Passions, however,
are not external, and do not require a doctrine of natural belief to carry
one to them beyond one's impressions. But a problem does arise with
other people's passions. Though they too are internal, they are internal
to others, and so how do we have access to them? Instead of modifying
his view of belief, Hume introduces the mechanism of sympathy: we
know other people's feelings by feeling them, i.e. by making them our
own. In his discussion of causal inference an idea is enlivened by the
impression with which it is associated and so achieves the status of
belief (or expectation). In sympathy, somewhat similarly, a mere idea
is enlivened by the ever-present 'idea, or rather impression of self', and
so achieves the status of passion.

What is the principle of sympathy? It is not yet another passion
alongside benevolence and the rest. It is a principle of communication.
'No quality of human nature is more remarkable, both in itself and in

its consequences, than that propensity we have to sympathize with others, and to receive by communication their inclinations and sentiments, however different from, or even contrary to our own' (*THN*, II, p. 316). Not surprisingly, opinions or beliefs of others can also be communicated by sympathy (*THN*, II, pp. 319, 427). (We shall not discuss here the importance of the principle of sympathy for Hume's moral theory; this task is well done by Árdal.) Our only initial access to other people's passions is through their outward behaviour.

> When any affection is infus'd by sympathy, it is at first known only by its effects, and of those external signs in the countenance and conversation, which convey an idea of it. This idea is presently converted into an impression, and acquires such a degree of force and vivacity, as to become the very passion itself, and produce an equal emotion, as any original affection (*THN*, II, p. 317).

This account calls for a source of 'force and vivacity' to convert the idea into an impression. (It also certainly calls for discussion of the theory of expression, and the notion that external behaviour can be read as signs of inner states independently of the ascription of beliefs. That discussion will come in due course.) The highly questionable 'idea, or rather impression of ourselves' is called in for the job (*THN*, II, p. 354). But there is an obscurity earlier on. What is the antecedent of 'this idea' in the passage quoted? Clearly it is not the external signs; they merely lead us to infer the presence of a passion in another. The original affection in the other is of course an impression, we merely infer to an idea. But what idea? Say the other person is proud. On Hume's own account he will be proud of himself. Will our idea of his passion be simply of pride or of his pride in himself (with *his* idea of himself as its object)? If our idea of a passion includes the fact that it is his (in the case of pride, this fact, deviously, is part of the cause and so object), enlivening the idea will not make the passion ours. (Cf. Passmore, 1968, p. 129, who muddles the point by treating 'sympathy' as a passion rather than a principle of knowledge by communication of passions.) And the fact does seem to be included: 'these movements appear at first in *our* mind as mere ideas, and are conceiv'd to belong to another person . . .' (*THN*, II, p. 319). In the case of pride the situation is complicated by the fact that the enlivening factor (idea of self) is also the standard cause of pride. But in general, can the passion communicated be the same as the other party's unless it has the same cause (and so object)? Do we share Hume's pride if we are not, like him, proud of Hume? Do we share Rousseau's fear, if we are not, like him, afraid of Hume? Of course not, but how can Hume's mechanism bring this about?

Presumably the original affection is an impression (of reflexion) and the idea which becomes an impression through sympathy is, like that original impression, simple. How does it get its object? According to our first reading of Hume the object would have to emerge by an original principle from our enlivened idea. On our emended version it would have had to have been part of the cause of that enlivened idea. On Hume's doctrine of sympathy the object presumably comes along with the simple idea which gets enlivened, though it itself remains an idea (it must in order to serve as object). In any case, Hume's principle must be more complicated and highly selective than it would first appear: the idea that it is the other's passion (i.e. associated with his idea of himself) must not be included, otherwise it admits too much; the idea which is the object must be included but not enlivened, otherwise it admits too little or the wrong sort of thing.

Though Hume modifies his account to accommodate the influences of comparison, resemblance, general principles, etc., in general two facts emerge: one's knowledge of another's emotional state is based on an inference to a feeling from external behaviour, and the knowledge consists in oneself experiencing a (perhaps weaker) version of that state. To avoid this second conclusion Hume would have to explain why sympathy does not act more widely than it does (given that the enlivening impression of ourselves 'is always intimately present with us'). And he would have to make this explanation without saying that the idea that the passion is another's is sometimes included in our idea of another's passion (for if it sometimes is, how would sympathy ever act in the way Hume claims?). This doctrine yields some further odd consequences. For one thing, one could not know another was experiencing a certain passion unless one had experienced it oneself. Not surprisingly, Hume remarks: 'Now 'tis obvious, that nature has preserv'd a great resemblance among all human creatures, and that we never remark any passion or principle in others, of which, in some degree or other, we may not find a parallel in ourselves' (*THN*, II, p. 318). But someone might well know and understand that someone else feels remorse or is ashamed (as opposed, say, to embarrassed) without ever having himself felt remorse or been ashamed. All he need grasp is concepts of loss and mistake in the one case, and of responsibility and guilt (roughly) in the other. No fine discrimination of sensations is called for and no personal experience of the passion is required.

Another apparent consequence seems to be that animals are susceptible to the same full range of passions as humans are. Hume discusses the pride and humility of animals (*THN*, II, i, section 12) and infers that they too experience the peculiar impression of pride. 'The very port and gait of a swan, or turkey, or peacock show the high idea he has entertain'd of himself, and his contempt of all others' (*THN*, II, p. 326). Perhaps attributing beliefs to the animal about the animal's own self-opinion might be acknowledged by Hume to complicate the picture, but essentially he sees no reason why animals cannot feel what we feel and so have the same passions we have. In Hume's view, of course, humans can speak, but their language only enables them to announce their passions in a way animals cannot, and that does not extend their emotional experience. However, to cite but one contradictory example, humans have an emotional life extended in time; and the reason, arguably, is that they have a language and time concepts. Consider Wittgenstein's famous remark: 'We say a dog is afraid his master will beat him; but not, he is afraid his master will beat him tomorrow. Why not?' (Wittgenstein, 1953, section 650). The dog could cower and so we could ascribe a present fear (directed to the immediate future), but what could the dog do that would show it feared an event in the (extended) future? Hume could say the dog has an impression which is fear of tomorrow's beating. But how does the impression (or the idea which is its object) get its date? (Is it a picture of a stick coming down? Of a stick coming down with a calendar with tomorrow's date circled?) And even if one could make an image do representative duty, what basis would one have for ascribing such a picture (as opposed to myriad others) to a creature without the ability to describe it (or discriminate it from others) in language? ('Language' here is not merely a matter of vocal cords.) Hume might regard this restriction as one merely of the causes of fear. He recognizes such restrictions on pride because we have to make

> a just allowance for our superior knowledge and understanding. Thus animals have little or no sense of virtue or vice; they quickly lose sight of the relations of blood; and are incapable of that of right and property; For which reason the causes of their pride and humility must lie solely in the body, and can never be plac'd either in the mind or external objects (*THN*, II, p. 326).

But the restrictions are not the result of narrowness of interests. Lacking certain conceptual equipment, animals *cannot* be concerned with relations of 'property'. If there is no appropriate way to ascribe such thoughts and such interests to them, it seems equally true that there are types of emotions that are not properly ascribable to animals at all, in virtue of the fact that the characteristic thoughts cannot be ascribed. Hume says 'When self enters not into consideration, there is no room either for pride or humility' (*THN*, II, p. 277). But what sort of fact is this? One cannot move from the 'very port and gait of a swan' to the claim that it has a concept of self. And if one cannot claim that, one cannot, in logic, claim that it feels pride. Indeed, even for humans, port and gait or other behaviour is only evidence of a particular emotion in the context of certain beliefs ascribed to the subject. As we shall argue, any behaviour (almost) can express any emotion. Even in a creature *capable* of a particular emotion (say, anger), a bit of behaviour which might usually be typical of that emotion (say, hitting), will only be an expression of that emotion under certain conditions, which include the thought behind it (see p. 138). The particular emotion being expressed (if any) will depend on the particular thought; just as the character of an action depends on the intention. Indeed, if the behaviour *can* be done intentionally (e.g. a scowl) it must be done intentionally if it is to count as expression (Wollheim, 1966–7, pp. 236, 243). So even if Hume's mechanism of sympathy were otherwise unobjectionable in its content and implications, it will not do because it does not show the place of thoughts in the meaning of behaviour, the place of problems of interpretation in the reading of external signs. 'Communication' of emotion is more complex, and less a matter of feeling, than Hume suggests.

13
Calm Passions

Hume makes a distinction between what he calls 'calm' and 'violent' passions. This distinction cuts across his other distinctions (e.g. direct *v.* indirect) and applies to the full range of passions.[8] In the first examples Hume gives ('the sense of beauty and deformity in action, composition, and external objects' – *THN*, II, p. 276), calm passions are modes of approval and disapproval. (See Kemp Smith, 1941, p. 167.) Reason, as a calm passion which can move to action, is 'a general calm determination of our passions, founded on some distant view or reflexion' (*THN*, III, p. 583). Of course, these calm passions, 'the sense of beauty and deformity in action . . .' can sometimes be violent, witness the 'raptures of poetry and music' referred to by Hume. Calm passions, then, generally are modes of approval and disapproval and arise from a distant view ('The same good, when near, will cause a violent passion, which, when remote, produces only a calm one' – *THN*, II, p. 419); but they need not always be, there are soft versions (low emotional intensity) of ordinarily violent passions (*THN*, II, p. 417, and see Árdal, 1966, p. 94ff.). Whether a given passion on any particular occasion is 'calm' or 'violent', depends on the 'disturbance in the soul' (cf. force and vivacity of an impression). Turbulence is not necessary to an emotion. We are led to classify certain passions as calm because they generally 'produce little emotion in the mind, and are more known by their effects than by the immediate feeling or sensation' (*THN*, II, p. 417). But almost any passion (not 'terror', or 'panic', or 'rage', or other emotions where high intensity is built into the description), could on some occasions be 'calm'. Because such passions 'cause no disorder in the soul' they are often mistaken for 'the determinations of reason' (*THN*, II, p. 417). Where Hume discusses the motivation of human actions (*THN*, II, iii, section 3) he is concerned to emphasize the contrast between such passions and reason, because he wishes to deny the power of reason to move. In fact, his examples of calm passions in this section are of desires or tendencies to action ('certain instincts originally planted in our natures, such as benevolence and resentment, the love of life, and kindness to children; or the general appetite to good, and aversion to evil, consider'd merely as such' – *THN*, II, p. 417). Hume also emphasizes that it is important not to confuse the calm/violent and strong/weak distinctions: these are different differences. 'Calm' and violent' are ends of a scale of inner turbulence, a measure of physiological tumult. (It is significant that Hume should recognize at all a 'calm' end of the scale, an end where 'real passions . . . are more known by their effects than by the immediate feeling or sensation'. This recognition contrasts sharply with his general view that an isolated impression constitutes the essence of each emotion; but we shall have to return to this.) 'Weak' and 'strong', however, are measures of strength of motive and this is the difference that matters in connection with action. ''Tis evident passions influence not the will in proportion to their violence, or the disorder they occasion in the temper. . . . We must, therefore, distinguish betwixt a calm and a weak passion; betwixt a violent and a strong one' (*THN*, II, pp. 418–19). The method of measuring motive is not clear, but because it is not just a matter of strength or intensity of sensation, or of violence of push, reason can enter in influencing passion and action. Where it enters in the form of a 'calm passion' we may expect connections between the description of the emotion (its specification or identity) and the description under which an action is motivated by it.

Calm passions are 'more known by their effects'. How is a calm passion, or for that matter, any passion, to be connected with behaviour? In the extreme case of calm passions, it seems that they are identified through their expression in behaviour rather than through feeling or sensation (which is 'in a manner imperceptible', *THN*, II, p. 276). But if an emotion is essentially an impression or feeling, what makes a piece of *behaviour* an expression of any particular emotion? Observed constant conjunction is the most likely Humean answer. But it is clear that this answer will not do for calm passions (where our access to, our awareness of, the 'cause' is through the 'effect'), and it is not clear that it will do at all. In his discussion of 'love and hatred' Hume comes close to recognizing the distortions introduced by treating relations which are conceptual as though they were simply causal. Desire connects passion with action, but, just as the simplicity of passions isolates the feeling from its object, it also isolates the feeling from its expression. So, for example, the desire for the good of the beloved is extraneous to the love itself: 'If nature had so pleas'd, love might have had the same effect as hatred, and hatred as love. I see no contradiction in supposing a desire of producing misery annex'd to love, and of happiness to hatred' (*THN*, II, p. 368). But in fact an apparent love would be rejected as love if we discovered that at the centre of the passion was a wish for harm to the putative beloved. We would say the feeling was ambivalent or redescribe the situation in terms of the subject's beliefs (e.g. that the 'harm' was not harm in his eyes). Hume himself notes:

> The passions of love and hatred are always followed by, or rather conjoin'd with benevolence and anger. 'Tis this conjunction, which chiefly distinguishes these affections from pride and humility. For pride and humility are pure emotions in the soul, unattended with any desire, and not immediately exciting us to action. But love and hatred are not compleated within themselves, nor rest in that emotion, which they produce, but carry the mind to something farther. Love is always follow'd by a desire of the happiness of the person belov'd, and an aversion to his misery: As hatred produces a desire of the misery and an aversion to the happiness of the person hated (*THN*, II, p. 367).

So Hume begins 'to be sensible, in some measure, of a misfortune'. But ultimately Hume takes the misfortune to amount to complications rather than a contradiction in his system. The immediate problem is an obvious lack of parallelism between love and hatred and pride and humility. That a desire should always be annexed to love and hatred, a desire in addition to an object (idea of another), is certainly a contrast with pride and humility. But why should it call for drastic measures? Why should it not be just another causal effect of the passion itself? Presumably, the answer is that a difference in subjective feeling provides no grounds (of the usual associative sort) for an additional effect. Difference in effect requires difference in cause (a sufficient reason). Love and pride exhibit the same quota of impressions, ideas, and associations upon analysis. Where can an additional impression of desire (this 'end' over and above 'cause' and 'object') come from in the case of love? The first possibility Hume considers is that it is not additional: 'the desire and aversion constitute the very nature of love and hatred' (*THN*, II, p. 367). He rejects this as 'contrary to experience. For tho' 'tis certain we never love any person without desiring his happiness, nor hate any without wishing his misery, yet these desires arise only upon the ideas of the happiness or misery of our friend or enemy being presented by the imagination, and are not absolutely essential to love and hatred' (*THN*, II, p. 367). The point, presumably, is that we can have the sensation of love without the sensation of desire, though if we *do* have a sensation of desire it *will* be for the happiness of the object of our love. The strange thing is that Hume's solution is to give the desires names (benevolence and anger) and say that they are conjoin'd with love and hatred 'by the original constitution of the mind' (*THN*, II, p. 368). But if the original contrast with pride was a problem, if there seemed to be an extra, (mechanically) inexplicable effect, why should saying nature makes it that way (sometimes, when the question of desire for another's happiness or misery arises at all) make it any less a problem?

Benevolence and anger raise the problems again: one wants to know how emotion is related to action. Are benevolence and anger simply desires? If they are, what is it that makes some desires emotions? What is the connection of benevolence with love? Hume's chemistry of impressions (*THN*, II, p. *366*) would seem to abandon the notion that impressions are distinct existences with only associative relations. But even if we accept the chemistry of impressions in order to make sense of benevolence's intimate connection with love, the problem of the relation of love to an 'end' is solved only by shifting it to benevolence. How is benevolence related to the desire for the happiness of another? Unless it just is that desire, why should the problem seem any less? That is, the desire is made by Hume somehow intrinsic to benevolence which in turn becomes contingently connected to love ('by the original constitution of the mind'). Is benevolence then still a simple impression? Perhaps it is simply the desire for the good of another, but then is desire simply a feeling or impression (as the passions are claimed to be)? To explore Hume's theory of desire would, however, take us too far afield.

We have already made some criticisms of what may be regarded as the Humean view of expression of emotion, as based on constant conjunction. At this point let us return to the calm passions and the special problems of their relation to action and behaviour.

14

Thought, Turbulence, and Action

Hume's recognition of the calm passions presents an important difficulty for his theory of the emotions. First, their existence seems incompatible with the demand that emotions be impressions. Second, Hume's description of their nature seems incompatible with his own doctrine of causation (which requires that cause and effect be independently possible, describable, and perceivable). The difficulty, however, is in Hume's system itself and not in the claim that some emotions are 'calm passions'. The distinction between calm and violent passions is crucial, I think, to the understanding of the emotions and possibilities for their guidance and control, and so of human freedom and happiness. This distinction requires clarification and defence, and we shall attempt both.

In discussing the calm passions, recognition of their motivating force (the feature that led Hume to attempt to give them a place in his scheme) is most important. It will also be pertinent to view the scales both within and among emotions (e.g. from animal objectless fear to intellectual fear, and from minimal physiological emotions to sophisticated cultural emotional responses) as continuous – so that calm passions

56

can be seen to have a place which is perhaps extreme but not isolated and mysterious in our mental life. Though calm passions are at the belief-impregnated end of the scale, emotions in general involve various forms of thought-dependence. We shall return to this theme in our discussion of Spinoza, who does much to clarify the connections.

But at present, I shall defend the distinction between calm and violent passions against a particular criticism, one that attempts to make too hard a separation between thought and affect and so tends to isolate the emotions from the influence of reason. Mary Warnock claims that the calm passions are not emotions at all (Warnock, 1957, p. 46). I am not concerned about the word 'emotion' and would be quite prepared to concede it to her. The dispute is only incidentally about classification, however. The important issue is the relation between the calm passions and the more generally recognized emotions (such as fear, anger, grief, etc.), in particular the importance of thought in their constitution and the level at which thought-dependence does form the ground of classification. Certainly there are differences between thinking and feeling, there can be dispassionate thoughts and attitudes, and it would be a mistake to assimilate emotion to thought alone. But it does not follow that all emotions must always involve a felt inner turbulence. (See Appendix B.)

How different as mental states are calm passions from those mental states which Warnock is prepared to recognize as emotions? The proper emotions 'have in common that they are all of them names for something in some degree agitating or disturbing' (Warnock, 1957, p. 46). It must be conceded that calm passions are not names for such exciting feelings, but that is the point of calling them 'calm'. What is the point of calling them passions? Basically the point, as Warnock herself recognizes, is that they often move to action.

Attitudes, which calm passions are thought to have more in common with than they do with emotions, do not move at all. At least, Warnock thinks that attitudes – basically long-term opinions (1957, p. 47) adopted towards general objects or to people or classes of people with whom one is in frequent contact – do not generally lead or lead directly to action. ('It may be that our actions reveal what our attitudes are, but our attitudes do not function as motives for action in the way that Hume lays down that passions do' – Warnock, 1957, p. 48.) In addition, attitudes are more readily ascribed to others than to ourselves, which also serves to distinguish them from passions. In any case, Warnock notes that 'any identification of the calm passions with attitudes must be wrong, since the calm passions certainly could be cited as one's reasons for acting, and were intended by Hume to be "influencing motives of the will" ' (1957, p. 49).

But in Warnock's view calm passions *resemble* attitudes and differ from violent passions in an important respect leading to differences in the criticism and justification of calm and violent passions. Warnock states concerning emotions (violent passions) 'that we attempt to justify them not by stating any opinion we hold but by trying to show that the object of the emotion is really of the kind which is commonly allowed to stimulate such an emotion' (1957, p. 58). The role of 'opinion' is crucial for the alleged difference then; attitudes and calm passions alike are matters of subjective opinion, while emotions are matters of objective agreed fact. In justifying calm passions, one appeals to the former, in justifying emotions, one appeals to the latter. Emotions are thus supposedly open to a narrower range of criticisms.

But Warnock's statement of her view does not seem to point the contrast she intended. For what do we do when we show that the object of an emotion is really of a certain kind but justify an opinion (the very thing Warnock wishes to deny)? She must be using 'opinion' in some sense narrower than that of 'thought' or 'belief', the sense in which I would have thought 'opinion' is essential to attitude and calm passion. That she does have some very special, subjectivist, sense of 'opinion' in mind is confirmed by another passage, which would also be otherwise difficult to interpret:

> It should be emphasised that to bring out the really hateful
> elements in an object is not to state a personal opinion of the
> object; or rather if it is that, it must be disguised. 'I hate him,
> because I think he is a blackmailer' would not be a proper form
> in which to cast a justification of hatred [a violent passion]
> (Warnock, 1957, p. 57).

I would have thought it to be a perfectly proper form. The normal implication of 'I think' is *not* that the opinion expressed is peculiarly subjective and personal. The statement 'he is a blackmailer' would (without further qualifications) serve as an objective statement of fact with the implication that I believe it, my adding 'I think' indicates explicitly that I believe it to be a fact; it may also suggest that I do not think I am in possession of the best grounds possible (conclusive grounds) for my belief, but *not* that my belief is somehow more personal than other beliefs. (Personal opinion aims at truth; it can be unconcerned only at the cost of becoming mere prejudice.) Would leaving out the 'I think' make Warnock accept the statement as a proper justification for an emotion? She says,

> The feeling can be justified only by being shown to have been
> caused by something which is generally permitted to inspire
> hatred, and therefore it must be cast in the form of an objective
> statement of agreed fact. This is a difference between justifying a
> feeling and justifying an attitude. For the justification of an
> attitude may quite openly rest on a personal opinion[9] (1957,
> p. 57).

Is there some special verbal 'form' or formula for objective statements of agreed fact? I doubt it. In any case, if 'I think he is a blackmailer' is not a justification for an emotion (of hatred), neither is it a justification for an attitude (unless the attitude is admitted to be irrational and so unjustified in any case). Even if Warnock could argue that subjective beliefs can justify attitudes though not emotions, I do not think she could show that calm passions are supported by such 'personal opinions'.

Perhaps love and hate are peculiar cases. Even though Warnock uses them as examples of violent emotions requiring objective support, she has earlier (1957, p. 51) cast suspicion on them: emotions, unlike moods and attitudes, may 'be extremely fleeting and momentary, though this does not seem to apply to grief, love, and hatred, which perhaps should not be classed as emotions, for this reason'. Perhaps these feelings, like attitudes, involve unusual amounts of stable belief. (But even the most fleeting emotions, e.g. amusement, involve beliefs; perhaps they are less liable to be wrong or open to correction because they have so little time to collect error. See Pears, 1962.) Indeed, love at least may appear peculiar from another direction. As Warnock notes (1957, p. 57), it seems peculiarly *unattached* to justifying beliefs, stable or unstable, objective or subjective. The heart has reasons of its own, that are allowed to be independent of reasonableness. But, as we have argued, though love may not need to be reasonable, it is still thought-dependent in the sense that concerns us. A special turbulence is not enough to make a feeling 'love'. What we are adding now is the suggestion that even without turbulence of any kind, a state may count as love, provided the appropriate beliefs, dispositions to behaviour, etc. are present.

But even considering cases other than love and hatred, we still do not get the desired contrast in varieties of justification. According to Warnock's concluding remarks, the proper form for a justification of emotion is 'to show that the object of the emotion is really of the kind which is commonly allowed to stimulate such an emotion' (1957, p. 58). But how does this differ from justifying an attitude, where 'to defend it or justify it is to point to the correctness of his opinion of that towards which he has the attitude'[10] (1957, p. 54)? And how does it differ from justifying a calm passion: 'Justification of a calm passion must consist in showing that what I feel to be virtuous does really and in a recognisable way deserve praise' (1957, p. 46)? In all these cases (omitting quibbles over irrelevant detail), I cite beliefs relevant to the emotion or attitude or calm passion and try to show that I have good grounds for holding those beliefs. Though the sort of involvement may differ, beliefs are involved in all, and justification is (largely) a matter of justifying those beliefs. But other dimensions of criticism (of emotions or attitudes or calm passions) exist. In the case of emotions, the beliefs may be justified, but may not be appropriate to the emotion one feels.

In these instances one's state of mind may have been misdescribed or confused, or otherwise inappropriate and unjustified. Or one's beliefs may be justified and one's feeling may be appropriate but felt to the wrong degree, too intense. These added dimensions also apply (with suitable modifications) to attitudes and calm passions. The last is least applicable to calm passions (though they may constitute too strong a motive in some cases), but that is partly why they are considered 'calm'. It is not an argument for not regarding them as passions. Degrees of turbulence provide a measure of intensity for emotions. If we say an emotion is too strongly felt, what may be meant is that it is out of proportion to the evidence for the relevant belief. The appropriate strength of the feeling may depend on the strength of the evidence ('too great a hope to build on such a slender reed'). More typically, for most emotions the type, rather than certainty, of belief will fix the appropriate strength of response. (If 'outrage' is a point on a scale of anger – though there is more involved than intensity of feeling – it may be justified by murder but not by certain lesser offences.) Most typically, if all we question is the appropriateness of strength of a feeling (and not the classification of the feeling as a type of emotion, etc.), we will be concerned with what is statistically normal. Consider the following statements. An inoffensive remark may cause an irascible man to lose his temper. The remark does not deserve the reaction, because in most people it would not produce it. Now both statements may be causal. They differ in that the first is associated with quantification over occasions in a particular man's life, and the second with quantification over men. In fact 'irascible' is definable in terms of deviation from the normal threshold of reaction. (Cf. 'the mild winter caused this sensitive plant to die' – I owe this point to David Pears.)

But Warnock does not focus on this sort of justification, even for violent emotions. As we have seen, to justify an emotion is 'to show that the object of the emotion is really of the kind which is commonly allowed to stimulate such an emotion' (1957, p. 57). Now what is 'commonly allowed' might depend on statistical regularities. But elsewhere she says that 'people are allowed by common ethical opinion to be angry in some reasonably well-defined situations' (Warnock, 1957, p. 56). And it is not clear that the permission of common ethical opinion does depend (merely) on what happens with observable regularity. Warnock also states 'the feeling can be justified only by being shown to have been caused by something which is generally permitted to inspire hatred, and therefore it must be cast in the form of an objective statement of agreed fact' (1957, p. 57). But this returns us to the contrast between 'agreed fact' and 'personal opinion', which was previously rejected. In fact, what is permitted or allowed to inspire hatred (or, the appropriateness of the object) may depend on the nature of hatred. The importance of characteristic beliefs to classification of mental states seems to enter into the justification of violent passions in as many ways as it does into calm.

For calm passions, Warnock claims that 'justification of one's calm passions would always consist in a description of the object of the passion, and an attempt to show that one's feelings were appropriate to their object' (1957, p. 54). In Warnock's type of feeling (in the narrow, turbulence, affect, or sensation sense) theory of emotions, to show that one's feelings are appropriate to their object *is* 'to show that the object of the emotion is really of the kind which is commonly allowed to stimulate such an emotion'. That, we have seen, is her formula for violent passions as well. The only sort of appropriateness in question is causal order, the order of natural law (statistical normality), and the danger to be averted is misnaming our feelings (we feel what we feel, but in certain circumstances we are more likely to feel what everyone else feels in such circumstances). The only other sort of failure amounts merely to eccentricity of feeling. Warnock herself puts differently the types of criticism of passions. Speaking of nameless emotions, unspecified agitations, she says we may be called on to defend them 'against the charge either of feeling any emotion at all, or of feeling too much' (Warnock, 1957, p. 55). The defence may be to describe the object which causes one to feel as one does or one may also try to specify more exactly what one feels. The justification may amount to an attempt to get the critic to share the feeling. But Warnock does not allow for other types of criticism and defence. She comes closest in the following passage:

> Let us consider a case now where the charge is that the emotion is unjustified or unwarranted or irrational (in the sense used of hope and fear). Here there may well be more of a genuine justification. We may try to justify feeling the particular emotion at all, by explaining further what the object of it is, by pointing out just exactly what it is which makes us angry or afraid. But in this case there may be further disagreement. I may not only point out to you what the hairdresser said to make me angry, but go on to argue that it is right, or at any rate all right to get angry if people make remarks of this kind. Here justification has gone beyond the mere specification or description of the object of the emotion; it has proceeded to the point of stating that the object is worthy of the effect it produced (Warnock, 1957, pp. 55–6).

And here is the oddity. How can a cause be 'worthy' of its effect? How can there be argument here? The effect follows or it does not. Warnock's example goes beyond the terms of her feeling theory and Hume's, for it requires a sense of appropriateness which goes beyond a regular relation of stimulus and response. And even if one can give 'worthy' a causal sense, as was done for 'deserve' in the case of the irascible man, and make it a matter of statistical normality, that will not work for all cases always; the principles of classification for mental states come into play (along with intensity, etc.). She gives an example of how the argument might continue: 'I may argue, for instance, that a remark of such and such a kind is worth getting angry about because it reveals a total misunderstanding, or because it is a threat to some well-established relationship, and so on.' I think she is perhaps right in saying that 'this is not an attempted justification of our behaviour, or our opinions, but of our feeling something or other on some specific occasion, perhaps only for a moment' (Warnock, 1957, p. 56). But it is not a justification for a feeling, exclusively. The feeling depends on a characteristic thought, and it is to that thought that charges of 'misunderstanding' etc. are relevant. To see this, imagine the argument taking a different course. I might stop at describing the hairdresser's remarks and say they constitute an insult, and then argue only about whether insults constitute appropriate objects of anger (leaving aside degree of anger, where Warnock's point about 'worthiness' may also have a place). Where someone is jealous, the justification of his emotion may just consist in justifying his opinion that he has been betrayed by one whose affections he had a right to believe were his own alone. Whether his behaviour and feelings might be shaken with his opinions is another and very large issue.

These points are also obscured because Warnock makes too much of the division between what she calls description and justification. She only concedes that we try to explain such feelings as love and hate 'by pointing out really lovable or hateful characteristics of the objects of the emotions, and this, as we saw, can sometimes be the first step towards justification' (Warnock, 1957, p. 57). But what she regards as the further steps required seem to go beyond the question of degree (is it normal to feel this strongly) to the issue of appropriateness (justifying having this emotion at all, having this one rather than some other), and this may be a matter of description. Justification may sometimes be description, especially where the criticism is that the emotion is out of place, inappropriate, or unwarranted, and especially where the description is of the grounds of the opinion that makes the emotion what it is. In this respect violent emotions are more like calm passions than unlike.

Warnock wants to contrast the role of opinion in attitudes and calm passions with its role in emotion: 'the most important difference between attitudes and emotions [is] that attitudes depend on some degree of thought, some assessment or appraisal of that towards which the attitude is directed' (1957, p. 52). We have been arguing that emotions, too, depend on thought of one type or another – the type of emotion depending on the content and nature of the thought involved – and assessment of the appropriateness of the object, or its influence on one's state, is of particular interest. In neither emotions nor attitudes need thought be restricted to some narrow form of 'personal opinion'. Warnock bases her contrast on the varying attacks that emotions, as opposed to attitudes, may be open to; but though we may admit that 'uncalled for' is out of place as a criticism of attitudes, that does not show that (more spontaneous) emotions do not involve thought. (For example, they can be unwarranted as well as merely excessive; the wrong emotion as well as too strong.) Warnock also suggests that because attitudes involve opinions they can be 'contradictory or illogical'; whereas emotions, not involving thoughts, cannot: 'At most they can be conflicting, but the conflict is between themselves' (1957, p. 53). Here one encounters the same problem we met in Hume: how can feelings be given vectors so that they can conflict? It is also unclear what the point of 'but the conflict is between themselves' is supposed to be. In the case of attitudes, where the conflict is presumably not 'between themselves', to say someone's attitude is contradictory or illogical 'means that what he professes as his opinion contradicts what one would infer his opinion to be from the way he behaves, e.g. "For a Communist, your attitude to the Public Schools is most illogical" ' (Warnock, 1957, p. 53). Here the conflict is presumably between opinions. But how is this story different from 'For someone who professes to hate her, your jealousy is most illogical'? The same tension between what is claimed in speech and what is revealed in action appears. The man who has an attitude need profess his opinion no more than one who has an emotion, and no more inference is needed to see that the opinion revealed by the behaviour of the man with an emotion yields a contradiction than that of the man with an attitude. For emotions, a conflict between professed opinion and behaviour of the sort described, may be more liable to be labelled 'insincerity' than 'illogicality', but the place of beliefs in emotions remains.

Hume himself allows reason (thought) small power to change emotions, mainly because he gives it no place in the nature of emotions. As we have seen, he isolated emotions as impressions of reflexion from the points where the place of thought can be most clearly seen: in connection with object and action. He says explicitly:

A passion is an original existence, or, if you will, modification of existence, and contains not any representative quality, which renders it a copy of any other existence or modification. When I am angry, I am actually possest with the passion, and in that emotions have no more a reference to any other object, than when I am thirsty, or sick, or more than five foot high. 'Tis impossible, therefore, that this passion can be oppos'd by, or be contradictory to truth and reason; since this contradiction consists in the disagreement of ideas, consider'd as copies, with those objects, which they represent (*THN*, II, p. 415).

It is a mistake to restrict thought to representation, but even with that restriction, it should be seen that thoughts have more of a role in emotions than they do in sensations. One's conception of one's state and of its causes are important elements in making one's state what it is and discriminating it from other states. Many errors can be made here, and these mistakes are open to correction by reason. According to Hume, however, there are very few points and ways in which reason can enter:

> passions can be contrary to reason only so far as they are *accompany'd* with some judgment or opinion. According to this principle, which is so obvious and natural, 'tis only in two senses, that any affection can be call'd unreasonable. First, When a passion, such as hope or fear, grief or joy, despair or security, is founded on the supposition of the existence of objects, which really do not exist. Secondly, When in exerting any passion in action, we chuse means insufficient for the design'd end, and deceive ourselves in our judgment of causes and effects. Where a passion is neither founded on false suppositions, nor chuses means insufficient for the end, the understanding can neither justify nor condemn it. . . . In short, a passion must be accompany'd with some false judgment, in order to its being unreasonable; and even then 'tis not the passion, properly speaking, which is unreasonable, but the judgment (*THN*, II, p. 416; cf. III, pp. 458–9).

An emotion being 'founded on' a thought, however, seems more intimate than its merely being 'accompany'd' by one. Within the passage the founding must bear a causal interpretation, and as we have seen, having certain sorts of causes can be essential to the identity of an emotion. If thoughts have no special place in emotions, then reasons should have no special place in emotions. And in that case criticisms based on the goodness or badness of a person's reasons for his emotion (warranted or unwarranted, justified or unjustified, reasonable or unreasonable) should have no more place with emotions than with sensations. But Hume acknowledges that such criticisms have some (though limited) place. And he cannot explain that place if the thought is merely an accompaniment, even a causal accompaniment, of the emotion. For then bodily sensations might be deemed reasonable or unreasonable in the same way. 'If my headache is caused by the belief that my fortune has been lost, no one would be tempted to judge my headache unreasonable on the grounds that my belief is so' (Pitcher, 1965, pp. 229–30). Even if reasons are (special forms of) causes, not all causes are reasons. Hume fails to reveal what is special about thoughts which cause emotions, and gives no hint at all that thoughts *about* what causes an emotion (our beliefs about the explanation of our state) are especially important.

In fact, Hume tries to deny that, *speaking properly*, emotions are reasonable or unreasonable, justified or unjustified, at all. If they really were mere sensations, it would make no sense to speak of them in that way. And, as Pitcher argues, this itself is ground for rejecting Hume's view: 'the View does not allow the notions of reasonableness and justifiability to gain any foothold in the concept of an emotion' (Pitcher, 1965, p. 330). Hume's account of the foothold it does in fact have in his theory is thoroughly confused. Cases of misjudging the means required to achieve an end when putting an emotion into action (e.g. revenge), are not cases of 'unreasonable emotion'. And the other sort of intellectual mistake he allows, a mistake about existence, is too narrow to cover the field. As Pitcher argues, one may be mistaken about the existence of an object, without the emotion's being unreasonable (one can have good grounds for believing something, but none the less be wrong). And more important, there are many other ways in which an emotion may be unreasonable, and however strictly one speaks, the emotion itself (as well as the judgment) may be called unreasonable. (In Pitcher's example of a spinster frightened of a nonexistent threat: 'her judgment is indeed unreasonable, but so is her fear. To be sure, the feelings of her stomach turning over and her heart racing cannot be called unreasonable, but neither are they her fear', 1965, pp. 330–1.) Pitcher catalogues some of the additional forms of unreasonableness (baseless or unfounded fear, irrational fear, superstitious fear, silly, vain or neurotic fear, abnormal or inordinate fear). There is no need to go through the matter in detail at this point. The Humean approach cannot account for the varieties of unreasonableness of emotions. It does not allow for the varieties of criticism and mistake that emotions are open to in virtue of involving beliefs, and so cannot allow reason an important place in changing emotions. This is especially clear where the emotion is inappropriate (e.g. fear of baby lambs) because the characteristic belief is absent or untenable.

It is perhaps worth repeating that a Humean, in the sense of causal, account of the emotion/object relation does not preclude all sorts of 'justification' for emotions. Some sorts are explicable within that scheme. (And I do not wish to object to that scheme except in so far as it is claimed to be a total account.) As with the anger of an irascible man, or exaggerated fear, we can make sense of an object's not 'deserving' a particular emotional response in terms of its being outside of the statistical norm. The response may be exaggerated in relation to how people usually respond to such provocations. Justification and appropriateness (in another sense) can also find place, as Hume suggests, if we bring in the creature's ends or purposes in action.

Consider first a non-emotional response. Suppose we ask whether or not a creature's behaviour in a particular situation is appropriate.

The criteria of appropriateness will be determined by the creature's ends of action. As an approximation, the behaviour will be appropriate to the situation if behaving in that way in that situation is likely to achieve the creature's ends. . . . Where emotional responses to objects are concerned, the criteria of appropriateness may sometimes be partly determined by reference to the responder's ends. Thus fear of an object is reasonable or appropriate if the object is likely to harm the responder in some way. Of course in the case of most emotions, the criteria of appropriateness are not wholly determined by reference to ends, and in the case of responses to works of art, perhaps not at all. Nevertheless, whether the criteria can be applied does not depend on the response being causally undetermined (Wilson, 1972, pp. 86–7).

I think Wilson's point is largely correct, but if it is really a point about a functional sense of appropriateness, he makes it in a misleading manner when he continues: 'Here is one difference between an emotion produced by a work of art and an emotion produced by a drug. A drug produces an invariant effect, so there is no room for saying that one effect is more appropriate than another' (1972, p. 87). It is not because the effects of art are erratic that there is room for appropriateness in art. (Indeed, the emotional qualities of art do not, in general, depend on its effects. A piece of music need not make *me* sad in order for *it* to be sad.) The effects of drugs, whether invariant or not, may be as *functionally* appropriate or useful as those produced by other causes. If drugs produce emotions, it can only be by producing appropriate beliefs. If the appropriate beliefs are not involved (whether produced by a drug or not), a state would not be a particular emotion. The emotion produced will not be invariant unless the belief is. There is a constraint placed on the causal manipulation of emotions by the cognitive element. This fact emerges clearly in the experimental work of Schacter and Singer (1962) and other psychologists. The state of mind a subject reports will depend importantly on his beliefs about its cause. Belief aims at truth, and certain explanations of how one came to be inclined to believe something are incompatible with one's regarding one's inclination as amounting to a belief (e.g. drug-induced belief) (Hampshire, 1967, cf. 1965, p. 87ff.). Any emotion depending on the belief being fully a belief will thereby be modified, and one's state will have to be redescribed as one dissociates from the 'belief' on which it depends.

Still there is a functional sense of appropriateness, at least where emotions involve inclinations to action or states of readiness. As one writer puts it: 'A man's emotions are reasonable when, in view of the man's beliefs, doubts, or conjectures, the form of readiness they involve is likely to be effective and necessary. When they involve inadequate or superfluous preparations, his feelings are unreasonable' (Thalberg, 1964, p. 222). As we shall see, this sense of appropriateness plays at least a part in Spinoza's notion of active emotion. But there are other ways in which emotions may be reasonable or unreasonable. This we have already seen, and it will become even clearer as we bring out further aspects of the classification of emotions and the importance of beliefs. So reason need not be merely the slave of the passions. It may be a part of them, a part that can move the whole.

HUME'S CLASSIFICATION OF THE PASSIONS*

PRIMARY
Sheerly instinctive passions arising from 'a natural impulse or instinct, which is perfectly unaccountable' (439) and not from precedent perceptions of pleasure and pain:

Violent (i.e. not calm): 'the desire of punishment to our enemies, and of happiness to our friends; hunger, lust, and a few other bodily appetites' (439)

Calm: 'benevolence and resentment, the love of life, and kindness to children' (417)

SECONDARY
(Impressions of reflexion) founded on preceding impressions of pleasure and pain:

Direct
Violent: 'desire, aversion, grief, joy, hope, fear, despair and security' (277) 'along with volition' (399, 438, 574)

Calm: 'the general appetite to good, and aversion to evil, consider'd merely as such' (417)

(Kemp Smith) moral and aesthetic sentiments as proceeding from the contemplation of actions and external objects 'the sense of beauty and deformity in action, composition, and external objects' (276)

Indirect
Arising from preceding impressions of pleasure and pain, but by conjunction with additional qualities:

Violent: pride, humility, love, hatred, ambition, vanity, envy, pity, malice, generosity, 'with their dependents' (276–7)

Calm: (Árdal) approval and disapproval of persons

* See Kemp Smith, 1941, p. 168; and Árdal, 1966, pp. 10–11.

II
Spinoza

When I speak of Spinoza's or the Spinozist view of the mind and the mental, I shall be referring to two main emphases: the importance of thought in the identification and discrimination of emotions and other mental states, and the importance of reflexive knowledge in changing those states. It is these two theses, and not some of Spinoza's more famous metaphysical doctrines, that I am concerned to explore.

Conatus and Unconscious Desire

Spinoza considers all emotions to be analysable on the basis of three basic or primary emotions: pleasure, pain, and desire. Each of these concepts must be understood in the special sense given to it within his system, and to understand that sense one must understand that system (to a certain extent) as a whole. Behind each of the three central concepts, and so behind all emotion, is the notion of the *conatus*. Spinoza tells us: 'Each thing, in so far as it is in itself, endeavours to persevere in its being' (*Ethics*, Part III, proposition 6). This endeavour is the *conatus*. Such a claim about an 'endeavour' ('tendency', 'drive', or 'effort') towards self-preservation might be seen as a straightforward empirical observation; indeed, in other authors it generally would be. But within the Spinozist system the *conatus* is far more than a Hobbesian 'first law of nature', it is a logical principle;[1] it applies to all things (not just men), and is in fact what distinguishes one thing from another ('actual essence').

But how can one deduce an 'effort' from a logic of individuation? The force of the argument is basically simple: What we have before us does not constitute a distinct individual unless it does exhibit a *conatus*, an effort to maintain itself as a coherent unit. The actual argument is more subtle and more difficult. In the *Ethics*, Part III, proposition 7, the argument equating essence with *conatus* seems to be that whatever we do (actively), which by the previous proposition is equated with the *conatus*, must follow from our nature or essence – following from our nature or essence is what it means for us to actively do. If desires constitute our essence, then our actions must flow from our desires (to be our actions, rather than passive responses). This argument puts the abstract point in words closer to our understanding of human behaviour. It also has the virtue of referring us back (for the proof of 'nor are things able to do anything else than what necessarily follows from their determinate nature') to an earlier proposition (*E*, I, prop. 29) where the distinction between *natura naturans* and *natura naturata* is introduced. (Incidentally, Spinoza tells us that emotions are part of *natura naturata – E*, I, prop. 31.) This distinction, I think, may make clearer how something static, as essence is traditionally thought to be, can yield dynamic effort. Perhaps essence and effort can be taken as two aspects or points of view, as part of a larger division under two aspects, of what is a single thing.

The nature of the *conatus* must, I am afraid, remain relatively obscure until its role in the system, in particular its relation to Spinoza's central distinction between the active and the passive, can be explained. Nevertheless, a bit more about the *conatus* and the endeavour of self-preservation can be said at this point.[2] The destruction of a thing is not something *it* can (actively) do to itself, it is something it must (passively) suffer as the effect of external causes (*E*, III, prop. 4). If its essence (and all *action* must flow from essence) included its destruction, it would be self-contradictory and could not exist at all. Given the essence, you must have the thing, so given the thing, you must have a thing which 'in so far as it is in itself, endeavours to persevere in its being'. Hence this 'endeavour' is simply another name for the 'given' or 'actual' essence of the thing. Though it might seem implausible that given a thing it must be maintaining itself, it will seem less implausible if we remember that the endeavour at self-maintenance just *is* the thing; and anything else, including possible endeavours at self-destruction, must be regarded as external (outside its essence). Without the endeavour at self-maintenance, one would not have a distinct thing, there would be no clear way of marking off the boundaries that individuate it. Without the *conatus*, all might collapse into a whirl of constant interaction, into a disorganized flux. The *conatus* fits into Spinoza's scheme of finite modes (particular things) within a single all-embracing substance. At a more concrete level, the *conatus* can be understood in Spinoza's terms as a balance of motion-and-rest, and in modern terms as, for instance, 'homeostasis'. Our concern is with the more abstract interpretation. As Hampshire explains it:

> Each particular thing, interacting with other particular things within the common order of Nature, exhibits a characteristic tendency to cohesion and to the preservation of its identity, a 'striving (*conatus*), so far as it lies in itself to do so, to persist in its own being' (*Ethics* Pt III. Prop. VI). This striving towards cohesion and the preservation of its own identity constitutes the essence of any particular thing, in the only sense in which particular things, which are not substances, can be said to have essences. Particular things, being dependent modes and not substances, are constantly undergoing changes of state as the effects of causes other than themselves; as they are not self-determining substances, their successive states cannot be deduced from their own essence alone, but must be explained partly by reference to the action upon them of other particular things. Each particular thing possesses a determinate nature of its own only in so far as it is active and not passive in relation to things other than itself, that is, only in so far as its states can be explained otherwise than as the effects of external causes; only so far as a thing is an originating cause – can any individuality, any determinate nature of its own, be attributed to it. Its character

and individuality depend on its necessarily limited power of self-maintenance. It can be distinguished as a unitary thing with a recognizable constancy of character in so far as, although a system of parts, it succeeds in maintaining its own characteristic coherence and balance of parts. (pp. 58-59) . . . Within Spinoza's definitions, therefore, it is necessarily true that every finite thing, including a human being, endeavours to preserve itself and to increase its power of self-maintenance. The *conatus* is a necessary feature of everything in Nature, because this tendency to self-maintenance is involved in the definition of what it is to be a distinct and identifiable thing (Hampshire, 1956, p. 93).

In the case of man, the *conatus* takes the form of desire. Joachim expounds Spinoza's reasoning with some clarity:

> Man is a particular thing, whose essence is constituted by modes of Extension and Thought. So far therefore as lies in him, man will tend to persist in his corporeal and mental being. And this 'conatus' is man's 'appetitus,' or 'will-to-be.' Thus man's 'appetitus' is simply his essence 'from which there necessarily follow all those actions which tend to his self-maintenance.' As man's essence is mental as well as corporeal, and as thought is by its very nature turned upon itself, this 'effort' in man is often an object of his consciousness: – i.e., man not only tends to maintain his corporeal and mental being, but is (or may be) also conscious of this tendency. In order to mark this characteristic of man's 'conatus,' Spinoza uses the term 'cupiditas' (desire) in preference to 'appetitus.' For the presence of self-consciousness, he thinks, makes no difference. 'Desire' – like any blind effort – is merely the tendency to self-affirmation which the essence of the desiring thing involves. Hence the term 'cupiditas' covers the whole range of human self-affirmation. It includes all so-called 'efforts, instincts, impulses, desires, and volitions.' (*E*, III, 9 S.; III, Aff. Deff., 1 Expl.) (Joachim, 1901, p. 193.)

In considering the relation between Spinoza and Freud (though we shall be more concerned with Freud as a crypto-Spinozist than with Spinoza as an anticipator of Freud) it is important to note that for Spinoza desire need not be self-conscious. When it is not, it is 'appetite'. Though Spinoza's system does not fit unconscious desires into a larger theory of unconscious mental processes that explains their origins and mechanisms, though he has no theory of repression and defence, still his system does leave room for the unconscious. Hume's, in contrast, does not. What sense can be made, in Hume's system, of unfelt feelings? In his terms, impressions of which we are unaware (and emotions are impressions) must be nonsense. Spinoza may not only leave room for the unconscious, he may even contribute to our understanding of the notion.

Since the place of unconscious desire in man, in Spinoza's system, can be seen as problematic, it is important to discuss it in more detail at this point. Unconscious desire or 'appetite' is a motive to action ('appetite is the essence itself of man in so far as it is determined to such acts as contribute to his preservation' – *E*, III, definitions of the emotions 1 explanation, and III, prop. 9, note); and in this respect Spinoza sees no difference between human appetite and desire: 'For whether a man be conscious of his appetite or not, it remains one and the same appetite. . . .' (It does not necessarily follow, however, that consciousness and thought about desire – even unconscious desire – cannot affect desire; this is a large matter to which we shall have to return.) Spinoza avoids defining desire solely in terms of appetite or determination to action in order to allow for the possibility of consciousness. But it might seem that, within Spinoza's system, that possibility is a necessity for man. 'Appetite' is a technical term in Spinoza, and though it may apply to some things other than men, it might be that men have only appetites of which they are conscious, i.e. desires. It seems, by Part II, prop. 23, that the mind is necessarily conscious of itself through the ideas of the modifications of the body. Spinoza, somewhat obscurely but still coherently, regards the human mind as the idea of the human body (*E*, II, prop. 13). Without further explaining or elaborating this famous mind–body parallelism and its relation to Spinoza's metaphysics and epistemology, we can also note that he believes that 'nothing can happen in that body which is not perceived by the mind' (*E*, II, prop. 12). The mind is necessarily aware of the body's modifications. But this 'awareness' (in the cases which concern us) still produces only appetite, which, Spinoza tells us (*E*, III, prop. 9, note), is one of those terms which relates to both mind and body. We do not, so far, have self-consciousness. For that, a further step is required, ideas of ideas. And that step, while always possible to humans, may not be necessary.[3]

Instead of defining desire, as he does appetite, as straightforwardly 'the essence itself of man in so far as it is considered as determined to any action', Spinoza complicates his definition by adding that desire is the essence 'in so far as it is conceived as determined to any action *by any one of his modifications*' (*E*, III, def. emo. 1 expl.). This definition thus includes reference to the cause or condition of consciousness of appetite. By Part II, prop. 23, the mind knows itself by perceiving the *ideas* of the modifications of the body. Though the ideas of the modifications of the body are part of the essence of the human mind, by the previous proposition, it is only the ideas of those ideas which constitute *knowledge* of the human mind, i.e. self-knowledge or self-consciousness or (in the cases which concern us) conscious desire. This second-order knowledge is always inadequate (*E*, II, prop. 29), but our initial question still remains: is it necessary? Can men only have appetites of which they are conscious?

It might still seem that Spinoza is driven by his definitions, against his deeper intentions, to answer 'Yes'. For according to Part II, prop. 21, the idea of the mind has the same relation to the mind as the mind itself has to the body and 'it follows . . . that the idea of the mind and the mind itself exist . . . from the same necessity. . . .' (This point is repeated at the end of the demonstration of prop. 22.) So it would seem that to have an idea would also be, of necessity, to have an idea of that idea – that is, to be self-conscious. So Spinoza does seem driven to deny that desires can exist unaccompanied by consciousness of those desires. But I believe that this position arises from incoherencies within the system, and I think an interpretation can be found which, while rejecting the inconsistent premises, preserves the central insights. The notion that the idea of the mind and the mind itself are equally necessary is mistaken. Spinoza says it follows from the fact that 'the idea of the mind . . . and the mind itself are one and the same thing, *which is considered under one and the same attribute*, that of thought'. This putative fact is supposed to derive from the corresponding fact 'that the idea of the body and the body, that is to say, the mind and the body, are one and the same individual which *at one time is considered under* the attribute of thought, and *at another under* that of extension'. (My emphasis.) While I find this last fact obscure, the corresponding putative fact is wholly unintelligible: how can one thing appear different when viewed from a *single* point of view ('under one and the same attribute')? Even were we to accept it (assuming we understand it), we could still doubt the apparent consequence that we are always conscious of our appetites; for this would presumably follow 'just as a person who knows anything by that very fact knows that he knows, and knows that he knows that he knows, and so on *ad infinitum*'. This endless reflexive awareness of knowledge is arguably illusory (Woozley and others give the arguments), but in any case cannot be meant to entail an infinity of thoughts. According to Spinoza, 'we can affirm an infinite number of things (one after the other, for we cannot affirm an infinite number of things at once)' (*E*, II, prop. 49, note). So the infinity of thoughts would have to be consecutive. But then it appears we would still be engaged on thinking elaborations of some first thought. And there is no alternative to consecutiveness. Even if Spinoza allowed it the thoughts could not be simultaneous, for so many thoughts would be unthinkable. Perhaps one could have recourse here to the claim that all the thoughts would be aspects of one individual and so really would be one and the same thing. But that claim remains unintelligible, for one must respond 'aspects of an individual what?' If the answer is an 'individual thought', additions of 'knows' and 'awareness' into the thoughts cannot leave them the same thoughts. One must then reject the iterated knowings on metaphysical, if not epistemological, grounds.

So perhaps all Spinoza is committed to (though his formulation would then be at the least misleading) is the openness of any idea or knowledge (of the body or otherwise) to awareness or knowledge, but not to the necessity of such higher-order awareness or knowledge. (That the claim is about potentiality may be marked by Spinoza's use of the word 'form' in the statement: 'the idea of the mind, that is to say, the idea of the idea, is nothing but the form of the idea in so far as this is considered as a mode of thought and without relation to the object . . .' – E, II, prop. 21, note.) Even mere openness will constitute a difficulty, however, when we shift the discussion to psychoanalytic theory. For how accessible an unconscious idea or desire is to consciousness must depend (to some extent) on one's theory of how it came to be unconscious in the first place, and it may require quite special techniques and conditions to make the potential knowledge real and effective.

2
Pleasure and Pain and the Spinozist Analysis of Love

Pleasure and pain (*laetitiae et tristitiae*) can be understood as passive mental states of transition, increase or decrease of power. The power (perfection or vitality) in question is basically the power of self-maintenance, i.e. the effectiveness of the *conatus*. In the case of man this would be the power of thought and the parallel power of action (change in one, within Spinoza's system, is inevitably also change in the other – E, III, prop. 11). He defines pleasure as 'man's passage from a less to a greater perfection' and pain as 'man's passage from a greater to a less perfection' (E, III, def. emo. 2 and 3). These states are produced as a result of the changing proportions of our thought, feeling, and behaviour that have explanations which trace back to our own nature, as opposed to external causes.

These notions of pleasure and pain are to be distinguished from those more specific types of pleasure and pain which relate to the body. Spinoza speaks of 'pleasurable excitement' (*titillatio*) or 'cheerfulness' (*hilaritas*) and 'painful suffering' (*dolor*) or 'melancholy' (*melancholia*). These latter notions are much closer to Humean impressions, and seem to name localized sensations or (more pervasive) moods. Spinoza, by making distinctions, is able to avoid the difficulties which arise from the Humean assimilation of all types of pleasure to impressions of pleasure. By treating pleasure and pain as states of the whole individual, Spinoza also leaves open how pleasure might be interpreted on closer analysis (i.e. as a form of attention, feeling . . .).

Pleasure, pain, and desire are Spinoza's three primary emotions. They are not primary or basic in the sense in which Hume takes impressions and ideas to be basic, for they are definable (as we have just seen). Rather, Spinoza's claim is that all other emotions can be explained as arising out of these three. A Spinozist account of an emotion looks very different from a Humean. For instance, in the case of love, Hume gives us a picture of a complex mechanism of double association of impressions and ideas producing a simple and undefinable indirect impression of reflexion which is the emotion. Spinoza tells us that love is 'pleasure accompanied with the idea of an external cause' (*E*, III, prop. 13, note; and def. emo. 6). The nature and implications of Spinoza's method of analysis can be better appreciated through a more detailed contrast with Hume's.

It will be recalled that pleasure and pain were central to Hume's approach. The following paragraph can serve as a brief reminder of their role:

> In outline the theory is simple. Pleasure and pain cause the direct
> passions of desire and aversion, hope and fear, grief and joy.
> When pleasure or pain is specially related to a particular person
> it produces an indirect passion, love or hatred if the particular
> person is someone else, pride or humility if it is oneself. The
> indirect passions are extended through sympathy to cover cases
> where the pleasures and pains are not our own. Finally, the
> variations in sympathy due to subjective factors and special
> circumstances are corrected by general rules, much as our
> judgments of colors, sizes, and shapes are corrected. Moral
> sentiments are species of love, hatred, pride, and shame, restricted
> to qualities of mind, extended by sympathy, and objectified by
> 'general rules' (Macnabb, 1969, p. 127).

As we have already noted, the sense of pleasure and pain involved is basically some specific sensation, in contrast to Spinoza's view. Also, there is no effort in Hume to construct more complex emotions out of more simple constituent emotions, for each emotion is already as simple as it could be; each emotion is in fact a specific type of pleasure or pain distinguishable only on the basis of feeling. In the Humean system pleasure and pain play a role in the causal history of the emotion (except where the emotion is one of the 'primary' emotions), and appear again as the form of the emotion itself. But in Spinoza, pleasure and pain are elements in the emotion – constituents – and the discrimination of emotions depends on the type of thought involved.

The role of causality in the analyses is also very different. The notion of 'cause' does not appear *in* Hume's analysis of the emotion itself, for in itself the emotion is not analysable at all, the causal relations are just among the attending circumstances. But causal beliefs appear inside rather than outside Spinoza's analysis, for the subject's idea of the external cause is an essential constituent of his love. One should be careful to distinguish ideas (beliefs, or thoughts) which appear *inside* emotions from ideas about emotions. The latter will be ideas of ideas, and even they do not correspond precisely to Humean impressions of reflexion. One should also not be misled by Spinoza's use of the word 'idea'. In Spinoza's sense, an 'idea' is not an image or feeling, and unlike a Humean impression or idea, it can express a whole thought or proposition. (This contrast is interesting in relation to Freud, who seems to hover in his use of 'idea' between some concrete, exorcizable, image and a more Spinozist notion corresponding to 'belief'.) Where Hume's system of external causal relations brings in an object of the emotion, it is an 'object' of the emotion only in being present and produced by it and therefore a concomitant object of attention. But as we have seen, the thought of the loved object cannot simply accompany some essential core of the emotion. The object, to be an 'object of emotion', must be thought of as in some way the object *of* love, a part of the explanation of one's state as a whole. In Spinoza's analysis, the object of love appears in the idea of the cause and so is in some sense internal to the emotion. The problem of clarifying this concept of 'object' of emotion and the form of internality or intentionality it involves, may perhaps be reduced to the more general question of the intentionality of the constituent beliefs. And, as Pitcher argues (1965, p. 339), to show that the problem is really part of a more general problem is, in a sense, to solve it. The important point for us is that Spinoza's approach brings out the dependence of the state, and our characterization of the state, on the subject's beliefs, in particular his beliefs about the state. This dependence is the main element of Spinoza's analysis that allows a role for reason in relation to the emotions. The place Spinoza gives to reason is perhaps the sharpest contrast with Hume, and the most illuminating in understanding the power and limits of Freud's technique.

Spinoza, like Hume, is interested in the laws of the working of the mind. For him there is a discoverable order to our emotions, and knowledge in this area is not only of intellectual interest, it is essential to our freedom and happiness. (Our beliefs about the nature of emotions may even affect what emotions we can have.) Spinoza, unlike Hume, does not confine himself to unanalysable impressions and a mechanical association of ideas in his discussion of emotions and their laws. Hume is so restricted by his epistemology. Spinoza accords association its place. He acknowledges that ideas follow on the appearance of ideas that have accompanied them in the past, or on the appearance of similar ideas (*E*, III, props 14, 16, which correspond to Hume's principles of association by contiguity and resemblance). As the result of such connections on the level of imagination, anything can come to seem a source of pleasure or pain (*E*, III, prop. 15). Hence, for example, we can come to love what is associated with something which is in fact associated with pleasure, though we may be mistaken when we take the first thing as the external cause of our pleasure. Spinoza in fact thinks that the succession of our ideas and emotions in accordance with the principles of imagination, the laws of association, is our normal (i.e. usual) condition. But he also thinks this suffering from our haphazard histories can, to some extent, be overcome. His epistemology provides for a contrasting state in which we are not the passive observers of impressions and ideas, the witnesses of our emotional lives. He derives from his distinction between inadequate ideas (imagination) and adequate ideas (intellect) his central distinction between active and passive emotion, a distinction that does not exist in the Humean scheme.

3
Active/Passive and the Intellectual Love of God

Descartes, in *The Passions of the Soul*, divides all thoughts into actions and passions of the soul. The will or desire, whether it has an abstract object or terminates in some motion of the body, is active. The ground for this classification is that 'we find by experience that [desires] proceed directly from our soul, and appear to depend on it alone' (Descartes, 1649, art. 17). All other thoughts, which are perceptions, are passive 'because it is often not our soul which makes them what they are, and because it always receives them from the things which are represented by them'. According to Descartes, we are necessarily aware of our desires, 'For it is certain that we cannot desire anything without perceiving by the same means that we desire it; and, although in regard to our soul it is an action to desire something, we may say that it is also one of its passions to perceive that it desires' (1649, art. 19). The emotions, or passions strictly so called, are treated very much as Humean impressions; Descartes regards them as perceptions relating to the soul alone 'whose effects we feel as though they were in the soul itself, and as to which we do not usually know any proximate cause to which we may relate them: such are the feelings of joy, anger . . .' (1649, art. 25). For Descartes, the emotions are one and all always passive.

Spinoza's distinction between active and passive is importantly different. A type of emotion (e.g. love) may in particular cases be sometimes passive, sometimes active. And the differences between Spinoza's and Descartes' distinctions can be seen to derive from deep metaphysical differences rather than superficial disagreements in terminology. For both, it may be said that actions are 'what I do'. But they differ in the notion of 'I' involved. Descartes identifies the person with his thinking element (*sum res cogitans*) or soul as opposed to his body. I am my thoughts, but most centrally I am my will, for that alone is totally within my control and depends only upon my soul. So only desires can be actions of mine, desires alone are attributable and ultimately explainable by reference only to my soul. Spinoza rejects Descartes' crude and unworkable mind-body dualism. Action, as opposed to passion, is still that which depends upon *me*, that which is ultimately explainable by reference to my nature, but my essence is no longer restricted to modes of the infinite attribute of thought, i.e. mind. The contrast is no longer between dependence on my soul and dependence on my body, but between explanation by reference to my nature as a person (an individual mind-body) and explanation by reference to causes in the external world. The will, far from being the centre of free activity, is dismissed by Spinoza as an illusion engendered by ignorance of causes. The contrast of volitions with other thoughts he considers illusory – all are part of the necessary order of thought. Explanation is never-ending; an emotion is active not if its explanation terminates in some act of will, but if the chain of causes includes nothing external to my nature.

The last formulation may seem misleading. For if I love or fear some particular person or thing, must not the particular object of my love or fear appear in any complete account of my emotion, and would not that object be external to my nature? How can emotion, then, ever be active?

Let us look more closely at the case of love. According to Spinoza, a man will be said to love a thing if he feels pleasure which he attributes to that thing as its cause. But a fuller understanding of the order of nature would reveal that he and the object are but limited parts of nature, and that the thing is just one member of an infinite chain of causes and only one of an indefinite number of conditions necessary to his pleasure (or there may even be unthought of sufficient conditions outside of the object). There is no one thing which is *the* cause, the belief that such a thing exists is the result of the working of imagination and an inadequate knowledge of causes. Love, where the pleasure involved is pleasurable excitement, may be excessive (*E*, IV, prop. 44) ; but the serious defect which arises from inadequate understanding is bondage to the passive play of fantasy in our emotional lives. When we imagine the objects of our emotions to be free and self-determining sufficient causes, we ourselves become the unfree victims of contingent external causes. This is our situation when our emotions are directed towards particular things as their objects. But an awareness of the necessary incompleteness of our knowledge of causes contains within itself the beginnings of the transformation of our emotions into active states. In so far as an emotion is constituted by the thought of an external cause, the rejection of that thought as false is the destruction of that emotion (*E*, V, prop. 2; III, prop. 48).

Within Spinoza's theory of knowledge, falsity is a matter of degree rather than (in his language) a 'positive' characteristic. The recognition of a belief as false depends upon its contrast with a more comprehensive and coherent thought, false ideas simply being partial and low-level perceptions of the truth. This notion of levels calls for explication, and the call becomes more urgent when we see the consequences of the epistemological position. In the case of love, the progressive addition to our idea of the cause and the decreasing inadequacy of that idea eventually transforms our pleasure from the love of a particular to the love of something else: ultimately, God or Nature. These interchangeable terms include the whole of the causal order, and in so far as we intuitively comprehend it (under the attribute of Thought) we, in our mental aspect (it is difficult to imagine what the necessary physical correlate would be), reflect and become assimilated to and identified with that whole. In this mystical state, what Spinoza calls 'the intellectual love of God', we are truly free and self-determining and our emotion is wholly active. But in order to become active our love has had to cease to be the love of a particular. In order to flow fully from our own nature, we have had to assimilate the whole of Nature (under the aspect of Thought) and become our own object. In this case the object, the cause, the mind, and the emotion are all free for they are all one. So it looks as though the whole of nature may be the only object of active emotion, despite the fact that Spinoza seems to imply that the active emotions could range more widely in their objects. It also looks as though active emotions may be limited to love, indeed, to this single mystical intellectual love. Spinoza has already argued (*E*, III, prop. 59) that 'amongst all the emotions which are related to the mind in so far as it acts, there are none which are not related to joy or desire' – in so far as we contemplate the whole of God or Nature our only response can be pleasure (for our power of thought is then at its greatest), and in so far as that is the only object of an active emotion that emotion must be love. So it would appear that the active emotional life of a free man would be a life without hate, jealousy, fear, etc., but also without hope, devotion, compassion, pride, shame, regret, benevolence, etc., or even love of particular things.

4

More Adequate Ideas and Activity

As a picture of the ultimate extrapolation of Spinoza's principles connected with active emotions the previous interpretation may be correct. But a closer examination of some of his central notions will reveal that his principles can be more helpfully applied to our own emotional lives if the impossible extrapolation to the case of the wholly free man is set aside.

Perhaps the most central concept is that of an adequate idea or cause. We can here concentrate on the notion of an adequate idea. It is tempting to over-rationalize this notion, to require the strong sort of necessity that Spinoza continually associates with it. An adequate idea has within itself all the marks of truth (*E*, II, def. 4). There is no need to check for a correspondence with some external object. From this criterion, the closest modern notion would appear to be logical or analytic truth. But this interpretation would, I think, be too narrow. Most importantly, Spinoza accepts degrees of adequacy and inadequacy, and logical truth is meant to be an all or nothing affair. In his clearest discussion of the distinction (concerning our knowledge of the sun) this point is well illustrated. Falsity consists in the privation of knowledge; the more comprehensive and coherent the theory of which an idea forms a part the less inadequate it is; the confused images of sensation and imagination being most inadequate of all:

> When we look at the sun, we imagine his distance from us to be about 200 feet; the error not consisting solely in the imagination, but arising from our not knowing what the true distance is when we imagine, and what are the causes of our imagination. For although we may afterwards know that the sun is more than 600 diameters of the earth distant from us, we still imagine it near us, since we imagine it to be so near, not because we are ignorant of its true distance, but because a modification of our body involves the essence of the sun in so far as our body itself is affected by it (*E*, II, prop. 35, note).

We can see in this passage that the displacement of inadequate ideas by more adequate ones (and so of passive emotions by more active ones) is not a simple process. Inadequate ideas are not baseless and passive emotions are not without strength. This discussion also presents the even more important consequence that the adequacy of our ideas and so the activity of our emotions depends on their relation to a more or less adequate system of beliefs about what we need or want as self-maintaining beings.

Perhaps absolute adequacy does require knowledge of what amounts to logical necessities forming an intuitive science; and so absolute freedom, as freedom from external causes, would also be freedom from emotions. But in striving for that (unattainable) state, freedom and adequacy must be matters of degree, and control of our emotional lives must depend on the requirements of human nature. So 'activity' is tied to our *conatus*, our desires and needs as self-maintaining individuals, and our more or less systematic beliefs about those desires and needs.

Spinoza's distinction between active and passive mental states derives directly from his epistemological distinction between adequate and inadequate ideas, and his understanding of the notion of 'cause' or 'explanation'. Inadequate ideas involve external causes – unlike adequate ideas, we have to look outside the order of our thoughts (our natures as thinking beings) for an explanation of their occurrence and truth.

Adequate ideas are the logical consequences of preceding ideas, they follow actively from our power as thinking beings.

> I say that we act when anything is done, either within us or without us, of which we are the adequate cause, that is to say (by the preceding Def.), when from our nature anything follows either within us or without us, which by that nature alone can be clearly and distinctly understood. On the other hand, I say that we suffer when anything is done within us, or when anything follows from our nature of which we are not the cause except partially (*E*, III, def. 2).

At this point, it can be seen that in so far as the mind is constituted by adequate ideas it necessarily acts, and in so far as it is constituted by inadequate ideas it necessarily suffers. An adequate idea is self-explanatory, or follows as a logical consequence of other adequate ideas, and so far as our mind is constituted by a succession of adequate ideas we do not have to look outside our own mental natures for the adequate cause of that succession.

But some complication is called for. Active/passive corresponds to the distinction between what one does and what happens to one. For Descartes, we do only that which follows from our will. For Spinoza, we do what depends on our nature alone (as finite modes, understandable under two attributes as mind and body). Adequate ideas are the actions of the mind, for they are explainable as elements in a series of logically related ideas and so dependent only on our nature as thinking beings. However, there are difficulties in identifying adequate ideas. First there is an ambiguity in 'ideas' – the term can cover single words such as 'motion' or complete thoughts such as 'the whole is not greater than the sum of its parts'. This ambiguity need not detain us because single words must be seen as functioning in sentences of an adequate theory; alone they are neither true nor false, and so neither adequate nor inadequate.[4] But, second, can one call an idea adequate without knowing whose it is and on what grounds he holds it? Here there is a genuine difficulty of interpretation. On the one hand, the answer is apparently 'Yes', because, we are told, adequate ideas bear their truth on their face; and further, all who have adequate ideas will thereby know and hence know that they know. But the answer is also apparently 'No', because, Spinoza indicates, we can have a thought (e.g. that involved in loving X) on either adequate or inadequate grounds. The thought remains the same. Thus the truth, even logical truth of a thought does not guarantee that it is an adequately grounded idea (e.g. a mathematical truth might be believed on authority). Though there are grounds for the former answer, I think that the latter, the view that it is not sufficient to have a thought (which is adequate for some people) for it to be adequate for oneself, is more compelling; this view is required by an understanding of the transition from passive to active emotion, by the wider interpretation of 'adequacy' we have argued for (as a matter of role in theory rather than logical truth), and by the fact that the possibility of knowing that one knows does not mean one always in fact knows that one knows (the possibility does not amount to its own realization). Even if it were the case that if a person does have an idea on adequate grounds, it necessarily follows that he knows the idea to be adequate, *inadequacy* would still depend on relation to the individual mind of some person (*E*, II, prop. 36). So one cannot tell that an idea is inadequate on its face, unless that face includes the owner's (which may happen where the idea is one that occurs to me and so the face is mine). The adequacy of an idea depends not only on its content, but also on whose it is and the grounds on which he holds it.

5

Transforming Emotions

In order to overcome fear, Spinoza prescribes that we 'often enumerate and imagine the common dangers of life, and think upon the manner in which they can best be avoided and overcome by presence of mind and courage' (*E*, V, prop. 10, note). Through doing this, we are able to get rid of the fear. What is objectionable in the emotion is the impotence associated with it – in the grip of fear one is disabled from action – and the impotence of mind of which it is a sign. Both *Timor* (def. 39) and *Metus* (def. 13) are sometimes translated as 'fear'; the quoted passage is concerned with the latter notion, which bears the sense of 'an inconstant pain arising from the idea of something past or future, whereof we to a certain extent doubt the issue' (and which becomes despair when the doubt is removed). Here freedom is properly freedom from. We wish to eliminate the emotion.

This is not to say that fear is always inappropriate: we may be confronted by something genuinely dangerous, something which might injure us by counteracting our efforts to maintain ourselves as thinking embodied beings. The more adequate our understanding of our natures and of what constitutes a threat (raging mobs do not help anyone's *conatus*) the more appropriate the fear will be; but the emotion itself can never be active. As a matter of definition, fear is painful and so the mind's power of acting is lessened or limited, and so fear cannot be active (see *E*, III, prop. 59). The notions of appropriateness and activity must be distinguished. For one thing, the thought and the affect are separable, so that an appropriate and adequate thought may be tied to an appropriate but passive affect. An emotion (as we have seen) may be appropriate but not active; the demands of freedom or activity of emotions are more stringent than those of appropriateness. An emotion may not be irrational and yet may still be painful and useless or ineffective from the point of view of larger purposes. We must distinguish between an emotion's being irrational and its being useless or ineffective, though there are systematic connections between them. Simply from the point of view of the discrimination and identification of emotions (about which Spinoza has a great deal to teach us) an emotion may be out of place; and it will then almost certainly (barring vast coincidence) be undesirable, because the thought and feeling are inappropriate or directed to an unreal situation. An active emotion will, of course, necessarily be appropriate. As we have seen, the notion of appropriateness can find no place in the Humean scheme, while he can give a sense to the 'reasonableness' of emotions in terms of their functional value. For Spinoza, appropriateness appears as a part (though only a part) of adequacy and activity.

So far we can see that for Spinoza, coping with fear and all of the emotions based on pain is a matter of eliminating them. Where they are based on true beliefs and so are appropriate, there will always be an active emotion incorporating those true beliefs (e.g. recognizing the danger but dwelling on the techniques of maintaining one's powers in the face of them) which will better enable one effectively to meet difficulties. (In this case of fear, the corresponding active emotion would involve 'presence of mind and courage', in the case of hatred, it is to be conquered by love or generosity.) It does, however, seem inevitable that where one does suffer pain and has more or less adequate beliefs concerning its sources that one will experience a passive emotion. Spinoza seems to acknowledge this in the case of hatred or anger, but points out, among other things, that if we appreciate 'that man, like other things, acts according to the necessity of nature, then the injury or the hatred which usually arises from that necessity will occupy but the least part of the imagination, and will be easily overcome . . .' (*E*, V, prop. 10, note). In effect, he is suggesting a revision of belief about the operation of causes, so that the object of anger will be seen as just an element of a necessary structure – a change which would inevitably alter the character of the emotion. And the intellectual activity, the search for and consideration of broader causes, is itself a pleasure and so alleviating.

But short of the elimination of useless or painful emotions and the development of an intellectual love of God, what happens when an emotion is transformed from passive to active through an increase in the adequacy of the associated ideas? Most basically, the object changes. The object, by contrast with Hume, is not merely an idea which occurs in conjunction with an impression, not even constant conjunction. The object is the believed cause of a change of state (*conatus*). Spinoza holds a strong thesis of intentionality: 'Modes of thought, such as love, desire, or the emotions of the mind, by whatever name they may be called, do not exist unless in the same individual exists the idea of a thing loved, desired, etc. But the idea may exist although no other modes of thinking exist' (*E*, II, axiom 3). The basic emotions of pleasure and pain may be exceptions (the only exceptions among the emotions). But though there is no reference to an object in their definitions, there are grounds for thinking that the intentionality thesis is all-embracing. For example, *E*, III, prop. 56 indicates that as passive states, pleasure and pain must involve inadequate ideas and so external bodies: 'The nature, therefore, of each passive state must necessarily be explained in such a manner that the nature of the object by which we are affected is expressed.' This does not guarantee a conscious thought of an object, but objectless emotions may turn out to be only apparently so (e.g. every time we are pleased, we must be pleased by something, and one should leave a placeholder for the object). It is not obvious in the case of desire and certain of its derivative emotions (e.g. regret, hope, emulation) that the object is the 'believed cause', but it is possible that these should not be regarded as central cases of emotions at all. And it is obvious that love and hatred (and the emotions defined in terms of them) and pleasure and pain do have believed causes as their objects (see *E*, III, def. emo.).

The sense of 'cause' involved is not Humean. It is not a case of constant conjunction or implied general statements. Spinoza tells us that an adequate cause is one 'whose effect can be clearly and distinctly perceived by means of the cause' (*E*, III, def. 1) and, more generally, 'From a given determinate cause an effect necessarily follows, and, on the other hand, if no determinate cause be given it is impossible that an effect can follow' (*E*, I, axiom 3). The cause of something is its explanation, its necessary (and sufficient?) condition. Within Spinoza's scheme, the premises of a deductive argument can be said to be the 'cause' of the conclusion, i.e. its logical ground. Though this extends the modern usage of 'cause', to assimilate 'cause' to 'logical ground' is actually part of a narrow interpretation corresponding to a narrow interpretation of adequacy. There is justification for it within Spinoza's scheme: 'the order and connection of ideas is the same as the order and connection of causes' (*E*, II, prop. 9, demo.) which derives from the claim that 'the order and connection of ideas is the same as the order and connection of things' (*E*, II, prop. 7) and ultimately from 'the knowledge of an effect depends upon and involves the knowledge of the cause' (*E*, I, axiom 4). (This last statement has other important consequences, notably that we cannot ascribe an emotion to ourselves unless we can ascribe an object to the emotion.) Though ultimately causes may have to be logical grounds, so that all effects can be seen as necessary consequences within an intuitive unified science, there is a wider interpretation, corresponding to our wider interpretation of adequacy. There are interim levels of understanding where the cause can be viewed as the explanation of the effect provided by the most comprehensive and coherent theory available in that area, or even merely the theory that someone happens to have.

Believed causes may involve false beliefs and the object of an emotion may not be the actual cause. Hence when our thought follows associative (mechanical) patterns rather than the laws of logic and science, our emotions may be misdirected. For Spinoza, the distinction between associative patterns and active thought is, of course, extremely important. His favoured word for a thought or belief involved in an emotion is 'idea'. He uses the word more widely than Hume ('By idea I understand a conception of the mind which the mind forms because it is a thinking thing.' – *E*, II, def. 3), and is careful to distinguish ideas from passive perceptions, and mental pictures or images ('dumb pictures on a tablet' – *E*, III, prop. 49, cor., note; cf. *Correspondence*, 1929, ed. Wolf, p. 289, on imagining *v.* conceiving God). Hence Spinoza can introduce grammatical complexity into 'ideas'; the 'idea of a cause' becomes ambiguous as it can mean the idea of an object which is a cause or the idea of an object as a cause (i.e. the thought that it is a cause). Where ideas are treated, in Humean fashion, as images, such complexity is not possible. So where our thought is in fact a succession of images, temporal and other discriminations become far more difficult. Hence Spinoza argues that 'a man is affected by the image of a past or future thing with the same emotion of joy or sorrow as that with which he is affected by the image of a present thing' (*E*, III, prop. 18). The tense, or temporal reference, is left out unless 'the image is connected with that of past or future time . . . the image of the thing considered in itself alone is the same whether it be related to future, past, or present time . . .' This quality of images has important psychological consequences, it enables us both to predict and to see why emotional reactions to memories and fantasies can be as strong as responses to reality. Recognizing a thought as a memory, as referring to the past, may change an emotion. Indeed, Spinoza suggests that such recognition weakens the hold of the emotion on us (*E*, IV, props 9 and 10). Contrast this notion that memories can be as powerful as present ideas with what one would expect on a Humean view, on which memories are treated as 'faded copies' – hardly likely to produce an impact comparable to live impressions. (Here the similarity of Freud to Spinoza is again noteworthy: Freud insists on the timelessness of primary process thinking and the pre-linguistic unconscious and on the equal efficacy of fantasies and memories. See Appendix C.)

The ambiguity in 'the idea of an external cause' remains unresolved in Spinoza, but, I think, the phrase is generally to be taken in the strong sense of an idea of a cause *as* cause. It is clear that to have an idea is to have a belief. Spinoza allows no sense to the Cartesian notion of assenting to an idea as an act of will. ('In the mind there is no volition or affirmation and negation except that which the idea, in so far as it is an idea, involves' – *E*, II, prop. 49.) So if one associates a particular object with one's pleasure or pain as its cause, one, in effect, believes it is the cause and it is the object of one's emotion. (Though there is no separate step of assenting to a belief, Spinoza would allow that one could dissociate from a thought – as in the sun case – as one comes to learn that it is not a belief properly grounded in evidences of truth. This comes closer to the sort of passivity of thought which Freud discusses, where one may suffer from an alien or obsessive thought, despite having dissociated from it or refusing to incorporate it.)

It is less clear what happens if there is an idea associated with one's pleasure or pain (if one thinks of it immediately before or following the change), but the idea is not thought of *qua* cause. Presumably, the emotion then has no object (even if it does have a cause), and according to the definitions of the emotions must be regarded as a different emotion. An emotion that would have been love becomes an objectless pleasure if left unexplained, and can be transformed into love by the ascription of a cause by the subject. Less radical changes result from the correction of less radical defects. For example, if we become aware of a multiplicity and complexity of causes, the emotion will have many objects and we will be less affected towards each than if we had regarded one alone as the cause (*E*, V, prop. 9). At the extreme other end of transformations, destruction of belief in the cause may destroy the emotion altogether.

This sort of transformation may be illustrated by Othello's situation. Were Othello to be convinced that Desdemona had in fact been faithful, and that the apparent evidence to the contrary was the result of the machinations of Iago, his jealousy would disappear. Of course, Othello has worked himself up into a state (sufficient to murder his wife) and there is no guarantee that that will automatically alter with the discovery of the falsity of his relevant beliefs (i.e. knowledge of the cause may not destroy all its effects), but the state will have to be redescribed. Even if the thought of Desdemona's unfaithfulness continues, it will not persist as a belief, and that it be *believed* is essential to Othello's state's being a straightforward case of jealousy. Given his new beliefs, he can no longer be simply jealous. The jealousy will disappear, as such, and (at worst) might continue in the form of pathological jealous thoughts. These may then be open to other forms of treatment. But rational argument certainly can take one part of the way. (There is no necessity to treat jealousy as though it were like a headache, something that comes and goes, but that there is no arguing with.) Given the following:

1 the recognition of the aetiology of the relevant beliefs, i.e. their inadequate grounding in the appropriate evidences of truth,

2 the conviction that the relevant beliefs are in fact false (i.e. one

could believe something which is true for bad reasons, so that a belief is ill-founded is not *sufficient* to show that it is false),

3 the recognition of the inappropriateness of the emotion given the new understanding of the beliefs or thoughts,

then the state of mind, both for Othello and other parties, must be redescribed because the state of mind essentially involved those beliefs, and was dependent on their being (full-fledged) beliefs. He can no longer be said to be jealous, though he may well still be in turmoil.

Spinoza displays particular psychological perspicacity in his discussion of the detailed structure of jealousy: 'hatred toward a beloved object when joined with envy' arising when 'I imagine that an object beloved by me is united to another person by the same or by a closer bond of friendship than that by which I myself alone held the object' (*E*, III, prop. 35). The componential analysis readily reveals why one might wonder whether the capacity for jealousy is a sign of insecurity or a sign of love, and how it can involve both.

One could say that the object of Othello's jealousy is Desdemona and her apparent lover (she being the object of the component hatred and he of the component envy) or their presumed relationship. In either case, the object would be what Othello believes is the source of his unhappiness and suffering. However, belief is essential to the character of his pain in two ways. First, facts must be mediated by perception, i.e. jealousy will arise only if one is aware of or believes in a provoking situation. But second, a certain type of belief is also a logical condition on the proper characterization of suffering being jealousy, and this condition is built into Spinoza's definition of jealousy. According to the first sort of thought-dependence, either Desdemona and her lover together, or their relationship alone, would not produce pain in Othello without some awareness or belief on his part in their togetherness or relationship. This does not mean that 'the belief that X is the cause of his jealousy' is itself the cause of his jealousy – that the emotion is self-fulfilling and this belief is its object. One must distinguish the jealousy and its component suffering, which is only properly characterizable as 'jealousy' one step further on. One must begin with 'the belief that X is the case' (where X is the Desdemona-Cassio relationship); this is the essential belief, the belief that is the cause of Othello's suffering. Given *this* belief, unhappiness will be produced in Othello. With an awareness of the causal connection, a new belief arises, 'the belief that the belief that X is the case is the cause of Othello's suffering'. So 'the belief that X is the case' and not 'the belief that X is the cause' is the believed cause of Othello's suffering, and it is this belief that makes his suffering jealousy. (See discussion of Thalberg *et al.* on thoughts as causes, and different senses of 'object', in Appendix A.)

One may not want to say, however, even in a technical sense, that any 'thought' is the object of his jealousy, because the thought is not the ultimate believed cause: there is an embedded object, the object of the causally efficacious belief, i.e. 'that X is the case' or 'X'. What is that object? To believe something is to assent to an idea, to entertain it (E, II, prop. 49). Once the will is discarded as illusory, as a universal faculty improperly abstracted from individual (volitions and) ideas, the will in belief cannot be said to operate on some further object other than the object of the idea. The object of belief is the object of the idea. 'A true idea must agree with that of which it is the idea' (E, I, axiom 6) and falsity consists in the privation of knowledge: 'in ideas there is nothing positive on account of which they are called false' (E, II, props 35 and 33). The object of an idea is *not* its cause (E, II, prop. 5 – in *Correspondence*, 1929, ed. Wolf, p. 341, Spinoza reaffirms that the object of an idea is not its efficient cause in reference to this proposition); the cause must be another thought because causal relations hold only between objects seen under the same attribute (Thought or Extension – E, II, prop. 6). And the relation of mental and physical correlates is some form of identity too intimate for causality. Hence the object of belief cannot be an object in the same sense as the object of emotion is, namely, a believed cause. The sense in which it is an object is obscure in Spinoza. He does offer a metaphysical guarantee that every idea will have a corresponding object in the realm of extension ('The order and connection of ideas is the same as the order and connection of things' – E, II, prop. 7). The ideas constituting the human mind have as their object the component parts of the human body (E, II, props 13 and 15). External objects are known through the modifications they work on the human body (E, II, props 16, 17, and 26). So we are carried to the ultimate objects of the emotions (though in cases involving ideas of ideas, the object of an idea may be another idea and so the object of an emotion may be an idea): the external objects.

We left Othello in turmoil. Assuming the relevant beliefs have dissolved, and that Othello's energies are not redirected as the result of new ideas (e.g. into hatred of Iago as the cause of unnecessary suffering and jealousy), we are left with a physiological residue, which will now, at the minimum, have a more complex explanation and so characterization. Following Spinoza, we have treated emotions as essentially characterized through thoughts. It is an important corrective to add that each of the ideas discussed is assumed by Spinoza to have a corresponding, though unspecified, physical correlate. Hume too was content to leave matters beyond the components of the mind, impressions and ideas, to 'the sciences of anatomy and natural philosophy'. But Hume's account gains much apparent plausibility from its appeal to feeling where Spinoza appeals to thought (here our central arguments have taken place) and its treatment of impressions and ideas as though they were themselves physiological rather than epistemological constructs. Emotions certainly are, in part, and on occasion, feelings.

Concerning the violent unbalance of bodily motion-and-rest we assume remains in Othello, Spinoza would presumably insist on a corresponding confusion of thought adding up to no definite emotion (unless pathological jealous thoughts continue to hold sway). What is important is not to deny the role of physiology, feeling, and affect, but to see how it differs from the role of thought. Following Spinoza in giving thought its place in the discrimination and identification of mental states puts us in a position to go further in understanding the power of reason in relation to the passions. Hampshire provides a helpful restatement of the central argument:

(1) The emotions and propositional attitudes are distinguished from each other principally by their actual and notional causes, where the notional cause is the subject's thought about the cause.
(2) The subject's thought of the object of the emotion (what he fears, is angry with and about) and of the propositional attitudes includes a thought about the cause or occasion: if his thought of the cause or occasion is substantially changed, his thought of the object will be changed; and if the subject's thought of the object is changed, his dispositions and behaviour are correspondingly changed.
(3) The subject of any emotion, or propositional attitude, which has an intentional object, has an authority, though not an overriding one, in determining what his state of mind is and what its object is (e.g., whether he fears and what specifically he fears): if he believes that he fears A, or is envious of B because of C, or that he is discouraged by D, or hopes for E because of F, this belief has to be included in any adequate account of his state of mind, even if the belief is erroneous. If the belief is erroneous, then his state of mind must be a confused and complex one (Hampshire, 1971c, p. 565).

The Spinozist approach is sometimes challenged on the basis of cases where we have a definite emotion but seem unable to find a similarly definite corresponding thought. We have argued that Hume lapses into self-contradiction and implausibility when he tries to make sense of the reverse cases, the 'calm passions', but his sort of feeling theory is on stronger ground when confined to the range of emotions he calls 'violent' (though even here certain general confusions seem unavoidable given Hume's approach). Can Spinoza's theory provide a structure and a language through which all emotions, even where they seem to be essentially affect alone, can be understood? However one ultimately deals with so-called objectless emotions (that is, whether they have very general objects, or unconscious objects, are derivative from fuller states, or whatever), there is no reason to believe that one must fall into contradiction in using Spinozist language to describe them. He enables us to see that there is a scale within fear, from highly articulate and well-formulated fears involving explicit thoughts, to very basic and perhaps incoherent fears involving inadequate and confused thoughts. Even should there be some states involving no thoughts at all, there is no reason why a Spinozist would be forced to deny them. But it is highly unlikely that there is anything which is properly describable as an emotion which is not thought-dependent in at least one of the two ways we have discussed.

It is worth noting that our lengthy discussion of objects had little to do with the involved nature of Othello's passion. The situation remains much the same for the apparently more straightforward case of fear of a raging mob: without an intervening awareness that there is a raging mob, there is no fear of a raging mob. Whether Spinoza over-intellectualizes the emotions depends in large measure on how much awareness is required for the emotion, in particular whether it must reach the level of (conscious) causal beliefs. It is important here to distinguish between the sufferer and third-party points of view. The victim may be afraid of, and known by observers to be afraid of, the raging mob. The victim may know himself to be afraid by all sorts of, perhaps 'felt', signs (including cold sweat, inclination to run, trembling, etc.) but if he does not ascribe these to the mob's presence he does not know that he is afraid of the mob (though that is what he is in fact afraid of, for it is the actual cause of his symptoms and behaviour). Such ignorance is unlikely in such a case, but often (especially for emotions like jealousy) he, like third parties, may have to depend on such clues (which may be understood as clues to his unconscious thoughts and fantasies) to discover what his state of mind is. Though it is not fully *his* state of mind till he makes the discovery – a discovery which may in turn transform it – and third parties may in fact be in a better position to tell.

Looking back to the case of love, we can consider the other sort of thought-dependence (mediation by thought, and characterization by thought and level of thought). Spinoza is not over-intellectualizing love by building in the idea of the cause. A loved object gives pleasure and is desired for its own sake; he is not introducing a utilitarian calculation of value, but bringing out the commitments in a claim to 'love'. It places constraints on the possible explanations one can offer for his state (though of course he may be wrong, even within the constraints), and on the explanations for desire and action he can base on the state.

6

Intellectual or Social Emotions

Spinoza's doctrines about the objects of the emotions reveal an intellectual (or social) dimension to our discrimination of emotions. In addition to the ranges within particular emotions (e.g. fear) from highly directed and thought-dependent, to apparently purely physio-logical and even objectless, there is a scale among emotions leading from the primitive to the highly thought-impregnated. To feel these emotions it is necessary to have particular beliefs. More accurately, the ascription of a certain state of mind to oneself or others depends on the existence in the subject of certain intellectual capacities (this is the element that suggests a new dimension) including: the discrimination of cognitive levels (hope and regret both require recognition of the difference between what is in doubt and what is, at least relatively, certain) and the having of certain concepts (there is no shame without 'responsibility'). This is very far from the Humean world where one feels what one feels, and there is no inherent reason in the nature of emotion why one person should have a coarser or more limited power of discrimination among emotions. For a Humean, the closest parallel would be an emotion-blindness somewhat like colour-blindness. Intel-lectual capacity and reason have no place.

We have already seen that change of belief can lead to more than change in object of emotion, the very character of the emotion can be transformed. In fact, our first example (p. 88) was of a change from objectless pleasure to love by the ascription of a cause. And every change in object is in a sense a change in emotion (see *E*, III, prop. 56). If this were not enough to guarantee the infinite variety and complexity of human feeling and emotion, Spinoza also points out that 'Different men may be affected by one and the same object in different ways, and the same man may be affected by one and the same object in different ways at different times' (*E*, III, prop. 51; see also prop. 57).

So it is foolish to ask 'how many emotions are there?' in expectation of a definite answer. An answer depends very much on the interest from which the question is asked, for there are an indefinite number of grounds of classification, none of which can exhaust all the differences. Over-concern with definition in this area is a symptom and cause of false precision. Spinoza concludes his own long series of definitions by saying that many emotions have no names, and the point of his list is to show how emotions can be understood (at least in their mental aspect) as variations arising from the three basic emotions of desire, pleasure, and pain, in accordance with his principles concerning the nature and operation of the mind. The confusion in the ordinary prin-ciples of classification makes the ordinary meanings of emotion words of little use in understanding the nature of the emotions. It is here worth recalling our initial observation that all the central words in the *Ethics* must be understood in the special senses provided by Spinoza. (Cf. *E*, III, prop. 52, note, and def. emo. 31 explanation.) Which does not mean that Spinoza is analysing some artificial constructs of his own rather than our emotional lives. Rather, he provides what can be regarded as the system behind our confused perceptions. And the system can allow for variations in accordance with the conceptual schemes and concerns of different times and different cultures. The principles of distinction, rather than the particular distinctions matter. The finer discriminations and subtleties that we should concern ourselves with here are embodied in Spinoza's definitions. Consider, for instance, his examples of 'notions of love or desire, which explain the nature of this or that emotion through the objects to which they are related' (hence voluptuousness, drunkenness, lust, avarice, and ambition, etc. are discriminated through their objects – E, III, prop. 56, note).

The difference between shame and repentance according to Spinoza is the difference between pain 'with the accompanying idea of some action which we imagine people blame' (cf. Hume on humility) and pain 'with the idea of something done which we believe has been done by a free decree of our mind' (see defs emo. 31 and 27, and E, III, prop. 30, note). The difference is a difference in belief. Shame arises if we imagine that we have given just cause for the hatred another bears us (E, III, prop. 40, note). The *capacity* to be ashamed depends on a prior understanding of blame (the pain with which a person turns away from another person's action, the purpose of which is to harm him). Without this concept, one could have no reason for thinking one was ashamed rather than merely repentant (which does not require awareness of our bad intention by another, the bad effects repented of might not even involve another). Even if we use 'shame' in its looser more modern sense, where it is assimilated to Spinoza's use of 'repentance', one could not feel shame (as opposed to, say, embarrassment, discomfort, or unease) unless one had concepts like 'guilt' and 'responsibility' and was able to apply them (even if misapplied on a particular occasion). One cannot feel shame *simpliciter*. That is, if one is unable to say of what one is ashamed, it cannot be proper to describe one's state of mind as 'shame'. If someone insists that he feels shame but can say no more, then an observer would have to conclude that either he does not know what shame means or (supposing there is evidence for understanding based on his use of 'shame' on other occasions etc.) that he has no reason for regarding his state of mind, his discomfort and unease, as 'shame' *rather than* any of a dozen other things. And the ascription of an object alone is not sufficient to justify the description of the emotion as 'shame'. If I merely insist that I am ashamed and, further, ashamed of, say, the ashtray before me, without being able to make any connection between the putative object and myself (other than the claim that it is the object), then the emotion remains unintelligible and it remains doubtful that I understand the word 'shame'. However my stomach may churn and hormones flow, and however the ashtray may obtrude itself on my consciousness, it is not enough to make my emotion shame (though it might be enough to make it 'fear'). But if I can tell a story, however implausible, suggesting or establishing the appropriate relations, then my emotion may become intelligible as shame: for example, I am an ashtray manufacturer and as part of a policy of planned obsolescence have so made the relevant object that it will disintegrate within a month, and therefore regard myself as responsible for its being defective. The shame may be unjustified, but it at least becomes intelligible as shame. I have reasons for describing my state of mind as 'shame' rather than in some other way, I have the sorts of beliefs (though the beliefs themselves may be unreasonable) which are appropriate to the emotion. (Consider a monkey making horrendous noises at a piano and wincing. Might it be 'ashamed' of its piano playing? Cf. Wittgenstein (1953, trans. Anscombe, section 250): 'Why can't a dog simulate pain? Is he too honest? . . .'). The social or intellectual end of the emotional scale is even more obviously open to change through change in belief than some of the cases we have considered, even more amenable to reason.

Change in belief should be sufficient to lead to change in emotion (the physical correlates should alter with the change in ideas, the order of things being the same as the order of ideas). However, the truth of the new thought is not necessarily the transforming factor.

> We know that, when we groundlessly fear any evil, the fear
> vanishes when we hear correct intelligence; but we also know, on
> the other hand, that, when we fear an evil which will actually
> come upon us, the fear vanishes when we hear false intelligence,
> so that the imaginations do not disappear with the presence of
> the truth, in so far as it is true, but because other imaginations
> arise which are stronger and which exclude the present existence
> of the objects we imagine, as we have shown in Prop. 17, Pt. 2
> (*E*, IV, prop. 1, note).

It is of course important to add that 'belief' has a normative aspect. If we know that a thought is inadequately grounded in evidences of truth, it is not fully a 'belief'. And where an emotion requires full-bodied belief (and not mere suspicion, or irrational fancy, or something else), reflexion on the source and grounds of a thought will affect that emotion. But Spinoza's remarks on the power of false intelligence, of fantasies and false beliefs are also important. Thoughts are important in emotions, but their importance may not depend on their truth. This has serious implications for our later discussions. We shall have to ask whether Freudian aetiologies must be true in order to be effective in changing emotional reactions, and even whether their effectiveness would be evidence of their truth. A Spinozist epistemology would suggest 'No' to both questions. Spinoza's own therapy must take these complications into account.

Ideas, even false imaginings, while not 'pictures on a tablet', are still entities and are not easily displaced. Their presence and persistence will usually depend on external causes. A passive emotion is, by definition, at least in part to be explained by causes outside our own nature and its power will depend on the power of those causes as compared with our own power (E, IV, prop. 5). Ultimately, 'an emotion cannot be restrained nor removed unless by an opposed and stronger emotion' (E, IV, prop. 7). But the first and most important step in changing a passive emotion is an understanding of its causes. Knowledge of the grounds of a belief changes that belief. If the grounds are adequate, the belief may stand but the explanation of its being held is complicated by the knowledge of its grounds. If the grounds are inadequate, that knowledge is the first step towards rejecting the belief. The belief, or more accurately, the thought, does not instantaneously disappear, for according to Spinoza there was nothing positive in virtue of which it was false, so the knowledge of its inadequacy leaves whatever was positive supported by its inadequate grounds, but we now know the grounds as inadequate and the belief is modified. Spinoza's discussion of the sun, cited previously in reference to adequate ideas, is again relevant:

> For example, when we look at the sun, we imagine his distance from us to be about 200 feet, and in this we are deceived so long as we remain in ignorance of the true distance. When this is known, the error is removed, but not the imagination, that is to say, the idea of the sun which manifests his nature in so far only as the body is affected by him; so that, although we know his true distance, we nevertheless imagine him close to us (E, IV, prop. 1, note).

Awareness of inadequacy does not drive out or destroy the idea, but the false belief gives way to an acknowledged imagination once we know the causes of the thought. The thought persists but it knows its level. In so far as such causal thoughts are constituents in emotions, changes in them are changes in the emotion. I may be in pain and regard Peter as the source of my pain, and so hate and be angry at Peter (anger, for Spinza, being 'the desire by which we are impelled, through hatred, to injure those whom we hate' – def. emo. 36). But if I learn that he is not the cause of my suffering, though the suffering may remain, my state of mind can no longer be hatred and anger at Peter (E, V, prop. 2). The removal of the suffering (the residue which remains once the beliefs which make it hate or anger cease to persist as beliefs) requires something more for its treatment:

> Whenever . . . the mind is agitated by any emotion, the body is at the same time affected with a modification by which its power of action is increased or diminished. Again, this modification of

the body (prop. 5, pt 4) receives from its own cause a power to persevere in its own being, a power, therefore, which cannot be restrained nor removed unless by a bodily cause (prop. 6, pt 2 [see also prop. 17]) affecting the body with a modification contrary to the first (prop. 5, pt 3), and stronger than it (axiom, pt 4). (E, V, prop. 7.)

Hence the total removal of an emotion requires another (opposed and stronger) emotion, but the correction of the understanding is sufficient for starting the process of transformation.[5]

7

Active Emotion and Action

Spinoza's general definition of the emotions at the end of Part III ('emotion . . . is a confused idea . . .') is actually a definition of the passions or passive emotions. Emotion need not depend on confused or inadequate ideas. Perhaps a totally free being would be free of all emotion (E, V, prop. 17); be that as it might, Spinoza, while not neglecting the vast difficulties on the road to freedom, insists that emotions can be active (see E, III, props 58 and 59). But it is not entirely clear which emotions are to count as active. Different points in the text suggest different readings. For example, fear of a raging mob, where it consists of a desire to flee, may well be rational – would it therefore be active? The argument in E, IV, prop. 15 suggests that where the desire springs from true knowledge of evil (danger to our *conatus*), it can be understood through our essence alone, and so follows in us in so far as we act. (The definition of fear or timidity in III, def. 39 is closest to this concept of fear, but it is more complex and via the notion defined at 13 involves doubt.) But to follow from true understanding of something (contrary to the implication of E, III, prop. 1), is not in itself sufficient for activity. E, IV, prop. 64 suggests that if the thing understood is evil, it cannot be understood adequately, or, more precisely, it cannot be understood through our essence alone. This is directly contrary to the claim of prop. 15, pt IV. Perhaps it will be sufficient to limit the earlier proposition in the light of the later. The later proposition (64) rests on the fact that passage to a state of less perfection cannot be understood through the essence itself of man (E, III, props 6 and 7). Pain is a passive state, and knowledge of evil, which is itself painful in so far as we are conscious of it (by E, IV, prop. 8), can only lead to passive states. (The desire to flee which we are discussing, unlike the fear, def. 13, discussed in E, IV, prop. 63, is not itself a painful state and so might be active if it did not arise from knowledge of evil.) It is easy enough to concoct a version of the desire to flee which will be active, say if it arises out of knowledge of what is

97

good, i.e. faced with a raging mob: fleeing (cf. *E*, IV, prop. 63, note). In general, 'to all actions to which we are determined by an emotion wherein the mind is passive we may, without the emotion, be determined by reason' (*E*, IV, prop. 59). But this should presumably be read as 'without the passive emotion'. Which emotions are active?

Can emotions of pleasure be active? Emotions of pain cannot be because pain is a lessening of the mind's power of acting, i.e. thinking (*E*, III, prop. 59) and because such lessenings cannot be understood through the essence itself of man (*E*, IV, prop. 64 and III, props 4, 6, and 7). Can changes in the other direction, increases in the mind's power of acting, be so understood? There are passages which suggest that states of change are passive in virtue of being states of change. Here we are troubled by those elements in Spinoza's system which, as we have seen, tend towards making the intellectual love of God the only active emotion. Spinoza clearly thinks pleasure can be active: e.g. 'in so far as pleasure is good, so far it agrees with reason (for it consists in this that a man's power of action is increased or assisted), and the mind is not passive therein unless in so far as man's power of action is not increased sufficiently for him to conceive adequately himself and his actions' (*E*, IV, prop. 59, dem.). But when determined by reason, Spinoza adds (in the same prop.) that we are determined 'without the emotion'. We have suggested an alternative reading ('without the passive emotion'). But where the emotion has a particular external object (i.e. where it is not the intellectual love of God and does not arise, as in *E*, III, prop. 58, from contemplation of one's own power of conceiving adequate ideas) must not an adequate understanding take into account the nature of that external body? (And pain is considered passive precisely because weakening of *conatus*, by *E*, III, prop. 4, brings external causes into account.) So it seems that activity should not be defined through explainability in terms of one's own nature. These matters are further complicated by Spinoza's view that perception of external causes reveals the constitution of one's own body. However I think we have already seen a way out. Activity is mainly a matter of adequate ideas, rationality rather than passive perception, ideas about one's own nature and the operation of causes. But these causes need not be confined to one's own essence because adequate ideas and their various associated emotions all lead to pleasure (*E*, III, prop. 58) in the contemplation of the adequate ideas and our power; and *this* pleasure is part of what makes the associated emotion active.

The emotions also have a dynamic aspect which may seem slighted by an emphasis on the role of thought. Why do we have emotions? Spinoza does not leave the having of emotions as a mysterious event in our lives, nor does he assimilate emotions simply to thoughts, so that our relation to the world must appear as entirely contemplative. We have already seen that functional value is an aspect of activity. The answer to why we have emotions is to be found by asking *what* we have when we have emotions. We do not simply have beliefs. Even if that were initially plausible, one would wonder what would differentiate beliefs that were emotions from intellectual beliefs (Hume has difficulties when he tries to work the assimilation the other way, i.e. treating beliefs as though they were emotions or feelings). (See Appendix B.) When one has an emotion, one has beliefs, but one may also have physiological affects, manifestations, expressions, desires, inclinations, motives . . . For Spinoza, the dynamic aspect of the emotions is provided by the *conatus*. Man's essence is desire and the ends of his desire are fixed in his nature. That which preserves and maintains him as a finite thinking embodied being is desirable. Emotion has natural expressions and is tied to action through desire.

Some emotions simply are desires (which does not mean that the desires are themselves simple). Hence Spinoza defines anger as 'the desire by which we are impelled, through hatred, to injure those whom we hate' (*E*, III, def. emo. 36). There is no mystery about why we are inclined to strike or harm those we hate. As Spinoza explains (*E*, III, prop. 39), to hate a person is to imagine him as a cause of pain, and pain always provides a self-explanatory (*E*, III, prop. 28) motive for the removal of its source. We may have other motives for harming another, but then we are not acting out of anger. And if we are angry we have a motive for action (it *is* the having of a motive for action). The crucial, and rather less clear, step is the one tying an emotion which is not itself a desire to one which is. Must we always be angry at those we hate? Other things being equal, the Spinozist answer is 'Yes'. The emotions themselves have an internal logic, a dynamic that moves us from one to the other and to action. Our *conatus* ensures (is) the endeavour to persevere in our being, and pleasure and pain are changes in the state of our ability to do this. Emotions are based on desire, pleasure, and pain; ultimately, *conatus*. Where the emotions are not themselves desires, Spinoza argues 'we endeavour to bring into existence everything which we imagine conduces to pleasure, and to remove or destroy everything opposed to it, or which we imagine conduces to sorrow' (*E*, III, prop. 28). The argument is based on the desire to increase and maintain the mind's power of thought and the body's power of action, i.e. the *conatus*. Pain and pleasure are motives for action, and in so far as emotions are based on pleasure and pain they contain motives for action – the precise nature of the appropriate action depending on the accompanying thoughts. What may make the suggestion that we are always angry at those we hate seem implausible is a confusion between being and feeling. We need not feel angry (the stomach need not churn, the adrenalin need not flow) in order to be angry (being 'furious' is different); but we must, of course, have the relevant desire (and 'feel' is sometimes used broadly to mean this, in which case we do 'feel' angry though we may lack any angry 'feelings'). We shall come to the sense in which we 'have' a desire when it is not a felt desire (though it need not be unconscious).

The expressions of emotional states in action do not necessarily follow from decisions, they follow from the states themselves.

> Thus the infant believes that it is by free will that it seeks the breast; the angry boy believes that by free will he wishes vengeance; the timid man thinks it is with free will he seeks light; the drunkard believes that by a free command of his mind he speaks the things which when sober he wishes he had left unsaid. Thus the madman, the chatterer, the boy, and others of the same kind, all believe that they speak of a free command of the mind, whilst, in truth, they have no power to restrain the impulse which they have to speak, so that experience itself, no less than reason, clearly teaches that men believe themselves to be free simply because they are conscious of their own actions, knowing nothing of the causes by which they are determined; it teaches, too, that the decrees of the mind are nothing but the appetites themselves, which differ therefore according to the different temper of the body. For every man determines all things from his emotion; those who are agitated by contrary emotions do not know what they want, whilst those who are agitated by no emotion are easily driven hither and thither. All this plainly shows that the decree of the mind, the appetite, and determination of the body are coincident in Nature, or rather that they are one and the same thing which, when it is considered under the attribute of thought, and manifested by that, is called a 'decree,' and when it is considered under the attribute of extension and is deduced from the laws of motion and rest is called a 'determination' (*E*, III, prop. 2, note).

If we would be free we must understand our emotions and rule them, or they will inevitably rule us.

An understanding of the way vengeance flows from anger sheds light on other relations between emotion and action. For example, consider the contrast in the ways Hume and Spinoza discuss the relation of love to desire. It will be recalled that this posed a serious problem for Hume's theory (*THN*, II, pt II, section 6) because the alleged simplicity of passions isolates the feeling from its expression. The desire for the good of the beloved must be regarded as extraneous to love itself, so the desire of producing misery could have been annexed to love without conceptual difficulty. But in fact we would regard apparent cases of love accompanied by harmful wishes as ambivalent or would redescribe the 'harmful' effects in terms of the agent's beliefs (which would, presumably, take the effects as not harmful). In the course of his discussion, Hume also denies that the desire for happiness is essential because we may not think about the happiness or misery of our friend at all. On this point he is of course correct, but then the initial problem of the incompleteness of love without the accompanying desire seems illusory – calling for neither his assimilation of the two nor appeal to 'the original constitution of the mind'. Spinoza, more accurately, first describes the associated desire and then accounts for its relation to the passion. He treats love as pleasure with the accompanying idea of an external cause, and (by *E*, III, prop. 13) argues that he who loves a thing necessarily endeavours to keep it before him and to preserve it. Hume's confusion stems from treating the desire as some sort of felt sensation, somehow identifiable as 'a desire of the happiness of the person belov'd, and an aversion to his misery', and then realizing that on some occasions (perhaps we are too absorbed in the object of our love to think of its happiness) we have no such feeling (though this would still leave him with a residual problem of accounting for its occasional presence). Thus Hume is like those 'authors who define love to be the will of the lover to unite himself to the beloved object, expressing not the essence of love but one of its properties' (*E*, III, def. emo. 6, explanation). The accuracy of Spinoza's observation can be seen in *his* account of the associated desire:

> I must observe, however, when I say that it is a property in a lover to will a union with the beloved object, that I do not understand by will a consent or deliberation or a free decree of the mind (for that this is a fiction we have demonstrated in prop. 48, pt 2), nor even a desire of the lover to unite himself with the beloved object when it is absent, nor a desire to continue in its presence when it is present, for love can be conceived without either one or the other of these desires; but by will I understand the satisfaction that the beloved object produces in the lover by its presence by virtue of which the joy of the lover is strengthened or at any rate supported.

Here will (desire) is given a readily intelligible criterion (satisfaction), and it becomes clear how the absence of certain feelings need not show the absence of desire. Though the feelings are not necessary, the desire (in this sense) is.

The expression of emotion in physical behaviour is important in understanding action by reference to emotions, and it is also important as a window into the mental life of others. We know another person's emotional life through its expression. That statement requires greater precision (Expression in what? – behaviour, action, speech . . . ? – What is revealed about emotional life? Does expression contrast with other manifestations or is it our only source of insight?) and hence qualification. But even at this crude level certain observations can be made.

We have seen that Hume's mechanism of 'sympathy' is implausible. We do not, in general, come to understand another's state of mind by having ourselves a weakened version of the same emotions (impressions of reflexion) on exposure to the visible manifestations of the real thing. Spinoza uses 'sympathy' in a different sense in connection with association of ideas, the displacement of feeling from one object to an associated one lacking the appropriate characteristics (*E*, III, prop. 15). (Spinoza specifically contrasts his use with an even earlier one where 'sympathy' was supposed to designate mysterious sources of attraction, a mysteriousness which Spinoza dispels with his associationist explanation.)

Spinoza's theory of 'imitation' is more comparable to Hume's mechanism of emotional transfer. The central proposition is *E*, III, prop 27: 'Although we may not have been moved toward a thing by any emotion, yet if it is like ourselves, whenever we imagine it to be affected by any emotion, we are affected by the same.' Unfortunately, this can be no more help in explaining our knowledge of other minds than Hume's mechanism (though, as in his theory, it can explain various emotional transitions), for that explanation would depend on how we come to imagine another to be affected by an emotion. The theory of imitation just provides a further consequence of such recognition (namely, the production of a like emotion in ourselves). And even the explanation for the phenomenon offered contains an unconvincing assimilation: the perception of an emotional state in another is taken to be itself an emotional state, in fact a duplicate of the state observed. The argument moves from the claim that the ideas of those modifications of the human body which are images of external things involve the nature of our own body and of the external body to 'If, therefore, the nature of the external body be like that of our body, then the idea of the external body which we imagine will involve a modification of our body like that of the external body'. But there is no reason to believe that the modification will be importantly 'like' the object perceived. Certainly there must be something in virtue of which a perception is a perception of one thing rather than another, but the mode of representation need not be picturing let alone reproduction. The suggestion that it is is immediately implausible, especially where the external expression of the emotion is at any distance from what might be regarded as its core (why should the perception of a scowl of anger itself involve a scowl?). Even where it is most plausible, because most vague and general, in the perception of pleasure and pain, the suggestion that the perception of pain is itself painful quickly becomes implausible once made precise. The pain of seeing a man afraid (a form of pain) need in no way be a form of fear. Admittedly, Spinoza confines his theory of imitation to cases like 'commiseration' and 'emulation' ('the desire which is engendered in us for anything because we imagine that other persons, who are like ourselves, possess the same desire'), but he offers no explanation of why the supposed mechanism does not operate more widely. The phenomena he discusses certainly occur, and his observations are often of interest, but the explanation he offers does not seem useful.

Spinoza offers a reason for not discussing what might be taken as the standard expressions of emotion: 'As for the external modifications of the body which are observed in the emotions, such as trembling, paleness, sobbing, laughter, and the like, I have neglected to notice them because they belong to the body alone without any relationship to the mind' (note before *E*, III, def. emo.). But if one follows Spinoza in recognizing that desires and dispositions to behaviour are built into certain emotions, one might be able to develop a theory of natural expression and gesture. Hampshire (1960c) does attempt to develop such a theory, treating natural expressions of emotion (shaking a fist in anger, etc.) as truncated actions. Indeed, he attempts to derive inner emotional life from dispositions to overt behaviour which become inhibited. The theory contains Spinozist and Freudian elements. Rather than considering it here, which would take us too far afield, I shall move on to the promised survey of psychological therapies, and return in the end to a brief discussion of the relation of Spinozist theory to Freudian theory.

III
Thought, Theory & Therapy

Therapies for psychological disorders can be ranged along a spectrum in accordance with the role and importance attached to the sufferer's thoughts or beliefs in the effectiveness of the therapy. That role will, in general, be correlated with the aetiological theory behind the therapeutic technique; if part of the problem is seen as ideogenic, then it is likely that thoughts will be assigned a role in unravelling the problem. This does not, however, determine the character of the thoughts that will be involved in the therapy: whether they need retrace the development of the pathogenic thoughts, be conscious or unconscious, be about the disorder itself or about other matters. In addition, the connection between aetiological and therapeutic theories, though strong, is not necessary. A therapy may be effective even though the theory that informs it is either false or non-existent. And, though what makes a problem or a disorder 'psychological' may be (partly) that it is ideogenic, the appropriate treatment might still be organic or 'physical'. Indeed, behind disputes about the aetiological role of thoughts may lie deeper differences about the nature of thoughts or, more broadly, 'the mental'. Thoughts themselves may be treated as epiphenomena (of no special interest), as mere events (even if causally efficacious events), or as interpretations (having internally elaborated structures).

1
Non-Analytical Therapies

Some therapies assign no role to thoughts; at this extreme end of the spectrum I would place certain drug and shock treatments. In so far as these suggest a model of mind, it is mind as brain; in so far as they are backed by an aetiological theory, it is the notion that somehow things (chemical or neurological) have become unbalanced. I do not wish to deny that such treatments work. It may well be that for certain sorts of problems (e.g. severe depression) the best thing one can do, the most effective treatment, is electric shock. This is an empirical question. But I do wish to suggest that when such treatment works, why it works must be regarded as a miracle. Things somehow get juggled back into place – we have no idea how. As with most miracles, however, we can expect the mystery to dissolve with the discovery of the causal mechanisms involved. What makes me place drug and shock treatments at the extreme non-thought end of our spectrum is that it seems unlikely that special thoughts or beliefs in the patient (especially beliefs about the nature of the problem) will be included in an account of the mechanisms.

There is a further question which I would like at least to raise. Are such non-thought treatments 'therapies'? Torture may produce psychological and behavioural changes, but it is not regarded as 'therapy'. This is partly because of the content of the treatment (pain, etc.), but more importantly because of its purposes and because it is not initiated by the patient or victim (the initiator having purposes of his own). It may also be in part because of the mechanisms involved. And if, for example, terror of the treatment itself is part of what contributes to non-thought 'cures', we may not wish to regard the changes as 'therapy'. Perhaps the terror of treatment forces the patient to overcome at least the overt manifestations of his problem. But is that 'cure' (even if the manifestations disappear permanently)? The treatment may produce change even when the patient does not desire it, or at least not because of a desire for change on the patient's part. Non-thought therapies (including behaviourist manipulations) are in a sense non-rational: they do not address themselves to the patient's thoughts and do not attempt to alter these thoughts through rational considerations. Whatever virtues they may have, non-thought therapies (that is, non-analytical techniques) do not treat problems in the terms in which they are problems for the patient; and, if the mechanisms are of certain kinds, their virtues may be thereby inherently limited.

2
Behaviour Therapy and 'Effectiveness'

Some therapies *apparently* assign no role to thoughts. Here I have in mind certain 'behaviour therapies'. Behaviour therapy is nicely illustrated, though perhaps caricatured, in Stanley Kubrick's film of Anthony Burgess's *A Clockwork Orange*. There Alex is conditioned against sex and violence (and, incidentally, Beethoven's Ninth Symphony) by being forced to watch certain films while nauseous from an injection. A similar actual treatment involved a man who attacked handbags: kept awake by amphetamine, he was presented with handbags and then made nauseous by injection of apomorphine, thus coming to associate handbags (as the conditioned stimulus) with an unpleasant response (Eysenck, 1965, pp. 182–8). Such treatments for behavioural dysfunctions use a model of mind I would describe as crudely behaviourist – the black box is at best an associative switchboard. But, again, I say this without wishing to deny that such treatment can 'work'. There is even something in the way of an aetiological theory to explain why it should work: there is a history of learning and previous conditioning which must be undone. But since the relevant learning theory holds that conditioning does not depend on thoughts, it holds that the treatment does not either. However, I would argue that we must assign thoughts a role, though rather a limited one (which places the therapy only a bit further along the spectrum), if we are to understand behaviour therapy.

Certainly its procedures are non-rational, in no way appealing to or addressing the patient's thoughts, but thoughts are none the less (at least minimally) involved. The behaviourists recognize that conditioning can involve delicate balances. Attacking handbags is dysfunctional in our society (the women and the police tend not to understand), but it would also be dysfunctional always to have to run at the sight of a handbag. So one needs the right *degree* of aversion. In addition, there are problems of stimulus specificity and generalization. Fine discriminations may be called for. For example, if one conditions a homosexual to avoid penises, what happens when he has to urinate? How do you condition the homosexual in relation to 'other penises' but not 'my penis'? The behaviourists have techniques for coping with such problems (Eysenck, 1965, p. 189ff., on conditioning a transvestite against only *himself* in women's clothes), but the conceptual question remains: 'How do you pick out *the stimulus* in the conditioning situation?' What is being conditioned? The behaviourists seem to assume this is given. But nevertheless there is a need to specify which aspects of the context are to be included in the stimulus. One cannot include *everything*, or the person's conditioning will relate to only this *particular* dress or this particular handbag (for example) in these particular surroundings – and so not carry over into his outside life, where his problem is. I think the specification of the stimulus must depend on the way in which the individual subject perceives the situation, and he or she can misperceive or, rather, perceive differently from the experimenters: Alex, for example, might respond only to the movie screen itself rather than to the images of violence on it (which he might *see as* abstract motions), or the transvestite might react to all women's clothes, and not just to himself in women's clothes, as the 'stimulus'. The subject must *selectively* respond to the stimulus object under a certain description, and 'we cannot control the property of a physical object to which an individual will respond' (we always present an object in a context, and so there is no 'objective' notion of 'the stimulus') (Taylor, 1964, pt II, and Chomsky, 1959, p. 553).

The conditioners are conditioning *something*, supposedly behavioural responses to environmental stimuli unmediated by thoughts. But if beliefs are not seen as influential factors, perhaps it is because the beliefs involved are, on the whole, *obvious*. People, in general, have similar interests and one can assume that the subject perceives the situation roughly as others (notably the experimenters) do – that is, the essential identifying description of the stimulus would be the same. However, it is clear that the response conditioned in the subject is a response to the environment *as he perceives* it, i.e. as he believes it to be. But it must be admitted that the subject's beliefs *about* the nature and source of his problem are left out, are taken to be irrelevant to the actual problem (which is a behavioural 'dysfunction') and to the treatment of it. The patient need not have *any* theory, let alone a correct one, about the nature of these problems. So though thoughts have a role, it is a limited one.

It is worth adding that the importance of thought in specifying the stimulus, aside from helping us place behaviour therapy on our spectrum, can form part of a more comprehensive critique of the aetiological and learning theory behind the therapy. For example, as Chomsky puts it, 'stimuli are not objectively identifiable independently of the resulting behaviour' (1959, p. 552, n. 5). If one ignores the mediating role of thoughts, one ends up discriminating 'stimuli' (and 'reinforcing conditions') through the 'responses' to them. Hence A is specified only as 'the cause of B'. And it is, of course, uninformative to be told that 'the cause of B' caused B. Consider someone who claimed that 'the desire to do X caused the doing of X'. If the 'doing of X' were the only criterion for 'desire' it would follow that people do only what they desire and that they desire whatever they do. Similarly, crude behaviourist definitions of 'stimulus', 'response', 'reinforcement', etc., create merely the illusion of understanding. If the notions are well and fixedly defined, then there are few (if any) lawlike relations between stimuli and responses (except for certain limited cases in rats – Chomsky,

1959, p. 551). There are few simple laws of input and output that can bypass problems of identification (i.e. specifying 'stimulus', etc., under a description), intermediary thoughts, etc.

There is a clinical objection to behaviour therapy, namely that it treats only symptoms, and that there will always be an underlying problem that will re-emerge elsewhere. This seems to me an empirical issue, and, whatever one's suspicions, the evidence is not yet in. I think this is all one can say *a priori* about the empirical issue, but I also think that there are several conceptual problems connected with claims of effectiveness about which at least a bit more should be said here. So I will again digress before moving along our spectrum.

The effectiveness of a therapy is no guarantor of the truth of the theory of the therapy. The therapy may work for reasons having nothing to do with the theory behind it (indeed, it may only *appear* to work because of extraneous forces that might otherwise have led to 'spontaneous' remission, or because of placebo effects). Or the theory of the therapy may show how pathological effects can be counteracted, without connecting that efficaciousness with a theory of the causal production of the symptoms (cf. drinking milk or surgical procedures which may alleviate the suffering from ulcers, but do not reverse the causal order or retrace the steps that led to the problem and *thereby* undo it. That is, it is 'symptomatic' rather than 'causal' therapy). The converse is often advanced against the claims of Freudian psychoanalysis. That is, it is argued that the ineffectiveness of Freudian psychoanalysis, or the indifference in effectiveness between it and other methods, reveals the untruth of Freudian theory.

First, what is 'effectiveness'? The notion of 'cure' is notoriously contentious, and the notion of 'cure rate' inevitably shares the infection. Many, especially those who regard 'neurosis' as 'behavioural dysfunction', equate cure, or success, or recovery with 'removal of symptoms'. This does not advance the discussion as much as it might at first appear to do. What constitutes a 'symptom'? This may vary from society to society and even from person to person (e.g. what is 'normal' for the man who vomits every morning, but is otherwise sound and wonders when asked about it, 'Doesn't everybody?' – a story of N. Reider told by Erikson, 1968, p. 18). Even if the nature of a 'symptom' was otherwise clear, it is not at all clear that all (or even most) patients entering psychoanalysis exhibit gross symptoms the removal of which constitutes 'cure'. Many come seeking release from inhibitions or a form of understanding (or something else) properly characterized in some way other than as the 'removal of symptoms'. And even where the notion of 'removal of symptoms' seems applicable, it may make a huge difference *how* the symptoms are removed. Psychoanalysis and behaviour therapy may not simply *contrast* in effectiveness, but actually be *incommensurable*. Wallerstein speaks of the distinction between the outcome goals of analytic therapy conceptualized in terms of observable behavior and relationship changes and the process goals of analytic therapy conceptualized in meta-psychological explanatory terms that posit at least implicitly a theory of therapy, of how analysis brings about change and reaches its outcome goals (Wallerstein, 1965, p. 768).

Process changes may simply be closed to behaviour therapy. In these terms even if behavioural symptoms disappear permanently and no new symptoms emerge, behaviour therapy may be inherently 'superficial'. Though various outcomes of analysis may be

> confirmable for the most part via observable behavioral referents, they nonetheless represent manifest end points, outcomes, of processes of intrapsychic, analytic change. Though phenomenologically similar, they are not dynamically identical with the same behavioral changes induced by other, non-psychoanalytic, means (Wallerstein, 1965, p. 754).

I will cite one example of treatment by rational alteration of desires (cited by Wallerstein for another purpose):

> Gill, in comparing true structural change in the ego as wrought by classical psychoanalysis with the change consequent upon the 'corrective emotional experience' in Alexander's usage of that term, stated that 'dependent behaviour is given up not because he has learned that if he acts too dependent he will be punished by a loss of therapy hours, but because despite the invitation to regress and the maintenance of the frequency of his hours he has come to feel and understand his dependency in such a way that he no longer needs it or wants it (1965, p. 751).

We should recall these contrasts when we come to discuss the cases of Little Hans (and Peter) and Little Albert, and the very different aetiologies and treatments they are associated with.

Returning to 'effectiveness', if we (despite hesitations) take effectiveness as a matter of cure rate (over the spontaneous rate), and we take 'cure' in the sense of 'removal of symptoms', one still must explain how to measure 'cure rates'. The length of time a treatment takes is, I think, irrelevant. There may be difficulties about degrees of 'alleviation' of symptoms short of total removal. These too I do not wish to consider. But differences in the character of the symptoms removed, and in the initial selection of patients, must be considered. We are sometimes offered gross statistics said to reveal that it is a matter of indifference whether one is treated for a problem by Freudian psychoanalysis, a psychoanalytic therapy informed by another theory, a non-psychoanalytic therapy, or even nothing at all. The cure and relapse rates are said to be roughly comparable. (Kline, 1972, ch. 11, provides a useful survey of the main empirical studies.) But what problem or condition is being cured? Different problems may be amenable to different methods, and these differences may be *concealed by the statistical categories*. Perhaps certain well-defined behavioural dysfunctions (e.g. phobias) are readily removed by conditioning techniques. Does this show that such techniques are equally effective in dealing with all the classical psychoneuroses? Do patients with such neuroses get treated by the conditioning techniques in the first place? Perhaps psychoanalytic institutes report cure rates roughly comparable to those of behavioural therapists. Here too there are problems in the nature and assessment of 'cure', and, as I wish to emphasize, initial selection of patients. (Even if all comers were taken, patients would to some extent be self-selected on the basis of their or their referring doctors' expectations from different techniques.) Such selection serves a variety of purposes. If one's aim were to produce the highest possible cure rate, careful initial selection of the patient population joined with treatment by the most experienced analysts could presumably produce as high a rate as one pleases. The facts are that we do not have the data we need for well-grounded judgment, and that the statistical categories tend to conceal problems and differences in the character of symptoms, and the nature and assessment of cures. Ideals of 'randomness' obscure just those issues that should be explored.

In addition, and most interesting for our purposes, the theories behind the therapies may differ in their ability to explain the effectiveness (whatever its actual extent once all the relevant factors have been clarified) of other therapies as well as their own.

3
Lévi-Strauss and Quesalid

I shall now focus on what I take to be the 'thought' end of the spectrum. Lévi-Strauss suggests that what is essential to the effectiveness of shamanism is the provision of a theory or conceptual scheme that enables the patient to reintegrate an otherwise alien experience. It does not matter that the understanding provided is 'mythical' or 'symbolic'. The shaman's theory need not be (literally) true, so long as the patient believes it and it is significant to him. The theory behind Freudian psychoanalysis might suggest quite other constraints on effective insight. In interpreting a symptom, an analyst is supposed to be retracing its actual history, i.e. its literal development. However, this appearance of extreme disagreement may be deceptive and should be further examined. When it comes to it, Lévi-Strauss would actually, I think, require at least 'structural' correspondences over and above coherence, for the effectiveness of symbols. And if we examine the role assigned to 'fantasy' in psychoanalytic theory, a number of questions can be raised (see Neu, 1973): Why should insight have any effect? Is literal truth necessary to the effectiveness of insight? Might 'fantasy' be as effective as reality? Why? Would it matter whether it was memory of (earlier) fantasy or (current) fantasy of memory? Why is insight (even where it includes literal truth as well as coherence) not enough? (That it is not enough is shown by the importance attached to abreaction, transference, and timing interpretations.)

First, let us see what Lévi-Strauss (1949) on the shaman can tell us about psychoanalytic theory, and what psychoanalytic theory can tell us about shamanism.

Lévi-Strauss tells the fascinating and instructive story of Quesalid. He was an unbeliever in shamanistic powers and undertook training as a shaman in order to refute their claims. But, much to his amazement, his use of the bizarre procedures – especially the technique of extracting a concealed tuft of bloodied down from his own mouth and claiming he had sucked out the pathological foreign body in the form of a bloody worm (1949, p. 175) – produced cures. And he became the most powerful shaman of all.

Now the initial undertaking, in so far as it was an effort to refute the shamans, is itself odd. It is not clear what Quesalid's failures could contribute that a collection of the failures of established shamans would not. Indeed, on the face of it, such failures promise far less. A man who set out to refute astrology would gain nothing by himself mastering the techniques of astrology. It could be claimed that his failures counted only against his practice, not against the techniques themselves. Similarly, if Quesalid had failed to cure, it would simply have shown that he had not mastered the techniques, that he was an inadequate shaman (not that shamanism was inadequate). This mode of defence would inevitably be open, and perhaps even more open for shamanism than astrology. Fellow astrologers might be sufficiently scientific in spirit so that they tried to replicate the critic's procedures with greater precision and success. The principles might be sufficiently objective, so that their application by the believers yielded the same results: false predictions. The shamans have an extra out. It may be one of the principles of the practice, that only a believer in the principles can effectively use them. Or if not a 'believer', someone infused with the proper 'spirit', one with a 'calling'. Quesalid's failure would only reveal him as a failed shaman, and not the failure of shamanism. Even if other shamans failed to succeed where he had failed, whatever explanations were normally available would still be so.

There is a problem about what distinguishes a routine failure from an 'anomaly', i.e. a failure arising in the context of a challenge or test of their powers. (What makes something a problem in what Kuhn calls 'normal science' rather than an anomaly leading to crisis and breakdown, and so revolution?) There are two things to notice: first, nothing is added to the confirmation or falsification situation by Quesalid's becoming a shaman, or an unbeliever becoming an astrologer. The same difficulties for the theory arise from the failures of its professionals. Second, if the usual outs used to explain failures seem *ad hoc* (and the juggling seems more *ad hoc* should Quesalid's failures receive special explanations: he lacks the spirit, etc.), one still has to explain what makes a change or adjustment in theory seem *ad hoc* rather than a natural development or articulation or elaboration. Every theory has to accommodate awkward facts. But sometimes the accommodations become more awkward than the facts. When there are too many epicycles and an alternative theory is available, a shift is possible. What exactly, however, makes a theoretical claim or shift in theory a 'simplification' rather than '*ad hoc*' raises many of the deepest questions in the philosophy of science (and some of the hardest disputes within scientific argument itself). I will leave these issues here. Quesalid did not manage a successful refutation of the shamans through failure. His was a different success, and raises different issues.

We should note that Quesalid's undertaking is much less odd if he hoped to *understand* rather than to *refute* the shamans. Indeed, many psychoanalysts claim that critics cannot understand the character of psychoanalytic claims or the nature of the evidence for them without themselves being psychoanalysed. It is not, however, necessary that critics themselves become psychoanalysts. But Quesalid was dealing with a practice that depends on concealment: to appreciate the character of magic it may well be necessary to practice it rather than simply to experience its effects.

4

Consensus and Curing

Lévi-Strauss tells the story of Quesalid mainly in order to emphasize the importance of belief by the community or group: cure by magic is a 'consensual' phenomenon (1949, p. 169). There are a number of separable claims which one might confuse under this description. The point here is different from that made by saying that what counts as a 'symptom' is a matter of the view of the society. Though that is (largely) true, once the character of sickness and health is fixed within a society, the transition from one to the other – or cure – may not be achievable by change in public opinion (or anyone's beliefs). There are limits to the powers of consensus: a myth (of converging rivers, etc.) will not mend a broken bone, and faith will not turn an aspirin into a birth control pill. The point Lévi-Strauss wishes to make he puts as follows: 'Quesalid did not become a great shaman because he cured his patients; he cured his patients because he had become a great shaman' (1949,

p. 180). Here, too, distinctions are necessary. We must distinguish group consensus in relation to the *status* of a sorcerer and in relation to the *power* of a sorcerer. Community belief may provide the criterion for a social role – this is a logical or conceptual connection. On the other hand, community belief may produce the power associated with a social role – this may be logical, but more interestingly may be an empirical connection. That social role and power can be separated is shown, in the cases of doctors and patients, by the fact that people may be able actually to heal or actually to suffer independently of the opinion of their society. Confirmation by the community does, however, help determine who we are, whether doctor, shaman, or patient.

In so far as this is a matter of social role, group consensus does indeed, meaning logically, determine who we are. This seems to be what is happening in the case of the Zuni boy who appears to become a witch in the course of his witchcraft trial (as he and his accusers come to believe he is). If the relevant community believes it, it is true. Their belief is part of what constitutes its being true. Who counts as a shaman, a doctor, a patient depends (in this way) on group consensus. But group consensus may also operate causally. It might be called the 'Genet Effect'. Told at the age of ten that he was 'a thief', Genet conceived himself in that way and decided he must become one, and did. He realized the label in his life (Genet, 1949). (Cf. the development of 'patienthood' as an identity, e.g. in Dora – Erikson, 1964, p. 173.) In the case of shamanism and healing, the mechanisms may be more complicated. The community's belief in the shaman's powers may help produce those powers, in quite various and complex ways. Before looking at some of those ways, I want to bring out, in another way, the contrast I have been trying to make.

Consider the case of a 'king'. All believe X is the king and therefore he *is* the king. But there may be place in the society for a distinction between *de facto* and *de jure* kings – e.g. there may be constitutional conditions for kingship (direct descent from previous kings and ultimately God) that will hold whether or not the community believes them to hold, and which the community cannot make hold by believing. The case of the 'shaman' is importantly different from that of the *de facto* king. If all accept X is a shaman he may therefore be a shaman, have the social role and have the social powers of the position. But unlike the king, all of whose powers are social, he may still lack the power to heal (though belief in that power may be what gave him community consensus to role in first place). That is, the doctor or shaman may not be the man who can heal; he is the man the community believes can heal. The title comes from belief in the power. The power, however, need not be a necessary condition of the belief, indeed, it may not exist prior to the belief. And it is possible that, in some cases, it arises as a result of the belief. If everyone believes 'X is king', he may have the power to rule *in virtue* of that belief. If everyone believes 'X is a shaman', he may still lack the power to heal. The interesting question is whether the acceptance can produce the power (where this is an empirical connection) and how.

Lévi-Strauss cites Cannon on the physiology of voodoo; and one can understand how the withdrawal of the community, the isolation a voodoo curse produces by virtue of the community's accepting it, might lead to physical collapse. (Consider models for self-fulfilling prophecies.) Freud himself recognized the professional importance of acceptance by the community. (Consider the use of the title 'Professor' in Vienna.) Such recognition increases the 'authority' of the physician, and may contribute to the effectiveness of his technique. But it is not in itself a sufficient explanation of effectiveness. As late as 1910 Freud could write:

> Hitherto, this authority, with its enormous weight of suggestion, has been against us. All our therapeutic successes have been achieved in the face of this suggestion: it is surprising that any successes at all could be gained in such circumstances. . . . I can only say that when I assured my patients that I knew how to relieve them permanently of their sufferings they looked round my modest abode, reflected on my lack of fame and title, and regarded me like the possessor of an infallible system at a gambling-resort, of whom people say that if he could do what he professes he would look very different himself. Nor was it really pleasant to carry out a psychical operation while the colleagues whose duty it should have been to assist took pleasure in spitting into the field of operation, and while at the first signs of blood or restlessness in the patient his relatives began threatening the operating surgeon. . . . Social suggestion is at present favourable to treating nervous patients by hydropathy, dieting and electrotherapy, but that does not enable such measures to get the better of neuroses. Time will show whether psycho-analytic treatment can accomplish more (Freud, 1910d, pp. 146–7).

Certainly co-operation from surrounding family and community is helpful and perhaps even necessary. Their belief, faith, recognition, etc., may yield such co-operation. But perhaps the essential element is the *patient*'s acceptance of the doctor's authority. And belief by the community, consensus, may contribute to producing belief in the individual patient. But perhaps such belief can arise independently and still be effective. (Quesalid himself attributed his first success to the patient's faith. The treatment worked 'because he [the sick person] believed strongly in his dream about me' – Lévi-Strauss, 1949, p. 176. Freud says that the patient need not enter treatment with any initial belief (1913c, p. 126). If it is necessary, it can develop in the course of treatment.) The question now becomes the relation of belief by the patient to the effectiveness of the therapy.

Lévi-Strauss, aside from emphasizing the consensual elements (without distinguishing the logical and causal) in shamanism, goes on to speculate about the mechanism by which shamanistic ritual and magical symbols produce cures. And he extends his account of the effectiveness of symbols to psychoanalysis. This account requires that one pay attention to the content of the rituals and symbols (not just to their acceptance by the community).

5
Structuralist Explanation: Coherence and Correspondence and Curing

There is ground for general suspicion of structuralist explanations: does being told that one thing we do not understand is similar in structure to another thing we do not understand help us to understand either? The nature of the 'similarities' must be specified. We must look to the details of each such explanation offered to see what, if any, enlightenment can be found. Lévi-Strauss offers parallels between the shaman and the psychoanalyst, and between the theories of both and physiological theory.

Quesalid effects cures through using the bloody down despite the fact that he knows this technique to be bogus; it is not connected with any known or believed aetiology ('sickness' is not really captured by bloodying a concealed tuft and Quesalid does not think that it is). But the method works and even enables Quesalid to expose 'impostors' (Lévi-Strauss, 1949, p. 178). His success reveals that the therapist need not believe in order for the therapy to work. We shall have to explore the natural implication of this: if belief by the practitioner is not necessary, then perhaps truth is not necessary either (which is not to say that the *content* of rituals and symbols and interpretations is irrelevant – even if truth as literal correspondence to an objective reality is).

Lévi-Strauss suggests that shamanistic therapies in non-Western cultures work because they provide a way of understanding problems and the world. The patient is given a theory, a set of terms and relationships that enable him to fit his experience into an intelligible order.

The system is valid precisely to the extent that it allows the coalescence or precipitation of these diffuse states, whose discontinuity also makes them painful [p. 182]. The song seems to have as its principal aim the description of these pains to the sick woman and the naming of them, that is, their presentation to her in a form accessible to conscious or unconscious thought [p. 195]. That the mythology of the shaman does not correspond

117

to an objective reality does not matter. The sick woman believes in the myth and belongs to a society which believes in it. The tutelary spirits and malevolent spirits, the supernatural monsters and magical animals, are all part of a coherent system on which the native conception of the universe is founded. The sick woman accepts these mythical beings or, more accurately, she has never questioned their existence. What she does not accept are the incoherent and arbitrary pains, which are an alien element in her system but which the shaman, calling upon myth, will re-integrate within a whole where everything is meaningful (1949, p. 197).

For Lévi-Strauss the beliefs need not be true, because in so far as the problem is one of *not understanding*, *any* coherent story or theory will solve it (though of course the story or theory must not fail to correspond at key points with known realities) and so end the suffering which is a *suffering from unintelligibility*. Psychoanalysis, in this view, may be the new mythology of our culture (1949, p. 183). Lévi-Strauss's point sheds a certain light. Coherence matters because patients are partly suffering from incoherence, the alien unintelligibility of their experience.

I think, however, that a Spinozist view of emotions and the mental would contribute much to a clearer understanding of how therapies which operate through beliefs can transform mental states. Emphasizing the importance of thought in the classification and discrimination of emotional states, the Spinozist view illuminates the consequent importance of reflexive knowledge in changing those states. If we acknowledge that emotions essentially involve beliefs, we can begin to see how changing beliefs can transform emotions. In the realm of the mental, understanding of the state becomes part of the state, because it is identified or specified through the associated beliefs. Where knowledge is self-reflexive, knowing can transform the thing known. This line of thought could reveal why insight is important, and perhaps why insight is not enough. Lévi-Strauss's theory, however, develops in a different direction.

Lévi-Strauss thinks symbols are effective, not because they are literally true and not because they change beliefs and so transform the associated mental state, but because they correspond with an underlying reality. The myth and the true account are similar in 'structure'. He speculates that the parallel in the case of a mythical incantation sung by the Cuna shaman to ease difficult childbirth is an underlying *physiological* reality. The myth is about a quest for the lost soul of the mother, a myth of passage through and over obstacles, and its elements correspond to or represent the vagina and uterus of the pregnant woman (1949, p. 188). He goes on to speculate that psychoanalysis too has a correspondence with the same physiological reality:

Given this hypothesis or any other of the same type, the shamanistic cure and the psychoanalytic cure would become strictly parallel. It would be a matter, either way, of stimulating an organic transformation which would consist essentially in a structural reorganization, by inducing the patient intensively to live out a myth – either received or created by him – whose structure would be, at the unconscious level, analogous to the structure whose genesis is sought on the organic level. The effectiveness of symbols would consist precisely in this 'inductive property', by which formally homologous structures, built out of different materials at different levels of life – organic processes, unconscious mind, rational thought – are related to one another. Poetic metaphor provides a familiar example of this inductive process, but as a rule it does not transcend the unconscious level. Thus we note the significance of Rimbaud's intuition that metaphor can change the world (1949, p. 201).

But this discussion pays too little attention to the elements on either side of the parallel, and to the nature of 'induction' and of what Lévi-Strauss calls 'reliving' or 'abreaction'. Again I would look to Spinoza for a better understanding of the power of metaphor, at least where the world changed is the mental world. But Lévi-Strauss means to explain how the myth can produce physical, organic, changes or cures.

He mentions that 'Freud seems to have suggested . . . that the description in psychological terms of the structure of psychoses and neuroses must one day be replaced by physiological, or even biochemical concepts' (1949, p. 201). That is true, but as the *Project for a Scientific Psychology* shows, the sort of reduction Freud had in mind was neuro-physiological. (To be fair, the *Project* was published a year after the original publication of Lévi-Strauss's essay.) And neurophysiology is rather different from gross physiology; our mental states may be embodied, but they are not precisely 'paralleled' on a gross level. Indeed, in the specific case of hysteria, no reduction to the physiological is possible. As Freud insists: 'Hysteria behaves as though anatomy did not exist or as though it had no knowledge of it' (Freud, 1893c, p. 169). And Lévi-Strauss does not notice the difference between 'reduction' and 'replacement'. The sort of *reduction* Freud envisaged did involve precise parallels, preserving psychoanalytic laws in different terms.[1] But the sort of biochemical basis Lévi-Strauss mentions (chemical basis for psychosis) would not provide parallels for psychoanalytic claims. Instead of reducing psychoanalytic theory, it would *replace* it. Indeed, it would leave the role of thoughts, their relevance, obscure. Why and in what way should ideas or thoughts provide a handle on to chemical forces? The term 'induction' covers the obscurity without clarifying it. How does 'inducing the patient intensively to live out a myth' help?

Lévi-Strauss calls this 'abreaction' (1949, pp. 182ff., 199), but this living or reliving is not the same as the early psychoanalytic notion (which involved 'energy discharge' and hence relief). In relation to the shaman's bloody-worm rituals, etc., Lévi-Strauss actually speaks of the sorcerer abreacting *for* the silent patient (1949, p. 183), which is without sense in psychoanalytic terms. And again, he does not explain why symbolic thoughts should provide a lever for producing physiological changes, except that the thoughts run 'parallel' to the physiology. But do they? And if they did, would that *explain* anything?

The difficulty may be brought out more clearly if we notice something Lévi-Strauss seems also to notice but then neglects. He acknowledges at one point that the complicated itinerary of the Cuna song 'is a true mythical anatomy, corresponding less to the real structure of the genital organs than to a kind of emotional geography, identifying each point of resistance and each thrust' (1949, p. 195). What he fails to emphasize is the implication that what is paralleled is not actual anatomy, but, as with hysteria, a fantasy anatomy. I am inclined to think that this therapy will be effective only if the difficulties are hysterical, i.e. ideogenic (Lévi-Strauss says the shaman cures 'true organic disorders' – 1949, p. 199). But the deeper problem in any case is that structuralist explanations here fail to explain. The general suspicion I mentioned earlier is here specifically realized: one process we do not understand is said to be similar to another process we do not understand, but this statement does not help us understand either of them. We cannot understand the process of psychoanalysis and the process of shamanism in terms of a third, underlying, process which they both parallel. We might begin to do so *if* there were an underlying physiological process common to them, but they each parallel fantasy physiologies, and there is no reason to expect that fantasy physiologies (unlike actual human physiology) will be the same for different cultures and individuals. Even if there were parallels to a common anatomy, how would this *explain* the effectiveness of either shamanism or psychoanalysis? Lévi-Strauss thinks these psychological treatments have direct physiological consequences, but does not explain how. He says, 'In our view, the song constitutes a *psychological manipulation* of the sick organ, and it is precisely from this manipulation that a cure is expected' (1949, p. 192). Why should telling a story, even if parallel with actual anatomy, 'work', e.g. make obstructions disappear? We can see how giving unintelligible physiological processes meaning may ease our psychological pain, but why should it alter the physiological processes themselves? The rhythm of the song might help (as a lullaby helps put a child to sleep) but this would not explain the relevance of the *content* of the song.

Lévi-Strauss's account is inadequate. Mere parallels do not explain why changes in one branch should bring about changes in the other. Even if there were the claimed parallels, why should there be a necessity to *preserve* the parallel (through bodily changes as the song progresses)? His account should be restricted to shamanistic cures of hysterical disorders rather than of physical disorders in general. Indeed, the fact that a disorder was curable by shamanistic story-telling, etc., might be part of what shows it to be 'hysterical' (along with the absence of organic causes, dissimilarities in pattern of disorder, etc.). Non-hysterical disorders may lack even fantasy parallels (and hence lack symbolic meaning).

Shamanistic cures are of three types, which are not, however, mutually exclusive.

> The sick organ or member may be physically involved, through a manipulation or suction which aims at extracting the cause of the illness – usually a thorn, crystal, or feather made to appear at the opportune moment, as in tropical America, Australia, and Alaska. Curing may also revolve, as among the Araucanians, around a sham battle, waged in the hut and then outdoors, against harmful spirits. Or, as among the Navaho, the officiant may recite incantations and prescribe actions (such as placing the sick person on different parts of a painting traced on the ground with colored sands and pollens) which bear *no direct relationship* to the specific disturbance to be cured. In all these cases, the therapeutic method (which as we know is often effective) is difficult to interpret. When it deals directly with the unhealthy organ, it is too grossly concrete (generally, pure deceit) to be granted intrinsic value. And when it consists in the repetition of often highly abstract ritual, it is difficult for us to understand its direct bearing on the illness. It would be convenient to dismiss these difficulties by declaring that we are dealing with psychological cures. But this term will remain meaningless unless we can explain how specific psychological representations are invoked to combat equally specific physiological disturbances (1949, p. 191).

But Lévi-Strauss's attempt to generalize from the text he considers fails. The fantasy anatomy that a psychoanalyst may confront may be different from the fantasy anatomy a myth deals with. So psychoanalysis is not parallel to shamanism (in this respect) for they are not parallel to the same third thing (actual anatomy). And many shamanistic cures are without 'correspondences' or physiological parallels at all. So Lévi-Strauss's account cannot be extended to cures in general. Even the particular symbolic treatment he discusses lacks a real physiological parallel (and even if it had it, the mechanism of change would not be clarified by merely pointing to the parallel). How a relation to fantasy anatomy allows effects on actual anatomy depends, I think, on the original disturbances in anatomy being hysterical (i.e. also depending on fantasies of anatomy – though perhaps different ones). The importance of thought in therapy should be clarified by the importance of thoughts in aetiology. Psychoanalysis tries to explain ideogenesis. Lévi-Strauss seems to deny or ignore it.

To summarize: Lévi-Strauss makes suggestions in terms of (social) consensus, (psychological) coherence, and (physiological) correspondence to explain the effectiveness of shamanistic symbols and magic, and extends his account to psychoanalytic treatment. Properly sorted out, I think the first two suggestions contain valuable insight, but that the third fails both for the particular case and in general.

6
Psychoanalysis and Shamanism: The 'Same Forces'?

Let us reverse the account. What can psychoanalysis tell us about shamanism? Erik Erikson suggests that the shaman is dealing with the 'same forces':

> In northern California I knew an old shaman woman who laughed merrily at my conception of mental disease, and then sincerely – to the point of ceremonial tears – told me of her way of sucking the 'pains' out of her patients. She was as convinced of her ability to cure and to understand as I was of mine. While occupying extreme opposites in the history of American psychiatry we felt like colleagues. This feeling was based on some joint sense of the historical relativity of all psychotherapy: the relativity of the patient's outlook on his symptoms, of the role he assumes by dint of being a patient, of the kind of help which he seeks, and of the kinds of help which are eagerly offered or are available. The old shaman woman and I disagreed about the locus of emotional sickness, what it 'was,' and what specific methods would cure it. Yet, when she related the origin of a child's illness to the familial tensions existing within her tribe, when she attributed the 'pain' (which had got 'under a child's skin') to his grandmother's sorcery (ambivalence) I knew she dealt with the same forces, and with the same kinds of conviction, as I did in my professional nook. This experience has been repeated in discussion with colleagues who, although not necessarily more 'primitive,' are oriented toward different psychiatric persuasions (Erikson, 1958, p. 55).

What is the meaning or place of this claim about the 'same forces'? Is this an advance on Lévi-Strauss's 'correspondences'? I think in some ways it is. Erikson's 'forces' may be less misleading than Lévi-Strauss's rather vague allusion to physiology and talk of 'induction'. But again one would have to discuss in detail the nature of the 'forces' involved. I will not do that here (though the quoted passage gives a place to start with the notion of 'ambivalence'), but rather I wish to suggest what it is that one would be looking to the details to reveal or confirm (and what sort of discoveries would be made). One way to bring out the sort of issues I have in mind is to point out that 'same' in 'same forces', like 'similar' in 'similar structures', is an incomplete predicate; and one must look to the accompanying noun ('forces', 'structures') to discover the criteria of applicability for the term. That is, 'similarity' is always 'similarity in a certain respect' or 'from a certain point of view'. One cannot say whether 'A is similar to B' is true or false until one is told in what respect they are thought to be similar. (Or rather, it will always be true for any A and for any B that there will always be some respect in which they are similar, *and* some respect in which they are not similar.) Part of the problem with Lévi-Strauss's claims is that the notion of 'structure' is itself insufficiently specific. It leaves unclear in what respect psychoanalysis and shamanism are said to be similar. When 'structure' is further specified (so the similarity or parallel is in terms of physiology), the details reveal the claim to be false or at least unpromising. Erikson too must specify what is the 'same' for the psychoanalyst and the shaman, i.e. they will be the same under a certain description or *qua* so-and-so, and here the 'so-and-so' is 'forces' (though these still need to be further specified in terms of 'psychic energies' and 'physico-chemical quantities' or, perhaps most plausibly, 'emotions'). I think 'forces' a more specific notion than Lévi-Strauss's. More important, both the psychoanalysts and the shamans are more likely to know about them (especially where they are understood in terms of 'emotions') than about physiology. Most important, discussion of 'forces' (especially emotional forces) is more likely to lead to an understanding of the role of understanding in producing change than is discussion of a mysterious 'inductive' process that connects change in one part of a parallel with change in another part (see p. 135). But I would like now to try to make my abstract point in another way.

What is Erikson saying when he says that the shaman and the psychoanalyst deal with the 'same forces'? Most simply, that they are using different words (and concepts) to talk about the same things. One must look to the details, i.e. to individual cases, to see whether this is true. One will not, however, discover that the terminologies *mean* the same – they do not.[2] Using Frege's distinction between 'sense' and 'reference', the shaman's system of terms and the psychoanalyst's have different senses but the same reference. The same object can be picked out under different descriptions, and one must indicate or specify under what sort of description they are the 'same object'. Consider Frege's own example of 'the morning star' and 'the evening star'. They refer to the same planet, Venus, which is a physical object that can be re-identified under different descriptions. The important point is that the discovery that they have the same reference was an *empirical* discovery. It could not have been achieved by an *a priori* analysis of the meanings of the relevant terms: the expressions in fact have different 'senses' (e.g. the morning star can be seen only in the morning, the evening star only in the evening) despite the fact that they refer to the same (astronomical) object. The criteria for identity here are provided by spatio-temporal continuity. To be sure that the shaman and the psychoanalyst refer to the same underlying forces, one would need some third way of describing the underlying 'reality',[3] or, if not a third description, at least a method for re-identifying the forces under the alternate shamanistic and psychoanalytic descriptions, for translating between them.

The question whether shamanistic and psychoanalytic vocabularies have a common reference despite their differing meanings is empirical, that is, it cannot be settled by *a priori* analysis of the meanings of the words, for the meanings *are* different. Even within a particular culture with a single common nosological vocabulary, words which apparently have a single meaning (e.g. 'phobia') may be tied to very different theories and so be importantly different. Psychoanalysts and behaviour therapists, for example, may, in some senses, be talking about different disorders. Diagnostic labelling is theory-laden.

7

Little Hans and Little Albert, Psychoanalysis and Behaviour Therapy: On Aetiology and Displacement

Will it turn out that everybody is talking about the same world and therefore really talking about ('referring to') the 'same forces'? *No.* (Our earlier contrast between *reductions*, which preserve entities and lawlike relations among them, and *replacements*, which displace prior conceptual and explanatory schemes, depended on the answer being '*No*'.) If the shaman and the psychoanalyst mean different things but refer to the same thing by their *different* words, one is tempted to say that the psychoanalyst and the behaviour therapist refer to the same thing but *mean* different things by their use of the *same* words. They may have a common nosological vocabulary, but the aetiological theories and the theories of change associated with it are so different that the phenomena covered may differ widely. The things referred to are the same only at the rather superficial level of 'behaviour' (here recall Wallerstein's point).

Consider the contrasting cases of Little Hans and Little Albert. Both boys suffered from animal *phobias*. There the important similarities end. As Freud tells it, Little Hans's fear of being bitten by horses was essentially a displaced fear of his father. It developed out of an Oedipal constellation of ambivalent feelings, and was intimately and intricately connected with the birth of his little sister, masturbation, his sexual theories (especially the universality of 'widdlers' and a faecal theory of birth), and other fears (especially of horses falling down and his mother having another child). Little Albert, on the other hand, did not develop his own fear of white rats, it was produced in him experimentally by Watson. Watson used Pavlovian conditioning techniques (sight or touch of rats followed by loud noise) to produce a phobic fear of white rats in Little Albert. The eleven-month-old child had previously been on quite friendly terms with the creatures. Afterwards, the fear response generalized to other furry animals, cotton wool, and even men with beards.

The two cases are extraordinarily different, but many behavioural psychologists try to assimilate them. They argue that Freud went, illegitimately, beyond what the evidence would support: namely, a behaviourist account of the formation of phobias. They suggest that Watson's conditioning model provides a more adequate alternative aetiology for Little Hans's problems, and makes 'desensitization' or 'deconditioning' a more appropriate treatment than 'interpretation' or 'analysis'. Unfortunately, the only thing they can see and so count as 'evidence' is 'behaviour' (narrowly described and conceived) and there are failures of understanding at every level.

Eysenck (1965, p. 107) refers to the critique of Freud's case of Little Hans by Wolpe and Rachman as 'a classic'. But it in fact contains so many misunderstandings that one hardly knows where to begin enumerating them. For example, their conclusion states:

> No confirmation by direct observation is obtained for any psychoanalytic theorem, though psychoanalysts have believed the contrary for 50 years. The demonstrations claimed are really interpretations that are treated as facts (Wolpe and Rachman, 1960, p. 219).

Evidence in psychoanalysis must be based on inference, given the nature of the claims (about unconscious processes, etc.). The crude demand for 'confirmation by direct observation' is as misplaced as a demand to be shown electrons.[4] And I suspect that behind it is an equally crude observational/theoretical distinction. 'Crude' because 'observations' and 'facts' are inevitably more or less theory-laden.[5] *Their* theory blinds them to the very rich evidence Freud provides.

This is not the place for a thoroughgoing examination of their 'critique', and so a few further examples will have to suffice. They attack the claim that, as they put it, 'Hans had a sexual desire for his mother', saying: 'That Hans derived satisfaction from his mother and enjoyed her presence we will not even attempt to dispute. But nowhere is there any evidence of his wish to copulate with her' (Wolpe and Rachman, 1960, p. 212). It is virtually incredible that they should use such a narrow notion of the 'sexual'. (I am leaving aside such evidence as the 'borer' fantasy – Freud, 1909b, p. 128.) In the very case under discussion, Freud goes to elaborate lengths to show that the 'sexual' desires of children are based on their own (sometimes bizarre) sexual theories, which in turn are based on their own level of bodily functioning. It would be remarkable if infantile sexual desires took the forms of normal adult sexuality (e.g. desire for genital union – few four-year-olds can conceive of such a union, let alone conceive of it as desirable). The sexual relations desired in Oedipal contexts must be understood more broadly. That they are none the less 'sexual' Freud demonstrates at length in his 'Three Essays on the Theory of Sexuality' (1905d).

A central theme in Freud's account is that Little Hans's fear of horses was displaced fear of his father. Wolpe and Rachman claim that 'there is no independent evidence that the boy feared or hated his father' (1960, p. 213). If true, this point would be damaging. It is worth pausing for a moment to examine why this particular point would be so damaging. The psychoanalytic notion of 'displacement' is rather more sophisticated in its application than what is sometimes thought to be its behaviourist equivalent: 'stimulus generalization'. When Little Albert's conditioned fear of white rats spread to other animals, the spread was said to be explained by *generalization* to 'stimuli resembling the conditioned stimulus' (Wolpe and Rachman, 1960, p. 216). This claim, though not false, is (without further specification) empty as an explanation. As we noted earlier, any two objects can be said to 'resemble' each other in one respect or another. It is not helpful to be told that the additional objects feared are feared because they 'resemble' the original objects. Every object 'resembles' the original object, and some (in some respects) resemble it even 'more' than the additional (generalized) objects of fear. Whatever objects had in fact become elicitors of the fear response, that they had become elicitors could have been 'explained' by generalization. So generalization cannot explain why one object rather than another becomes an object of fear (by relation to a conditioned or unconditioned stimulus). Therefore 'generalization' is void of any explanatory value. Something that would explain everything explains nothing. It leaves out any significance in the further objects beyond 'association by resemblance' – which is too widespread and non-selective to be of any use. The notion of 'displacement', however, is more informative because it places more stringent constraints on explanations involving it. A change can be seen as *displacement* (rather than mere 'change') only against a background of continuity. The continuities required in the case being considered are of at least two kinds: if Little Hans's fear of horses is to be displaced fear of his father then (a) he must fear his father (or have feared his father), and (b) he must somehow identify horses with his father. Notice that (b) is required to make horses suitable substitution objects, and 'identification' is a stricter notion than 'resemblance'. This sort of connection is also required because Hans's fear of horses might otherwise be merely *another* fear (in addition to his fear of his father) rather than a *displaced* fear. There may also be further background constraints, e.g. (c) motivation for a change which is to count as displacement may have to be of a special sort (e.g. ambivalence toward the first object). (Note that the behaviourist notion of 'generalization' shares the obscurity of 'stimulus'. Was Hans's father a 'stimulus' generalized by 'similarity' to horses? Again I suspect that behaviourist conceptualizations will yield only vacuous descriptions and explanations.)

Now let us return to the charge that the first condition is not met, that 'there is no independent evidence that the boy feared or hated his father' (1960, p. 213). Wolpe and Rachman notice (and reject) only one bit of evidence, Hans's symptomatic act of knocking over a toy horse (1960, p. 213). They rightly regard this as an 'interpreted fact' involving a variety of assumptions, including that the horse represents Hans's father. They fail to see that both the underlying assumptions and the claim itself are supported by a number of other acts and correlations, and that there is an intricate and complex web of evidential support. As evidence for hostility, there are scenes where Little Hans alternately butts, bites, then strokes and kisses his father (a picture of ambivalence – Freud, 1909b, pp. 52, 125). For identification, Hans tells his father not to 'trot away from me' (1909b, p. 45), parents are expected to have widdlers 'as large as a horse's' (1909b, p. 10), and his father had in fact played at being horse for Hans (1909b, pp. 126-7). The identification with animals and hostility merge in the fantasy of the crumpled giraffe (1909b, pp. 37ff., 123). The beautiful and subtle richness of Freud's account, its coherence, is lost on Wolpe and Rachman. On the horse representing Hans's father they say:

> Hans consistently denied the relationship between the horse and his father. He was, he said, afraid of horses. The mysterious black around the horses' mouths and the things on their eyes were later discovered by the father to be horses' muzzles and blinkers. This discovery undermines the suggestion (made by Freud) that they were transposed moustaches and eye-glasses. There is no other evidence that the horses represented Hans' father . . . (1960, p. 213).

The claim about 'no other evidence' is simply false (see above). And the 'discovery' that they say 'undermines' Freud's suggestion in fact *confirms* it. It specifies more clearly those particular features which make particular horses more fearful than others for Hans; and they are precisely those features which make them resemble Hans's father more closely (by corresponding to his moustache and glasses – 1909b, pp. 42, 123). What better evidence for unconscious identification or symbolization could one have? If the muzzles and blinkers show something else, what is it? Why should muzzles and blinkers otherwise be significant? (Why should they be picked out as significant features in the total 'stimulus' situation?)

This brings us to a final point about Wolpe and Rachman. Their alternative behaviourist account suggests 'that the incident to which Freud refers as merely the exciting cause of Hans' phobia was in fact the cause of the entire disorder' (1960, p. 216). To suppose that Hans's witnessing the fall of the horse which drew the bus could explain everything is to take a much too simple view of Hans's 'entire disorder'. It leaves too much out of account. But without going into the subtle interconnections that Freud elaborates, the behavioural conditioning explanation raises more questions than it answers (the latter number is very small in any case). What makes the horse's falling down 'traumatic'? There is no suggestion that an experience or event that gets singled out might be connected with Hans's own interests, desires, and development at the time it occurred. If they do not matter, why shouldn't such incidents be traumatic for everyone, and why shouldn't other incidents (e.g. a friend cutting his foot – 1909b, pp. 58, 82, 126) have been traumatic for Little Hans? Why, too, did the symptom 'generalize' from horses 'falling' to horses 'biting'? Is this choice of one 'generalization' and rejection of others to be explained by 'resemblance'?

8

Nosology and Anthropology

I shall return to the connection between these alternative aetiological theories and the theory of psychoanalytic therapy and to the role of interpretation in producing change. But first I would like to connect the contrast I described between behaviourist and psychoanalytic aetiologies for 'phobias' with certain general points about nosology.

Freud calls his case of Little Hans 'Analysis of a Phobia in a Five-Year-Old Boy'. But it is clear that he conceives of 'phobia' very differently from Wolpe and Rachman. They regard phobias as 'conditioned anxiety (fear) reactions', resulting from the accidental (i.e. meaningless) association of a 'neutral' stimulus with an occasion of fear (unconditioned stimulus) (Wolpe and Rachman, 1960, p. 216). Freud sometimes epitomizes his view of phobia by saying 'it is nothing else than an attempt at flight from the satisfaction of an instinct' (Freud, 1920g, p. 42). To show how this formula applies to Little Hans would require more detail than is possible here. But we can now raise the question: Does 'phobia' as used by Freud mean the same as 'phobia' as used by the behaviour therapists? (Cf. The question whether the uses of 'hysteria' in ancient Egypt and Greece (when symptoms were traced to physiology, a 'wandering womb'), in the early Freud, in the later Freud, and in contemporary psychoanalytic theory, are the same use. Note that even the womb theory suggests a connection with sexuality, whatever its other aetiological and treatment implications.) We should now see that the content of one's answer to this question matters less than having clear understanding of the differences and similarities that would justify an answer. These same differences and similarities, here discussed in relation to 'meaning' or 'sense', would also be what gives body to dispute about changing 'realities' or 'worlds'.

I have suggested that the psychoanalytic and behaviourist accounts of 'phobia' have only their reference to avoidance behaviour in common. Do they refer to the 'same disorder'? (Same 'disease' might provide different criteria for 'identity', but it also raises too many further questions.) How many mental disorders are there? Both these questions and their answers are indeterminate, at least until one makes clear from what interest they are raised. What counts as a distinct type of 'disorder', like what counts as a distinct 'sense' of a word in general, may be illuminated by Wittgenstein's discussion of the 'uses' of hammers:

> Do we use a hammer in two different ways when we hit a nail with it and, on the other hand, drive a peg into a hole? And do we use it in two different ways or in the same way when we drive this peg into this hole and, on the other hand, another peg into another hole? Or should we only call it different uses when in one case we drive something into something and in the other, say, we smash something? Or is this all using the hammer in one way and is it to be called a different way only when we use the hammer as a paper weight? – In which cases are we to say that a word is used in two different ways and in which that it is used in one way? . . . (Wittgenstein, 1958, p. 58).

Perhaps it will appear that the case of 'phobias' is different because the differences in 'sense' would attach to different implications for 'treatment'. But, similarly, perhaps someone would count a use of a hammer as 'different' only if it implied differences in design. One might design a hammer used as a paperweight differently (e.g. more flat surface) than one used for banging in nails. And then, one might design a hammer used for banging in wooden nails (a mallet) differently from one used for banging in metal nails. Each of these might therefore be a 'different use', but at least one's system of classification would have a clear rationale. What counts as a significant difference depends on one's purposes, whether the design of hammers or the treatment of mental disorders. Things do not come with labels on them. The world is not unequivocally divided into types of things. If we are to make sense of our classifications of diseases or mental disorders, we must recognize that it is *we* who do the classifying. There may be 'natural kinds' (certain common or overlapping groupings of features) that make one system of classification more suitable (a 'better fit') than another. That we must choose does not mean our choice must be arbitrary. We must pay attention to our rationale (whether explicit or implicit) for regarding certain differences as justifying or relevant to differences in classification.[6] We must divide the world in accordance with our interests, and in dividing up diseases and mental disorders there are (as elsewhere) alternative competing and complementary rationales; we can divide them according to (for example) symptomatology, aetiological and developmental theories, prognosis, or the treatments they are amenable to. These alternative schemes may overlap, or similar cases may fall under different names if we change the basis for our nosological scheme. What is important is to be aware of what we are calling what and why.

I said earlier that only the behaviour is the same in the psychoanalytic and behaviourist uses of 'phobia'. Wittgenstein may again be helpful:

> To the question 'How do you know that so-and-so is the case?',
> we sometimes answer by giving 'criteria' and sometimes by
> giving 'symptoms'. If medical science calls angina an inflammation
> caused by a particular bacillus, and we ask in a particular case
> 'why do you say this man has got angina?' then the answer 'I
> have found the bacillus so-and-so in his blood' gives us the
> criterion, or what we may call the defining criterion of angina.
> If on the other hand the answer was, 'His throat is inflamed',
> this might give us a symptom of angina. I call 'symptom' a
> phenomenon of which experience has taught us that it coincided,
> in some way or other, with the phenomenon which is our defining
> criterion. Then to say 'A man has angina if this bacillus is found
> in him' is a tautology or it is a loose way of stating the definition
> of 'angina'. But to say, 'A man has angina whenever he has an
> inflamed throat' is to make a hypothesis (Wittgenstein, 1958,
> pp. 24–5).

Wittgenstein states a distinction we have been using all along, and so puts us in a position to ask whether behaviour gives us 'symptoms' or 'criteria'. I will not here explore the role of 'behaviour' in relation to 'phobias', but will mention two further points. To label a disorder as 'hysterical', or 'phobic', or 'neurotic', in the way we use the terms, does have a hypothesis built into it. The 'facts' (here too) are theory-laden. There is no neutrally describable set of behaviours (that is, bodily movements) which is, as such, 'hysterical' or 'phobic' or 'neurotic'.[7] In explaining a neurotic symptom psychoanalytically we show it to be a *neurotic* symptom; i.e. if its explanation were purely physiological (for example) it would not be 'neurotic'. The sort of explanation possible (available) determines what the thing to be explained is. The character of the thing to be explained is not 'given' independently of the possibilities of explanation (the explanation we offer). This connection of descriptions with explanations brings us to my second point. In deciding what are symptoms and what are criteria, we should beware of being too rigidly operationist in fixing our definitions. Discoveries about empirical correlations and new explanations may give us good grounds for shifting our definitions. Definitions themselves can function as correctable hypotheses. (See Putnam, 1962a, and consider Freud's difficulties with early definitional objections to the 'unconscious mind'.) Wittgenstein himself is aware of the need for flexibility here:

> In practice, if you were asked which phenomenon is the defining criterion and which is a symptom, you would in most cases be unable to answer this question except by making an arbitrary decision *ad hoc*. It may be practical to define a word by taking one phenomenon as the defining criterion, but we shall easily be persuaded to define the word by means of what, according to our first use, was a symptom. Doctors will use names of diseases without ever deciding which phenomena are to be taken as criteria and which as symptoms; and this need not be a deplorable lack of clarity. . . . We are unable clearly to circumscribe the concepts we use; not because we don't know their real definition, but because there is no real 'definition' to them. To suppose that there *must* be would be like supposing that whenever children play with a ball they play a game according to strict rules (1958, p. 25).

Charges of shift in meaning should not be allowed to become obstacles to empirical discoveries. Awareness of differences and similarities should replace insistence on sharp divisions.[8]

Appreciation of these points may help clarify certain problems within anthropology. For example, Hildred Geertz (1968) suggests there is a paradox raised by Latah in the Javanese. 'Latah' is described as a psychological disorder with quite specific symptoms and limited distribution. The symptoms include involuntary obscenities, compulsive imitation, and compulsive obedience when teased, etc.; and seem to be confined to older women of the lower classes. The symptoms seem to be related with extraordinary directness to (and so be explainable by) certain features of Javanese culture: 'the value for elegant and polite speech, the concern over status, sexual prudery, and the dread of being startled'. So it would seem one could explain the pattern of symptoms as a meaningful response to certain rigidities in the social structure. But Latah also seems to occur in cultures widely different from the Javanese – so the culture-dependent aetiology that seems plausible for Java does not seem to hold for the disease in general.

Geertz suggests that one must look for some broader cultural or sociological similarities to resolve the paradox. But perhaps the problem is of a different sort: as we have seen in the case of 'phobia', behaviourally similar symptomatologies may have quite different aetiologies (as different as aversion behaviour arising from behavioural conditioning and from Oedipal conflict). Perhaps 'Latah' does not denote the 'same disease' (in *this* sense) in the different cultures; so the fact that Latah also occurs in different cultures need not count against its culture-dependent and perhaps culture-specific aetiology in Java. The same point could be made by saying that similar symptoms may have different 'meanings' in different cultures. The word 'meaning' can cover all the ambiguities (and then some) that we have indicated as different dimensions or rationales of nosology. So the problem may be one of nosology rather than requiring for solution the finding of common cultural or sociological patterns in apparently diverse societies. So the distribution of what appears a single disease in diverse cultures is not necessarily paradoxical. Both within a particular society and cross-culturally, apparently similar patterns of behaviour or symptoms may be produced by very different mechanisms and circumstances and so, depending on one's nosological principles, may 'really' represent or constitute 'different' diseases or disorders.

It is worth emphasizing that differential diagnosis can be extraordinarily difficult, even within a particular society or culture, and even within a particular theory (say, psychoanalytic) of mental disorder within that culture, and even when the diagnosing is done by medical people rather than anthropologists or philosophers. A patient suffering from stomach cancer, for example, may look very like a case of *anorexia nervosa*. Apparent diversity of symptoms also produces complexity: different observable patterns of disorder may be manifestations of the same mechanisms. Looking cross-time rather than cross-culture for our example, the person who exhibits classical hysterical conversion symptoms and the 'new hysteric' (e.g. the woman who fails to derive feelings of pleasure despite open and promiscuous sexual activity) may exhibit the same underlying processes in these (apparently) very different forms. Historical changes in culture may be related to changes in patterns of disorder in a way as revealing of the role of culture in mental disorder as are the correlations of contemporary differences in culture with the character and distribution of disorder. Finally, we should be alert to the possibility that the same psychological mechanisms operate on different cultural materials in different ways (in part at least determined by the material itself) so as to produce the same (apparent) results. *Globus hystericus* can arise from a variety of circumstances, each suitable to its production in its own way. Here the search for broader similarities may well find a useful place.

9

Psychoanalysis and Behaviour Therapy: The Effectiveness of Interpretations

The treatment of Little Hans by his father, in consultation with Freud, consisted mainly of interpretations plus 'enlightenment' about various sexual matters. One of the strands of the analysis took up the 'lumf' theme (Freud, 1909b, pp. 126, 131). It turned out that Little Hans equated his faeces with a child, and the whole complex was connected with the fear of his mother becoming pregnant again and producing another rival. He was cured.

Little Hans is not the only case where clearing up excremental and reproductive confusions has had dramatic impact. The confusions are in fact quite typical and the 'cures' quite common. Erikson reports the case of Little Peter. Peter was a four-year-old with an extraordinarily severe case of constipation:

> this little boy had a fantasy that he was filled with something
> precious and alive; that if he kept it, it would burst him and that
> if he released it, it might come out hurt or dead. In other words,
> he was pregnant. . . . I felt 'surgical' action was called for. I came
> back to his love for little elephants and suggested that we draw
> elephants. . . . I asked whether he knew where the elephant babies
> came from. Tensely he said he did not, although I had the
> impression that he merely wanted to lead me on. So I drew as
> well as I could a cross section of the elephant lady and of her
> inner compartments making it quite clear that there were two
> exits, one for the bowels and one for the babies . . . he had a
> superhuman bowel movement after I left (1950, p. 50).[9]

On a behaviourist understanding, clearing up the facts of reproduction should be of no value in relation to a horse phobia. So why should such interpretations have any effect? Why should 'insight' matter? First, not all interpretations do have effects. Pointing out that a phobic object is not genuinely dangerous (e.g. Hans need not fear horses) will not dispel the fear; that is part of what makes a 'fear' a 'phobia', it is out of proportion to the danger and unreasonable. But some interpretations do have effects. How were the very dramatic effects we have just mentioned produced? In these cases the fear was reattached to its original object. The fear that was inaccessible to reason in its displaced form, became manageable when correctly interpreted. So the content of the interpretation obviously makes a difference. On the behaviourist account this should not be so. Wolpe and Rachman suggest:

> Hans's recovery from the phobia may be explained on conditioning
> principles in a number of possible ways. . . . The interpretations

may have been irrelevant, or may even have retarded recovery by adding new threats and new fears to those already present. But since Hans does not seem to have been greatly upset by the interpretations, it is perhaps more likely that the therapy was actively helpful, for phobic stimuli were again and again presented to the child in a variety of emotional contexts that may have inhibited the anxiety and in consequence diminished its habit strength. The *gradualness* of Hans's recovery is consonant with an explanation of this kind (1960, pp. 217–18).

But this behaviourist account does not offer the beginning of an understanding of why little Hans's gradual improvement was so directly correlated with the contents of the various steps in the progressive analysis, or why at certain points the changes were so dramatic. Again, the behaviourist approach disregards the intricate subtlety of the neurosis and Freud's understanding of it. And it implies what is plainly false, that interpretations consisting of reassurances about the manifest phobic object would be as effective as interpretations uncovering the 'real' object and the reasons for the displacement. The contents of the thoughts matter to the process.

But, though we know that insight matters, we have not yet established *why* it should. A proper answer would require a more thorough discussion of the role of thoughts in the aetiology of neuroses (see Neu, 1973). Non-thought theories will not illuminate the role of thoughts where their *content* makes a difference. (I am putting aside for the moment those cases where the content does not make a difference, and also those cases where actual truth may seem necessary in addition to belief or acceptance as truth.) Why should clearing up excremental and reproductive confusions help clear up neuroses?

The process may seem as 'magical' as the shamanistic cures. According to Freud,

the psychoneuroses are substitutive satisfactions of some instinct the presence of which one is obliged to deny to oneself and others. Their capacity to exist depends on this distortion and lack of recognition. When the riddle they present is solved and the solution is accepted by the patients these diseases cease to be able to exist. There is hardly anything like this in medicine, though in fairy tales you hear of evil spirits whose power is broken as soon as you can tell them their name – the name which they have kept secret (1910d, p. 148).

Of course, mere psychoanalytic diagnostic labelling does *not* have the magic power (of 'Rumpelstiltskin') to make the problem named disappear. In a way, however, interpretations can be seen as enormously elaborated 'diagnosis' (we have already seen that even the apparently descriptive diagnostic labels themselves already contain commitments to aetiological theories). One reason why they should have force is suggested by the beginning of the quoted passage. If what lies behind psychoneuroses are instincts and desires which have been repressed and which emerge in distorted or displaced form, we can begin to see why discovering their original objects should help. We are then in a position to reattach our desires to their ends, to redirect our energies realistically, and to pursue the objects of our real needs. Recognizing the demands of our nature and condition can put us in a better position to meet them. This is another reason why I find Erikson's reference to 'forces' more promising than Lévi-Strauss's notion of 'induction'. 'Induction' leaves the nature of therapeutic changes magical.

We have not thoroughly explored the nature of 'insight'. On a Spinozist account, thoughts may be effective even though not 'true'. We can overcome someone's fear of a harmless creature (if based on the belief that the creature is harmful) if we convince him that the creature is not dangerous. But this would happen whether our information were true or not. The content of interpretations is important, but interpretations are not effective in virtue of being true (though that may be what makes them acceptable and their being accepted is what makes them effective). Truth may contribute enormously to the acceptability of a belief, but the belief may produce changes in virtue of its acceptance rather than its truth. Here Lévi-Strauss's emphasis on a coherent narrative (which at least parallels the truth – that is, at no important point fails to correspond with what is known) seems vindicated by a closer look at the mechanisms of transformation. One should consider whether Freud would in fact have insisted that his therapy works because the theory behind it and the theory it provides for the patient (they overlap but are not the same) are both true. That the contents of interpretations matter is in any case clear.

10
Insight Is Not Enough

But insight is not enough. On rare occasions, Freud thought that once an emotion was understood, once the unconscious was made conscious, it *must* dissolve:

> Was there any guarantee, he [rat man] next enquired, of what one's attitude would be towards what was discovered? One man, he thought, would no doubt behave in such a way as to get the better of his self-approach, but another would not. – No, I said, it followed from the nature of the circumstances that in every case the affect would be overcome – for the most part during the progress of the work itself. Every effort was made to preserve

135

Pompeii, whereas people were anxious to be rid of tormenting
ideas like his (Freud, 1909d, p. 177).

This is too optimistic. It follows from making the unconscious conscious
that forces which previously moved unconsciously are now surveyable;
and so the conflict has become, in a sense, 'normal'. But there is no
guarantee that it will be happily resolvable, or even that control will
be possible. Beliefs are built into the nature of emotions, therefore
reason is not powerless in the face of the passions, but it is not therefore
omnipotent. Spinoza saw that sometimes only an emotion can overcome
another emotion. Knowledge may put you in a position to become free,
but circumstances may place limits on your freedom.

In discussing Little Hans, Freud suggests that when impulses
become conscious, we can substitute conscious control for unconscious
repression. Even this is not a guarantee that the now-recognized
energies will be liberated, the needs satisfied. But once rational control
is substituted, some satisfaction may now be allowable where unconscious repression had been total and precluded recognition and so any
(but distorted) satisfaction. And the suffering (in addition to that of
unsatisfied desires) produced by distorted compromise symptoms may
thus be eliminated. The actual amount of satisfaction possible depends
on reality. As Freud said (very early on):

> When I have promised my patients help or improvement by means
> of a cathartic treatment I have often been faced by this objection:
> 'Why, you tell me yourself that my illness is probably connected
> with my circumstances and the events of my life. You cannot
> alter these in any way. How do you propose to help me, then?'
> And I have been able to make this reply: 'No doubt fate would
> find it easier than I do to relieve you of your illness. But you will
> be able to convince yourself that much will be gained if we
> succeed in transforming your *hysterical misery into common
> unhappiness*. With a mental life that has been restored to health
> you will be better armed against that unhappiness' (Freud, 1895d,
> p. 305, emphasis added).

Of course, this does not mean that psychoanalytic patients must resign
themselves to unhappiness, or some other adaptation to given conditions. Psychoanalytic therapy can be a prelude to releasing energies
for transforming the external world (Freud, 1910d, pp. 150–1).

But still, insight is not enough.

Freud observed, in his theoretical essay on 'The Unconscious', that
'If we communicate to a patient some idea which he has at one time
repressed but which we have discovered in him, our telling him makes
at first no change in his mental condition' (Freud, 1915e, p. 175). And
elsewhere he says,

If knowledge about the unconscious were as important for the
patient as people inexperienced in psychoanalysis imagine,
listening to lectures or reading books would be enough to cure
him. Such measures, however, have as much influence on the
symptoms of nervous illness as a distribution of menu cards in a
time of famine has upon hunger (Freud, 1910k, p. 225).

To discover why insight is not enough, I would examine what more is
needed. Freud's theory of abreaction offers some possible answers and
while ultimately inadequate is worth considering for a moment here
(for greater detail, see Neu, 1973).

The early abreaction theory calls for affect. In the course of repression,
while an idea is supposed to be weakened and removed from consciousness, the associated affect (which could not be discharged in the usual
ways) is supposed to remain, in the case of hysteria, to be 'converted'
into symptoms. So it is not enough for cure that the repressed idea only
be retrieved, the affect must be reattached and then discharged. It is
therefore the role of psychoanalysis to bring affect and idea together,
again. It is of course important that the conditions that kept the affect
from being discharged in the original situation are not duplicated in the
analytic situation (hence analyst must be accepting, etc.). There are
theoretical difficulties presented here, connected with the identification
and re-identification of the energy involved in symptoms and abreaction.
(Some of these difficulties might be compared with those we have discussed in relation to the Humean attempt to explain the identification,
discrimination, and nature of emotions in terms of simple felt impressions.) But here I wish to explore another aspect of the notion of
abreaction.

What sort of 'discharge' of emotional energy is 'abreaction'? Is the
connection of energy involved in discharge behaviour to the emotion
such that the emotion is the 'motive' of the behaviour? Must it be a
conscious 'motive' or may it be unconscious (i.e. is abreaction necessarily conscious)? These questions can be approached through another:
Is 'abreaction' a species of 'manifestation' or of 'expression' of emotion?

That difference rests, I want to claim, on the intentionality of the
behaviour. Expression *must* depend on the subject's thoughts. The
problem is whether those thoughts may be unconscious or must be
conscious. One can *manifest* an unconscious emotion (meaning that the
thought involved is unconscious – whatever the status of the 'affect')
in all sorts of ways: e.g. Elisabeth's love of her sister's husband manifested itself in somatic hysterical symptoms (especially localized in
pains in the left thigh), intrusive thoughts ('Now he is free again and
I can be his wife', at sister's deathbed, Freud and Breuer, 1895d,
p. 156), and significant behaviour (e.g. overzealous defence of his

appearance, Freud and Breuer, 1895d, p. 158). The emotion could be said to be 'expressed' in as many ways, where 'expression' here equals 'manifestation', but *she* is not *expressing* the emotion on these occasions. For that to be true, she would have to know that she loves him, and intentionally do the relevant actions because of that love. Behaviour, if it can be intentional, must be intentional to count as 'expression' (see Wollheim, 1966–7). To bring this out, imagine that 'A hits B'. Suppose that is all you know of their behaviour. What emotion is A expressing? One might be inclined to say 'anger' and perhaps 'jealousy' and other emotions in that range (unpleasant and hostile). But why not, say, 'gratitude'? Perhaps A is grateful to C who hates B, and expresses that gratitude by hitting B. Perhaps A is grateful to B, but B has strange ways of deriving pleasure (or at least A believes B derives pleasure in those strange ways). Any bit of behaviour, neutrally described, could be used to express (almost) *any* emotion. But to know what emotion is being expressed, you must know the thought behind it, why the agent is doing it, you must know the intentional description of it as an action (see MacIntyre, 1971).

'Catharsis' might seem a matter of the discharge of neutrally described energy; but as embodied in the 'abreaction' theory, such an account cannot be adequate. Catharsis and abreaction as treated by Freud seem to be species of expression (despite many misleading statements), in the sense in which expression requires conscious intention. Because you do not discharge *that* particular energy, you do not abreact that particular emotion, unless your behaviour is intentional action (where the relevant intention involves expressing *that* emotion). Otherwise running around the block or other activity (or conversion into a symptom) should always be sufficient 'discharge' of any emotion. But it is a central claim of the abreaction theory that strangulated affect *cannot* be discharged in just any way, most particularly not by symptomatic actions. Incompatible ideas must be reintegrated back into consciousness, and reattached to their original affect, before the affect can be adequately discharged. General release of energy (e.g. from running) may bring relief by lowering the vitality of the entire system, and so lowering the level of suffering along with it, but it does not discharge the particular troublesome energy. To tell what emotion is being discharged or abreacted you must go through the patient's thoughts.

Our question was whether those thoughts may be unconscious. We have seen that they must be conscious for the emotion to be expressed rather than merely manifested, and it seems that 'abreaction' requires the thought to be conscious because it is a species or type of 'expression'. It might seem an empirical claim of the abreaction theory that the energy is not discharged unless discharged in connection with (the appropriate) conscious thought. I hope it is now clear that that is actually a conceptual point: we do not know what *the* energy is (what emotion is being expressed rather than merely manifested) except through the conscious thoughts. We identify the energy through the behaviour, which in turn we identify through the intention. That abreaction is a species of expression is a consequence of how we tell what emotion is being discharged or abreacted.

We can not discharge the energy of strangulated affect, unconscious emotion, until the associated idea is made conscious because 'discharge' really means 'express'. Symptoms can manifest unconscious feeling. But even if symptoms disappeared without the thought becoming conscious, the emotion would not have been 'abreacted'. This discussion, of course, still leaves open the whole question of the nature of unconscious emotion, but it should be clear that understanding of that must come through understanding of the nature of unconscious thought.

In exploring why insight alone is not enough, it would also be worth considering what factors go into the proper 'timing' of an interpretation. It is not sufficient for the issuance of an interpretation that the analyst believe it to be true. The discovery of what makes an interpretation effective, the timing good, should reveal the non-rational or non-thought factors in psychoanalytic transformations. Unfortunately when one turns to psychoanalysts to learn what the relevant factors (outside of truth) in timing are, one is usually told only that one gives an interpretation when the patient is 'about to see it for himself'. The patient must be ready if insight is to take place. (Cf. Marxists on social readiness for change and overcoming 'false consciousness'.)

At this point, an examination of the roles of transference, fantasy, anxiety, developmental theories, 'instruction', etc., in psychoanalysis would be necessary in order to take our understanding further. But I cannot do that here. Let me just suggest (again) that a Spinozist view of the nature of the mental can help us understand how it is that knowledge makes us free, or at least 'freer'. If our state of mind has to be redescribed in accordance with changes in our understanding of its causes (and so objects), we can see how changing thoughts or beliefs can transform emotions. Sometimes we reason with an angry man, and show him that the object of his anger is somehow inappropriate or its degree exaggerated, in the expectation that convincing the man will change his emotion. One should also not neglect that the study of mind may itself be a joy and so replace the suffering it examines.

11
Freud's 'Theory' of the Emotions

Freud's speculations about the nature of mind started from neurophysiology and with assumptions about psychic energy. In the early writings, emotion is treated as simply equivalent to that psychic energy. Emotion or affect is simply a quantity of energy, or cathexis, attached to an idea. This is open to many problems, including those of the identification and reidentification of psychic energy. There are other problems with the notion of 'psychic energy' (see, e.g. Shope), but even independent of them, it cannot be correct to equate emotion with psychic energy in general. There is more that goes on in the mind. There are instincts (drive cathexes) and thoughts (bound cathexes), which even assuming an underlying energy system, it would be only confusing to assimilate to emotions. It is better to recognize the special intimacy of idea and affect in those affectively charged ideas which constitute emotions. Freud himself recognizes the importance of fantasy as the wish-fulfilling representative of instinct, and this is a part of giving thoughts their proper place in emotions. And we have already seen how giving thoughts their proper place can help clarify our understanding of 'abreaction' of emotion and other aspects of the therapeutic process.

If one insists on extracting a general theory of the emotions from Freud, one must turn to his middle and later writings. There he equates emotion not with a quantity of psychic energy, but with the discharge of such energy:

> I am compelled . . . to picture the release of affects as a
> centrifugal process directed towards the interior of the body and
> analogous to the processes of motor and secretory innervation
> (Freud, 1900a, pp. 467–8).
> . . . ideas are cathexes – basically of memory-traces – whilst
> affects and emotions correspond to processes of discharge, the
> final manifestations of which are perceived as feelings (Freud,
> 1915e, p. 178).

Hence felt affect requires that energy reach a threshold level of intensity (Brierley, 1937), that is, a threshold of discharge, and that its effects, mainly interior, be distinguished from those of other sorts of drives to action. When other forms of discharge are prevented, when there is conflict (whether with reality or internal conflict), affects serve as safety-valves. But again, felt discharge of energy can only be made sense of in terms of emotion if thought is given its proper place.

Rapaport (1953) points out that there is a third stage in Freud's theory of the affects. Freud's new theory of anxiety, the perspective of ego psychology, allowed that energy could be bound in such a way that affects could serve as 'signals' rather than 'safety-valves'. We may take these 'tamed' passions to correspond (in some ways) to what we have called 'calm' passions. Their influence on behaviour can be great and need not be disorganizing or disruptive. In any case, 'Freud, in his development of the signal theory of anxiety, abandoned the theory of instinctual discharge as characteristic of all affects' (Pulver, 1971,

p. 350). (I should perhaps note that Rapaport's discussions of Freud's theory of affects – 1942, 1953 – are not particularly helpful from our point of view. He is more concerned with the effects of feeling on thought processes than with the role of thought or cognition in feeling processes. And he in general takes the economic point of view, talk of cathexes, countercathexes, and hypercathexes, too seriously; that is, more seriously than the theory requires or the evidence warrants.)

On a descriptive level, one can move to unconscious emotions quite readily if one starts from emotions in which feelings, as such, are unimportant. For example, we sometimes say that someone is afraid when they react immediately to a perceived danger by fleeing, even though *at the time* they might claim to be feeling nothing in particular, indeed, they might be too afraid to feel anything until after they stop running. We can come by this route (that is, cases of delayed affect) to distinguish between being afraid and feeling afraid (Mullane, 1965). The non-experiential aspects of emotional states are sometimes sufficient for their identification; and such emotions may be descriptively unconscious or preconscious. It is enough that we would experience the feeling under certain conditions, that it requires only an effort of attention to make us aware of it (see Pulver, 1971, pp. 350–1, for more examples). But what of a repressed emotion? Sometimes our unawareness of an emotion is the result of conflict of psychological forces, of defence. Sometimes there are distortions in behaviour and thought that will allow us to infer to (or which may be interpreted in terms of) unconscious thoughts and emotions. Little Hans's fear of horses masked his unconscious fear of his father. An affect may be displaced if felt at all. In some cases, we would feel anxious if our defences were weakened, if the unconscious were allowed to emerge, but if defences are lowered in the right context, e.g. where the therapeutic alliance provides supporting strength, anxiety may be released and we may actually feel relieved. The development of insight in a particular area, in the context of an ongoing project of understanding, may help us to strengthen the ego in general (that is, in its general efforts to confront present reality rather than a world distorted by archaic emotions and fantasies).

We cannot really explore the realm of unconscious emotions properly here. But a few points can be made. If Freud followed Hume, the existence of unconscious emotions would seem senseless. Unfelt feelings can find no place in a Humean epistemology. As Freud puts it:

> It is surely of the essence of an emotion that we should be aware of it, i.e. that it should become known to consciousness. Thus the possibility of the attribute of unconsciousness would be completely excluded as far as emotions, feelings and affects are concerned (Freud, 1915e, p. 177).

But, of course, he immediately rejects this:

But in psycho-analytic practice we are accustomed to speak of unconscious love, hate, anger, etc., and find it impossible to avoid even the strange conjunction, 'unconscious consciousness of guilt', or a paradoxical 'unconscious anxiety'. . . . it may happen that an affective or emotional impulse is perceived but misconstrued. Owing to the repression of its proper representative it has been forced to become connected with another idea, and is now regarded by consciousness as the manifestation of that idea. If we restore the true connection, we call the original affective impulse an 'unconscious' one. Yet its affect was never unconscious; all that had happened was that its *idea* had undergone repression. In general, the use of the terms 'unconscious affect' and 'unconscious emotion' has reference to the vicissitudes undergone, in consequence of repression, by the quantitative factor in the instinctual impulse. We know that three such vicissitudes are possible: either the affect remains, wholly or in part, as it is; or it is transformed into a qualitatively different quota of affect, above all into anxiety; or it is suppressed, i.e. it is prevented from developing at all. . . . We know, too, that to suppress the development of affect is the true aim of repression and that its work is incomplete if this aim is not achieved. In every instance where repression has succeeded in inhibiting the development of affects, we term those affects (which we restore when we undo the work of repression) 'unconscious'. Thus it cannot be denied that the use of the terms in question is consistent; but in comparison with unconscious ideas there is the important difference that unconscious ideas continue to exist after repression as actual structures in the system *Ucs.*, whereas all that corresponds in that system to unconscious affects is a potential beginning which is prevented from developing (1915e, pp. 177–8).

One can perhaps give some sense even to unconscious affects as such (see Pulver, 1971). But here I wish to note only that Freud follows Brentano in what I have been arguing is also the Spinozist analysis of psychological states as composed of idea and affect, with idea providing the object of the state. In relation to emotions, it is also important to note that the associated idea is generally concerned with the cause of the state and is essential to the discrimination of the state from other states. Thought and feeling, idea and affect, can be separated off. They can have independent histories. (Both are taken by Freud to be instinctual representatives, and according to the early theory of anxiety later abandoned by Freud, the affect may be transformed directly into an emotion of anxiety – 1915d, p. 153.) It should be clear, at any rate, how an emotion could be unconscious in virtue of the associated idea being unconscious. And it is arguable that the whole complex could be unconscious (see Pulver, 1971), though it is unlikely that it could then maintain its structural integrity (Freud, 1926d, p. 142n.).

Even at the catharsis or abreaction stages of Freud's theorizing, we have seen that thought is essential. It is essential in determining which affects are felt and which repressed, and essential in identifying which emotion is being 'expressed' or 'abreacted' when there is 'discharge'.

It is only if we understand the role of thought that we can understand how fantasy and memory can have the consequences they do in symptom formation, and how interpretations in terms of fantasy and memory can be effective in the relief of emotional and psychological disorders. An understanding of the role of thought, including unconscious thought, could help us see the place of unconscious emotions in our lives, and how displacement, repression, reaction formation, and other mechanisms operate and how our lives might be led without the suffering that such defensive manoeuvres can bring. The recognition of the forces that govern our lives is the first step to discovering how we can control them (if we can), to discovering how we can be more active, self-determining, and free.

12

Unconscious Fantasy and Emotion

We have repeatedly noticed ways in which the capacity for certain emotions may depend on conceptual or linguistic capacities. A limit on one can be a limit on the other. Freud offers a fascinating speculation on the broader connection between the capacity for consciousness and linguistic capacity, on the connections of language with consciousness (Freud, 1915e, pp. 196–204). He suggests that the conscious and preconscious presentation ('Vorstellung') of an object consists of a presentation of a word and a presentation of a thing ('memory-images'). When the word-presentation becomes detached, the thing-presentation and so the idea is unconscious. To become conscious or even preconscious a thing must be connected with the word-presentation corresponding to it (Freud, 1923b, p. 20). This in turn connects well with an interesting speculative explanation of certain features of primary process (i.e. unconscious) thinking. That such thinking is free of time and contradiction, but subject to displacement and condensation may be due to the role of language:

It is language which builds up time and contradiction. Without spatial, verbal, and social bearings, comparisons of time length are uncertain. Outside language there are no *contradictory* terms or relationships, but different terms, different relationships, and that is why there is no time and no contradiction in the unconscious. Conversely, displacement and condensation exist *in* language itself.

Trope, metonymy are displacements (etymology is in great part the history, 'diachrony' (Saussure, 1915) of such displacements), concepts and metaphors are condensations or both condensations and displacements. And that is why displacements and condensations are seen as positive attributes of the unconscious, since language uses them, whereas time and contradiction are seen as negative since they are built up by language (Bénassy and Diatkine, 1964, p. 172).

If the unconscious were without words, without language, it would not be surprising that it is not subject to those laws which depend on language.

But if the discrimination of emotions depends on distinguishing thoughts, and distinguishing thoughts depends on their expression in linguistic form, how can one distinguish unconscious thoughts which precisely lack linguistic form? The question gives one an additional ground for expecting unconscious emotional structures to be unstable. And even were it answered, it might not make the speculative connection between consciousness and verbal forms especially helpful in relation to understanding the contrasts between conscious and unconscious emotions, at least in so far as unconscious emotions depend on unconscious affect or feelings (as such). Freud himself says that we

> come to speak, in a condensed and not entirely correct manner, of 'unconscious feelings', keeping up an analogy with unconscious ideas which is not altogether justifiable. Actually the difference is that, whereas with *Ucs. ideas* connecting links must be created before they can be brought into the *Cs.*, with *feelings*, which are themselves transmitted directly, this does not occur. In other words: the distinction between *Cs.* and *Pcs.* has no meaning where feelings are concerned; the *Pcs.* here drops out – and feelings are either conscious or unconscious. Even when they are attached to word-presentations, their becoming conscious is not due to that circumstance, but they become so directly (Freud, 1923b, pp. 22–3).

In all of which Freud may simply mean that affects are never, as such, unconscious, and to understand what it means to call emotions unconscious one must refer to the associated ideas, or the ideas which may have become detached in the course of displacement or some other process. Looking to the place of 'thing-presentations' might help us understand some of the constraints on effective insight, why telling alone is not enough (why word-presentations are not enough). Richfield (1954) connects the constraint on insight, the special force of the acknowledgment needed for effective insight, with the contrast pointed by Russell's distinction between knowledge by acquaintance and knowledge by description. And one might explore how this might be connected with the special therapeutic importance attached to interpretations concerned with the patient's immediate situation, i.e. transference interpretations (see, e.g. Strachey, 1934). But we must leave these problems here.

With them we also leave the problem raised by the question of discriminating unconscious thoughts. That question of course depends on the nature of the unconscious, the form of the unconscious, what it means for something to be unconscious. It also depends on the principles of inference by which one moves from conscious, or observable, 'manifestations' to the contents of the unconscious. That is a huge problem, but I would like to say just a bit here to help locate it.

How does one get, for example, to the notion of an unconscious fantasy? What happens when the notion of day-dream fantasy gets extended to the unconscious, where it becomes 'unconscious fantasy'? It is not a simple transposition. Starting with a conscious day-dream and subtracting the feature of consciousness does not yield Freud's notion of unconscious fantasy. A day-dream once totally forgotten, is not unconscious, it simply is not. A day-dream that remains recallable when no longer current, is not an unconscious fantasy either. Stored memories, whether of perceptions or day-dreams, are merely descriptively unconscious, i.e. preconscious. The evidence for the existence of a descriptively unconscious day-dream is its emergence in conscious memory. The assumption is that the day-dream continues to exist in some more or less unaltered form (unconscious memory) available to consciousness when called for. The assumption is on a level with that which we make when we assume that the table we are perceiving continues to exist even when unperceived by us, i.e. that it does not go out of and return to existence with our blink. The case is of small interest because the peculiarity of unconscious fantasy (like unconscious emotion) is that it is thought to be active, that it exerts an influence on our observable thought and behaviour rather than sitting in cold (preconscious) storage. But to say that *it* is active precisely when we are unaware of it, leaves us wanting to know what form *it* takes.

In order to refer to a particular fantasy, that is, in order to describe its content, to discriminate one unconscious fantasy from another, we must put it into words. ('I gotta use words when I talk to you,' *Sweeney Agonistes*, T. S. Eliot.) It does not follow that that is the form the fantasy takes in the individual's experience. The problem is that, where the fantasy is unconscious, the fantasy is not (consciously) experienced at all. How then can we know what form the fantasy takes, or that it exists at all? Clearly we must make an inference. This does not necessarily make unconscious fantasies any worse off than a vast range of highly respectable (non-mental) entities such as electrons. It is indeed arguable that there is no 'given', and that even if not everything is known by inference, nothing is known without mediation (in one form or another). But such an argument would not solve any of our problems with unconscious fantasies. Even if there is no sharp division to be made between theoretical terms and observational terms, psychoanalytical claims about unconscious fantasies (especially claims about pre-linguistic fantasies, of the sort made by Kleinians) stand in need of support (both from above – theory – and below – observation), and that all statements may (from some point of view) require support provides them no special comfort. We have noted that in order to speak of particular fantasies we must verbalize them, but that it does not follow that those or any words represent the form in which the fantasy is had. Freud makes a number of suggestions (e.g. topo-graphical and functional) concerning the character of unconscious ideas, but perhaps the most interesting is the one that we have looked at briefly, namely, that they are precisely non-verbal, that unconscious ideas or fantasies involve thing-presentations detached from word-presentations. We have already mentioned that this suggestion con-nects with an interesting speculative explanation of certain features of unconscious processes, and with certain other interesting notions (and there are other connections as well, for example, Freud relates his suggestion to the detachment from objects and over-valuation of words in schizophrenia). I am afraid that we cannot explore the suggestion, or its connections, or its problems, here. There is no easy route, I think, from the manifestations of unconscious fantasy to its form and content. But I do believe that there are routes and that a full-scale consideration of unconscious fantasy and unconscious thought is called for. It is necessary to a proper understanding of unconscious emotion. That it is necessary is one of the things I hope we have brought out in empha-sizing the importance of thoughts (whether conscious or unconscious) in the understanding of conscious emotion.

13
Spinoza: 'The Philosopher of Psychoanalysis'

It could be said that Freud does not himself have an explicit theory of the emotions. What is sometimes called 'psychoanalytic theory of affects' is more about undifferentiated states of energy charge or energy discharge than about the emotions as they are commonly understood. Freud offers no systematic discussion of the classification and discrimi-nation of emotional states as such. Though he does pay some attention to certain particular emotions, e.g. guilt, love, jealousy, his general theoretical writings tend to centre mainly on undifferentiated states of anxiety. Emotion, when it appears under that heading, tends to be assimilated to generalized anxiety, finer discriminations not receiving theoretical treatment. But, more importantly, much analytic interpretation is concerned with the patient's understanding or explanation of his states, with uncovering the meaning (in emotional and other terms) of symptoms, thoughts, and behaviour. The central analytic effort is to transform the emotional life of a patient through an understanding of its causes and meanings. And the faith that knowledge will make you free here depends on something like a Spinozist view of the emotions.

There are a number of points at which an understanding of Spinoza can illuminate the theory of mind that underlies or makes intelligible the role of analysis and self-knowledge in therapy. In particular, it is fruitful to consider the important role Spinoza gives to thoughts in the discrimination of mental states, especially emotions (and the consequent importance attached to reflexive knowledge and its peculiarities in changing those states) in relation to psychoanalytic theory. An appreciation of the place of thoughts in the nature of the emotions can help one understand how the 'correction of the understanding' can help make one free, or at least freer. If beliefs are built into emotions, uncovering the levels of childish impulse and fantasy embedded in present emotions may help to transform those emotions and their accompanying inclinations to action. In both the Spinozist and Freudian views, reason can be seen to have a place in our efforts to control and to live actively our emotional lives. It makes sense to ask that our emotions be reasonable, i.e. appropriate to the realities with which we must cope; and an understanding of our nature, our situation, and the forces which move us can be a step towards making our emotions reasonable. We need not passively suffer our emotional lives, in Humean fashion, or as though all our experience and behaviour were the thoughtless product of conditioning (and amenable only to further conditioning), in behaviourist fashion.

Having seen that thoughts are involved in emotions (especially thoughts about the causes of our states of feeling and our inclinations to action), and having appreciated some of the various ways in which this is true, we are in a better position to examine those states with a view to possibly changing them. Knowing where we start, recognizing fantasy or imagination as fantasy or imagination, puts us in a position to correct our understanding and, with it, our emotions. Our thoughts must know their own level. As we have seen, it may be necessary that a thought be a full-fledged belief for the accompanying state to be a particular emotion (say, regret). (See also Gordon, 1969, and Thalberg, 1973.) If we recognize the grounds of our thoughts as inadequate, those thoughts cease to operate as full-fledged beliefs and our state must be redescribed. (If, after rejecting a belief characteristic of fear, a person still insists that he is afraid, this cannot be simply true. Not because it must be simply false, but because his state of mind must be complex.)

Where beliefs or thoughts constitute or place constraints on our emotions, appreciation of the sources and character of our thoughts may help liberate them. Spinoza points out that, in certain contexts, diverse types of thoughts, memories and current perceptions, can have equal impact. Indeed, mere imaginings, mere fantasies, may have consequences comparable to those of perceptions of reality. We have seen that this contrasts sharply with what the Humean view of memory as faded copy would suggest about forcefulness (see also Appendix C). (Spinoza also seems to suggest that the operation of association in producing emotions depends upon the production of a memory which is not recognized as memory, or is indistinguishable from a perception of present reality – E, III, prop. 14.) Clinical observation and theory confirm Spinoza's suggestion: according to Freud, fantasy may be as aetiologically important as reality (Neu, 1973). The Freudian extension of thoughts to an unconscious level is also an extension of our understanding of the emotions. In virtue of the role of thoughts in emotion, it can help us to understand how the underlying dynamics of emotion and emotions themselves can be unconscious.

> any individual is a psycho-physical organism with a quantity of undifferentiated energy that appears in consciousness as desire and, below the level of consciousness, as appetite. This is the instinctual energy that must find its outlet, however deformed and deflected it may be by its interactions with the environment. Desires and appetites are projected upon objects, as objects of love or of hate, in accordance, first, with the primary economic needs of the organism, as objects promoting or depressing its vitality, and secondly, upon objects that are derivatively associated, through the complex mechanisms of memory, with increase or depression of vitality. Following this conception of a person's undifferentiated energy of self-assertion, Spinoza's account of passive emotions, and of the laws of transference that govern them, is very close to Freud's mechanisms of projection, transference, displacement, and identification, in forming the objects of love and aggression (Hampshire, 1960a, p. 205).

The movement from confused ideas and passive emotion to more adequate ideas and active emotion through the 'correction of the understanding' is very much like the movement towards freedom and self-determination through making the unconscious conscious.

Comparisons between Spinoza and Freud are possible on many levels, ranging from their observations on particular emotions to broad sympathies of approach. I would here like to mention a few specific comparisons, adding cautionary qualifications. Spinoza does anticipate Freud's doctrine of ambivalence, the possibility and importance of contrary emotions felt towards a single object. (We have seen that Hume can find no room for the notion in his system.) But he does not explain the possibility of ambivalence in terms of conflict between the conscious and unconscious. Spinoza leaves room for unconscious desires, and the operation of confused and inadequate ideas, in his terms, is very like the operation of unconscious ones, but he does not have a theory of repression and the unconscious. Passive emotions may be due to (unconscious) processes of association, and ideas may be determined by other ideas of which the mind is not aware (*E,* III, prop. 2, note), but it is not clear that Spinoza is operating with anything more than the notion of the not-conscious, rather than the unconscious. The latter is not a simple or isolated notion that might or might not have occurred to Spinoza, Descartes, Leibniz, or other philosophers. It is tied to a complex theory of mental functioning, to a theory of repression and defence and of primary process thinking.

Spinoza's psychology, like Freud's, is importantly dynamic. Indeed, the *conatus* has often been compared with Freudian *libido* (Rathbun, 1934; Hampshire, 1956, pp. 106–7). The comparison has point, but must be understood within limitations. Spinoza's doctrine of the *conatus* or impulse towards self-preservation is comparable to libido, *if* one takes libido (as Rathbun and Jung seem to) as including sexual and *all* other impulses. The two notions both mark the main driving forces behind human action, and fit into comparable economic models of mind as a homeostatic system seeking to maintain equilibrium in its interactions with the world outside its finite boundaries. But they cannot be simply equated. Spinoza's *conatus* is, within his system, a unitary force (the only inner driving force). Freud, however, insists on distinguishing sexual libido from (what he calls) the ego or self-preservative instincts – at least he so insists in his early theory. And Freud's instinct theory, despite its many changes, remains always determinedly dualistic (see Bibring). Dualism provides the key to inner conflict and inner conflict provides the key to neurosis. So, at first, Freud placed ego instincts beside libido. As libido expanded to cover ever more and more, so that eventually it came to represent all the life forces, the theory continued to provide for a second set of instinctual forces to oppose and conflict with it. In the end, beside the life instincts stand the death instincts. And Spinozistic *conatus* does not include a death instinct, indeed, Spinoza specifically excludes it (drives towards self-destruction must be outside man's essential nature).

Frustration of our central desires produces pain. Both Spinoza and Freud connect states of pleasure and pain with the power of instincts in action. Spinoza recognizes painful emotions (but these emotions are passive and do not amount to a death instinct). Spinoza treats pleasure as an increase in *conatus*, whereas Freud regards increase in libido (in instinctual tension) as painful (see *Project,* 1950a). Freud does this for a number of reasons, including his belief that

Sensations of a pleasurable nature have not anything inherently impelling about them, whereas unpleasurable ones have it in the highest degree. The latter impel towards change, towards discharge, and that is why we interpret unpleasure as implying a heightening and pleasure a lowering of energic cathexis (Freud, 1923b, p. 22).

Nevertheless the contrast here is relatively superficial. Freud apparently reverses Spinoza, but his notion of tension is, I think, meant to be more literally physiological than the *conatus*. When Spinoza speaks of pleasure, he means increase in vitality or capability of action (not psychic tension), and though this undoubtedly has a physical embodiment, that is not the point. In any case there are problems one could raise with Freud's account. For one thing, increase in tension (e.g. in sexual tension) is not always experienced as painful. Furthermore, if Freud wishes to insist that *all* emotions are discharge phenomena, then 'discharge' should be taken as 'change of charge', because there are painful emotions, and pain (on his account) involves increase (not discharge) of charge. Perhaps there is some other way to distinguish the sort of discharge which is pleasure and the sort of discharge involved in unpleasant emotions. In any case, if emotion is a process of discharge, the internal aspect of discharge must be emphasized, for if one is not careful to distinguish types of discharge emotion might seem to be involved in all action (assuming all action involves discharge).

I will not here review the place of thoughts in Spinoza and Freud, and the ways in which psychoanalytic concepts (and shamanistic concepts as well) can help give one's emotional life an intelligible order and open the possibility of reordering. We have seen that part of one's suffering may be the passive subjection to unintelligible and seemingly alien feelings. The roles of coherence and acceptance (as well as truth) in the effectiveness of interpretations call for further exploration, as do the roles of non-rational factors (including transference and anxiety) in analytic therapy in general. There are also other suggestive parallels of detail (e.g. Freud's notion of the ego as primarily a body ego and Spinoza's notion of the mind as the idea of the human body) that one might explore.

Freud himself never refers to Spinoza's thought in any of his published writings. But from the beginning Spinoza was a presence in psychoanalytic thought. Lou Andreas-Salomé calls him 'the philosopher of psychoanalysis'.[10] In particular, she emphasizes the concept of physical and mental manifestations as 'representations' of one another, which she regards as a step beyond parallelism and beyond Freud who 'has developed throughout a method of its own for the one of these two worlds, which can be grasped psychologically'. She emphasizes also the psychoanalytic concept of 'overdetermination':

This insight, that everything is, nay *must* be psychically overdetermined if only one pursues it far enough, reaches far beyond the usual logical concept of determination, splits its one-sided concatenation, and ultimately turns it into a principle of universal reciprocity (Andreas-Salomé, 1964, p. 75).

The naturalism of Freud and Spinoza extends beyond the physical realm into the psychological. But the notions of 'determination' and 'determinism', let alone 'overdetermination', are in fact problematical, and especially problematical in relation to the thought of Spinoza and Freud (see Hampshire, 1960a, p. 199ff.). The models of explanation and role of thoughts in explanation really need to be carefully considered. In any case, Freud insists that no psychological state is without meaning (which may not be the same as saying that it has a 'cause' in a narrow Humean sense). And while Freud maintains a faith in an underlying neurophysiological reality, he recognizes that psychological phenomena must receive psychological explanations, at least until a reduction of the laws of psychology to material laws, or their replacement by such laws, is possible. ('Our psychical topography has *for the present* nothing to do with anatomy; it has reference not to anatomical localities, but to regions in the mental apparatus, wherever they may be situated in the body' – Freud, 1915e, p. 175.) Spinoza treats mind and body as two aspects of what is in fact a single substance. The sense of this requires consideration. But in any case, explanation of thoughts must be done in the order of thoughts. Freud and Spinoza operate with common or at least overlapping notions of psychical determinism, and yet they recognize the power of understanding and of reflexive knowledge in relation to human freedom. Making the unconscious conscious may be compared in some ways with transforming confused ideas into adequate ones. Correcting our understanding can contribute to correcting our emotional disorders.

I do not wish to claim that Spinoza was an historical influence on Freud. My interest has been to show in what ways Spinoza provides a philosophical foundation for much in Freud. What I have mainly been trying to argue is that if Spinoza is close to the truth about the mind and the mental, then he offers us the beginning of an argument to show that Freudian, or more generally, analytic therapies, make philosophic sense. Spinoza is 'the philosopher of psychoanalysis. Think far enough, correctly enough on any point at all and you hit upon him; you meet him waiting for you, standing ready at the side of the road' (Andreas-Salomé, 1964, pp. 75–6).

In Summary

Hume and Spinoza are the most systematic representatives of two opposing traditions of argument about the relation of thought and feeling in the emotions. The Humeans treat emotions as essentially feelings (impressions or affects) with thoughts incidentally attached. The Spinozists say roughly the reverse, treating emotions as essentially thoughts ('ideas' or 'beliefs') with feelings incidentally attached. It is argued that the Spinozists are closer to the truth, that is, that thoughts are of greater importance than feelings (in the narrow sense of felt sensations) in the classification and discrimination of emotional states. It is then argued that if the Spinozists are closer to the truth, we have the beginning of an argument to show that Freudian or, more generally, analytic therapies make philosophic sense. That is, we can begin to understand how people's emotional lives might be transformed by consideration and interpretation of their memories, beliefs, etc.; how knowledge might help make one free.

I

Hume

Hume, as a physicist of the mental, attempts to explain all of our mental life on the basis of atomistic impressions and ideas and laws of association among them. He treats emotions as discrete and simple feelings with a complex causal history: that is, as impressions of reflexion (1). Pride, for example, is said to be the product of a mechanism of double association between the idea of the subject of pride and the idea of its object (self) and between the impression of pleasure occasioned by the source of pride and that pleasure which is pride itself (2). It is argued that this mechanism misrepresents the phenomena and even Hume's genuine insights, which are conceptual, and that his meagre materials are inadequate to a reconstruction of emotional, let alone the rest of mental, life (3–14). The simplicity of emotion impressions is incompatible with the operation of the principle of association by resemblance (4). If genuine comparison is to make sense, it will have to depend on features of the impressions outside of their simple essence (5). But then we could not learn to identify and discriminate emotions in the way we do, at least not if we restrict ourselves to their simple essence, which is meant to be all that is essential to the learning of emotion concepts and the classification of different emotional experiences (4–5). Hume's mechanism for producing pride requires association between pleasant impressions and so requires an initial impression of pleasure. It is argued that though the sources of an emotion may all involve pleasure, pleasure cannot be treated as an impression (6). The double association mechanism also requires an association between the idea of the subject of pride and its object.

The 'idea of self' is problematical (7), and it could not in any case *emerge* as the object of pride. It is involved in the idea of the cause and so is already present, so the object is not the *effect* either of the emotion itself or of whatever causes the emotion (8–9). The object collapses into part of the cause of the emotion despite Hume's views on conflict of emotion (10), and places conceptual constraints. Without the association of ideas, the double association mechanism in turn collapses back into reliance on association of (simple) impressions, which in any case (even if possible) could not explain the production of uniform emotion impressions. That is, the feeling of a particular emotion (the meaning of an emotion concept) would vary with each of its causes (8, 10). The special relation of emotion to object helps bring out the thought-dependence of emotion (10–11). The 'causal' force of objects is mediated by thoughts, and the classification of one's state (often) depends on one's beliefs about its cause. By not taking proper account of the role of thoughts, Hume comes to give a misleading picture of our knowledge of other minds, including those of animals (12). He does recognize that emotions may involve very little felt turbulence, but he cannot really explain the nature of calm passions (13). Because the simplicity of impressions isolates emotions (violent as well as calm) as rigidly from their consequences in behaviour as from their objects, Hume cannot within his scheme account for the expression of emotion in action (13). But there must (*contra* Warnock) be place for calm passions, and if one understands that place, and the place of thought in emotion in general, one can see how reason can be more than the slave of the passions (14).

II
Spinoza

Spinoza reconstructs the logic of the emotions on the basis of three primary emotions: pleasure, pain, and desire. All three must be understood in relation to his notion of the *conatus*, or the essential striving for self-maintenance by individuals (1, 2). Desire and appetite, within the system, leave room for the notion of unconscious desire (1). A Spinozist analysis of an emotion (love) is contrasted with a Humean, especially in terms of the nature and place of pleasure and desire, and the notions of object and cause (2, 7). Emotions are treated as complex, rather than simple, and as essentially involving thought, especially thoughts about their causes (or explanation) (2). Emotions are distinguished on the basis of thoughts, and depending on their character and source the thoughts are adequate or inadequate and the associated emotions active or passive (3). There are elements within Spinoza's system that might lead one to take 'the intellectual love of God' as the only wholly active emotion, but Spinoza can be interpreted so as to allow for degrees of adequacy of thought and activity of emotion in relation to particular objects. One's emotional life can become more active, the individual more free, through the correction of the understanding (3, 4). Various mechanisms for transforming emotions, particularly through correcting our beliefs about their objects and recognizing the level (the sources and grounds for) our thoughts, are considered (5, 6). These mechanisms become especially clear if one considers the intellectual or social dimension of emotions made possible by the role of thought (6), and if one considers the connections of emotion to action made intelligible if one does not isolate emotions (as though Humean simple feelings or impressions) from their behavioural consequences or constituents (7).

III
Thought, Theory and Therapy

Western therapies for psychological disorders can be ranged along a spectrum in accordance with the role they assign to thoughts. At the extreme ends can be placed drug and shock therapies, where no thoughts are involved, and Freudian psychoanalysis, where the patient's understanding of his suffering is essential to 'cure' (1, 9, 10). In this context, shamanism is especially interesting because it seems to involve thoughts, but thoughts and a theory which need not be true. Is mere belief enough? Lévi-Strauss's story of Quesalid and analysis of shamanism are examined (3, 4, 5). His suggestions in terms of social consensus (once sorted out – 4), and psychological coherence (in so far as suffering is suffering from unintelligibility – 5, 9) are found valuable, and extended to psychoanalysis. But his physiological-correspondence account of the effectiveness of symbols fails. The underlying physiology is a fantasy physiology, and in any case merely pointing to parallels or correspondences would not constitute an explanation. Here a general suspicion of structuralist explanation is realized (5). In connection with a claim of Erikson's, it is brought out that whether there is a common underlying reality, physiological or otherwise, referred to in different cultures and in different theories of psychological disorder, must be an empirical issue and cannot be settled by *a priori* analysis of the meanings of the terms used in the languages of the different cultures and theories (6). Later, general nosological issues are considered and some of their implications for cross-cultural understanding of psychological disorder brought out (8).

Some of these themes are further explored by contrasting the theories informing psychoanalysis and behaviour therapy. It is argued that behaviour therapy must involve thoughts in at least some minimal way, obscured perhaps by the obviousness of their content, and that in any case its place on our spectrum may limit its explanatory (if not its therapeutic) force (2). Various difficulties in assessing effectiveness and explaining change are explored (2, 9), and it is brought out that common nosological terminology (e.g., 'phobia') may conceal important differences (7). A critique of a behaviourist discussion of the analysis of a phobia (Little Hans) is offered, and the richness of the psychoanalytic notion of 'displacement' as opposed to 'stimulus generalization' is argued (7). The relations of description to explanation, explanation to effectiveness, and effectiveness to the content of interpretations are discussed at various points.

Though Freud does not himself have an explicit theory of the emotions, except perhaps for certain inadequate general claims about quantities of psychic energy and the discharge of such energy, the central analytic effort is to transform the emotional life of a patient through an understanding of its causes and meanings, of how the past distorts the present. To appreciate how fantasy and memory can have the importance they do in symptom formation and the shaping of emotional life, and how interpretations in terms of fantasy and memory can be effective in the relief of emotional and psychological disorders, a Spinozist understanding of the role of thought in the nature of emotions is indispensable. We cannot understand claims even about the 'abreaction' of emotion or the 'discharge' of energy, let alone notions like displacement and unconscious emotion, unless thoughts are given their proper place in the analysis of emotions and emotional life (10, 11). Freud offers an interesting speculation about the nature of the unconscious, as the realm of non-verbal thing-presentations, which connects with certain other interesting claims, but which also raises large problems connected with how one can discriminate unconscious thoughts and fantasies and so unconscious emotions (12). Certain comparisons of Spinozist and Freudian doctrine are considered and it is argued that they come together in their purposes and in the concept of mind which makes room for reason in the therapy of emotions (13).

Throughout, the advantages of a Spinozist theory of mind in understanding the role of thought and insight are emphasized. It is particularly the Spinozist doctrines of the importance of thoughts in the classification and discrimination of emotional states, and the consequent importance of reflexive knowledge in changing those states – rather than some of Spinoza's more famous metaphysical doctrines – that are emphasized. In fact, the Spinozist view of the emotions can be seen as at the extreme thought end of a spectrum of theories of the emotions: it emphasizes the cognitive element in the emotions rather than treating them as blind sensations or physiological responses. And I would like to suggest that this second spectrum, this spectrum of philosophies of mind, may stand behind and help explain the spectrum of therapeutic theories. For both spectrums, the one of philosophical theories of emotion and the one of psychological theories of therapy, correspond to varying views of the nature and importance of thought-dependence.

Appendix A
On Objects and Causes

Hume's argument for the distinctness of object and cause, as we have seen (part I, section 10), is a bad argument, based on an unrealistic picture of conflict of emotions. There are other arguments to show that the object of an emotion could not be its cause. I wish to look briefly at a few of them, not in order to give a definitive analysis of 'object', indeed, not to insist that the object of an emotion *is* its cause, but only to show that *these* arguments are not sufficient to show that the object *could not* be a cause. And, more importantly, I wish to show that thoughts may play a causal role in thought-dependent states, even though thought-dependency generally refers to the classification and discrimination of mental states and is therefore a conceptual point. (I will not attempt to disentangle in just what way 'objects' are given in thoughts. But I would agree with Green, 1972, that between thoughts, desires, and other thoughts, they are indeed given.)

I may have a psychological response to a situation or object that does not, in fact, exist. 'We can be as pleased by what we only believe to be the case and is not, as by what we know to be the case. Thus I may be pleased because (as I suppose) I have inherited a fortune, when I have not' (Williams, 1959, p. 225). But causes, to be effective, must exist; so if one is to give a causal analysis of 'I am pleased because I have inherited a fortune' in those cases when I have not, the causation must be mediated by my belief: either the object or some thought or belief about it is the cause of the feeling. But if I am responding to my belief in those special cases (of ill-founded emotions), I must be responding to it (or through it) in all. My beliefs do not suddenly become efficacious in virtue of being false, in order to do duty for the missing reality. 'The causal account must hold that it is *always* my belief that is the cause, or at least the proximate cause, of my pleasure; and that the statement "I am pleased because I have inherited a fortune" must be taken to mean "I am pleased because I believe I have inherited a fortune" ' (Williams, 1959, p. 227). Where my psychological state depends on what I am aware of, the effects of reality (whatever it may be) are mediated by my awareness. As Williams argues, if it was ever the belief that caused the pleasure it was *always* the belief that caused the pleasure, even in those cases in which the thing I said I was pleased at really existed. For if not, the statement 'I am pleased because I have inherited a fortune' would express a causal hypothesis different from, and incompatible with, the hypothesis expressed by the statement 'I am pleased because I believe that I have inherited a fortune.' But it is evident that at the time of believing in the inheritance, I could have no grounds whatever for preferring the second of these hypotheses to the first, since it is logically impossible for me to distinguish between what (as I believe) is the case, and what I believe to be the case. Hence there will be two incompatible hypotheses about my pleasure which in principle I shall not be able to distinguish. But it is clear that my retrospective description of the situation as my 'being pleased because I believed . . .', and anyone else's description of it in these terms, are just based on my sincerely thinking or saying at the time 'I am pleased because I have . . .'; thus it appears that a necessary condition of the assertion of the true hypothesis would be my previous belief in or assertion of a false one, and this is absurd (Williams, 1959, pp. 226–7).

Green, however, distinguishes objects of emotion and what he calls 'occasions' of emotion. His concern is with the contrast between those cases in which the belief on which an emotion is founded is true and those cases in which it is false (Green, 1972, p. 36). If the object of my emotion does not exist, obviously it cannot be the cause of my emotion. So in these cases the cause of the emotion must be a thought about the object, the belief that it exists or is the case or whatever. As we have seen, the thought then must always be given a causal role. (If Jones had not believed such-and-such, he would not feel so-and-so.) Green calls the thought the 'occasion' of the emotion. But when I am pleased I believe I have inherited a fortune, the *belief* is not the object of my pleasure. And where the object of my emotion does exist, it may be causally relevant to producing that belief which is in turn the occasion of my emotion; but the two remain distinct:

Where we have a description of an emotion of the form 'A φd x because p,' the object of the emotion may be non-propositionally indicated by x, while the thought which is the occasion of the emotion is expressed in the 'because'-clause. In such cases, object and occasion are clearly distinct. Where we have descriptions of emotions of the form 'A φd that p', the 'that'-clause may both propositionally specify the object of the emotion and set out the thought which is its occasion. This does not mean that in such cases object and occasion are the same, however. If an M.P. is indignant that his bill was not passed, it is his thought that his bill was not passed which is the occasion of his emotion; but he is indignant, not that he thinks that his bill was not passed, but that the bill was not passed (Green, 1972, p. 37).

If my belief ever plays a causal role it would appear that it must always play such a role. But can it ever play such a role? Thalberg (1964, p. 215) argues that the thoughts on which emotions are founded cannot 'cause' those emotions because 'you must be able to gather evidence of the effect which is logically independent of your evidence of its putative cause' and, he continues, one cannot do this for emotion and thought because 'it appears that if we prove he is vexed that tickets are gone, we also prove that he thinks (believes, conjectures, doubts) that tickets are gone; therefore we cannot claim that his emotion is the effect of his thought'. Put more generally, causes and effects must be independently describable, otherwise it may not be logically possible (as a Humean account of causation requires) that one should have existed and not the other. That is, there may not be two distinct items to be causally connected.

Wilson points out that 'if I am afraid of a dog, the dog and my fear are distinct items in any sense of the word' (1972, p. 27), so object and emotion may be causally connected. He restricts objects to existing items (well-founded emotions); but my thought has the same object as my emotion, and even where I am afraid of something which (in fact) does not exist, my thought is certainly identifiable independently of my emotion. I describe my thought independently of any emotion it might be claimed to cause. (The same thought that in some circumstances might be associated with anger or fear, in other circumstances might produce neither.) The difficulty (over logical independence of cause and effect) is more acute for causal theories of the relation of desire and action. It is sometimes claimed that there is a straight tautology of action: one cannot identify a desire without reference to the action of which it is the putative cause, the cause is not describable independently of the effect. (If the only criterion for a desire to pick a flower is the actual picking of the flower – given the opportunity, etc. – then it looks as though the existence of the cause depends on the existence of the effect and so one may not have two independent items.) It is arguable that we do have other handles on to desires to act, other than through the actions they putatively cause (see Pears, 1966–7), and it is in any case clear that Wilson is right that thoughts or objects and emotions are separable items. But these points are not fully adequate as a reply to the general difficulty. That objects are clearly independently describable meets only the demand that the cause be describable independently of the effect. But the effect must also be describable independently of the fact that it is caused by its cause. This is more difficult. One must show that the effect (the emotion) is describable independent of the claim that it is caused by its object (or thought). If a relation to a certain object or thought is a logically necessary condition of the emotion being the emotion it is, how can the two be causally related?

The difficulty as raised by Thalberg is parallel to what has been called the 'backward tautology of action': desires cannot be causes of action because a bodily movement is not an 'action' unless it is produced by a desire (Hamlyn, 1953). 'Action', as opposed to mere bodily movement, is not (it is claimed) identifiable independently of desires; i.e. one must attribute a (desire) cause in specifying the (action) effect. By appealing to *prolepsis*, however, one can see how such specification is possible, and so reply to the backward tautology of action (Pears, 1966–7, pp. 92–3). Just as we can say that a man married his wife on such-and-such a day because his 'wife' can be independently identified under some other description (she is a 'woman', whether or not she becomes a wife), so we can say desires cause actions because the effect can be neutrally (i.e. independently of its cause) described as 'bodily movement which may or may not be an action'. Now the question becomes whether there is an alternative underlying description of the emotions parallel to Pears's description for actions. If there is, then one could reply to the backward tautology argument in terms of prolepsis. Now 'vexation which may or may not be vexation that tickets are gone' will not do, because in so far as it is not clear what is the determining thought it is not determinate what is the emotional state. The specification of the state at this point and at this level does depend on the thought. Whether it is 'vexation', as opposed to 'irritation', 'embarrassment', 'annoyance', . . . may depend on the precise content of the thought. When Thalberg says an emotion is 'founded' on a thought, he means that the thought is a constituent in the emotion (if the thought is merely a reason for the emotion, then he says it 'grounds' it – but we are saying that emotions are always 'founded' on their reasons through thoughts, i.e. I may have various grounds for a belief on which my emotion depends). Perhaps a broader description will do: 'mental state which may or may not be an emotion'. This gets closer to Pears's model: when the causal theorist says that thoughts cause emotions, he means that they cause mental states, which because they are so caused, are the particular emotions they are.

Pears's neutral description for the case of desire/action was 'bodily movement which may or may not be an action'. He could have added '. . . and which, if it is an action, may or may not be the particular action specified through the desire'. Exactly similarly, the man's vexation might be given any of the three following neutral descriptions: 'mental state which may or may not be an emotion', 'and which, if it is an emotion, may or may not be vexation', 'and which, if it is vexation, may or may not be vexation caused by that particular thought'.

Reference to the desire involved is necessary to fully specify an action, and reference to the thought is necessary to fully specify an emotion. Indeed, sometimes one would have to refer to the thought in order to determine even the type of emotion. But one could individuate both action and emotion, identify them in the sense of pick them out, short of saying anything about their causes (e.g. 'the emotion had by Jones at 3.01 p.m. . . .').

The situation may even be more complex for emotions than for actions, in a way that is helpful to the causal theorist. Every action involves at least one bodily movement, and bodily movements are of a (relatively) uniform character. The notion of 'mental state' is very broad (and 'state' even broader), and encompasses all those components of an emotion exclusive of the thought which make it identifiable as the emotion it is (given the addition of the thought). These may be very diverse: e.g. involuntary and invisible bodily changes, involuntary bodily behaviour, sensations, inclinations to action and intentional behaviour, and associated thoughts and feelings. Even if a thought is a logically necessary or essential constituent of an emotion, it will make sense to say it 'causes' the emotion if it causes the *rest* of the emotion, i.e. the other constituents. If E consists of P, Q, R . . . and P causes Q, R . . . then one can say, quite properly, that P causes E. For example, 'the cause of the pile-up on the M4 was Smith's absent-mindedly running his car into the back of Jones's car', or 'the bombing of Pearl Harbor was the immediate cause of the war between the USA and Japan'. (These examples are from J. M. Shorter.) In these cases, the cause is part of the effect. It would not have been quite the same pile-up (or war) if it had been started in a different way, but the *other* features of the two effects are none the less contingent consequents of the first event. In these cases we secure the contingency required for a causal analysis by omitting an element; and this will work for emotion even where a thought is part of what constitutes an emotion, provided it is only a part. If the thought is not itself a constituent, but gives one of the (causal) conditions of the state being described as a particular emotion, prolepsis allows us to fall back on a more generic description. As Green puts it,

> many descriptions are applicable only where a certain causal
> relation is supposed to hold. The causal relation is built into the
> meaning of such descriptions. Where this is the case, the fact that
> a logical connection obtains will not preclude the existence of a
> causal connection. For example, a burn is by definition an injury
> caused by contact with heat; thus, where there is a burn, of
> course there is contact with heat, but this hardly means that
> contact with heat is not the cause of the burn. The case of emotion
> words is similar: a given emotion word can be partially defined

as an affective state caused by a thought of a certain sort. 'Fear', for example, is an emotion word which can be partially defined as an affective state caused by the anticipation of some danger. This being the case, there is no reason to suppose that the logical relation between emotions and thoughts precludes a causal connection (Green, 1972, p. 38).

The point is quite general, and J. R. S. Wilson makes it with great persuasiveness in his book, *Emotion and Object*:

> Sometimes two concepts are related in that any item which falls under one has a certain relation to some item falling under the other. Thus any item falling under the concept father has a certain relation to some item falling under the concept child; any item falling under the concept cause has a certain relation to some item falling under the concept effect. In some such cases it may be true that someone who did not know of this relation would not possess the concepts in question (Wilson, 1972, p. 25).

The conceptual connection of emotion of a certain sort with thought of a certain sort does not preclude the thought causing the emotion, any more than the conceptual constraints on 'fathers' and 'effects' precludes their being causally related to 'sons' and 'causes'.

> What one can establish on conceptual grounds is that *if* any item belongs to one type, say T1, then it must have a certain relation, say R, to some item belonging to another type, say T2. That is, it may be necessary that *if* x is of type T1, then there is some y such that y is of type T2 and xRy. But to establish that x *is* of type T1 [fear, burn, father, effect, wife. . . .] one must establish that there is some other item of type T2, and that the relation between the two items is of the right kind, and to establish *this* may be a matter of induction (Wilson, 1972, pp. 25–6).

Even where establishing these points is not a matter of induction, this does not mean that the relation is not causal (despite the claims of Williams, 1959, p. 227, and others). I may not need induction to know that I am vexed because (I believe) the tickets are gone, or that I am amused by a particular remark, and the absence of induction does not detract from the causal force of these claims. First-person reports of psychological states may be privileged in certain ways and still be reports with a causal force. A claim about a causal relation need not itself be a claim about how it came to be known, and it may have come to be known in a variety of ways.

The important commitment is to a general (or law-like) statement. This statement must be open to the evidence of induction, that is, it is refutable by the evidence of negative parallel instances. But it may be considered causal even if it is not based on the evidence of similar instances, or any 'evidence' at all. Sometimes one can assert physical causal statements without inductive evidence:

> in order to know that a singular causal statement is true, it is not necessary to know the truth of a law; it is necessary only to know that some law covering the events at hand exists. And it is far from evident that induction, and induction alone, yields the knowledge that a causal law satisfying certain conditions exists. Or, to put it differently, one case is often enough, as Hume admitted, to persuade us that a law exists, and this amounts to saying that we are persuaded, without direct inductive evidence, that a causal relation exists (Davidson, 1963, pp. 93–4).

Induction is not the only path to causal knowledge. What is important, what matters in terms of the knowledge being causal is not the path to it, but the commitment to a general statement. Hume saw this and tried to bring it out in terms of 'constant conjunction'. Without such conjunction, it is difficult to see how one would distinguish between the claim that one event followed another and the claim that the later was caused by the earlier. Davidson discusses the commitment in terms of causal laws or general statements; making the useful point that if one event causes another, there must be descriptions of these events which figure in a true causal law, but that these descriptions need not be the descriptions under which you originally pick out the events (see Wilson, 1972, ch. II). The general statement need not be a generalization about the events as described (ultimately, the law may hold only, say, on a neurophysiological level). All one need be sure of is that there is *a* law covering the case, even if one cannot state it at the moment. And this assurance need not arise from consideration of similar instances. But it will of course be open to the challenge of negative parallel instances, even if induction is not needed to establish it.

Causal claims do not require induction, nor do they require certain sorts of corrigibility or openness to error. But these points are well developed by Pears (1962) and Wilson (1972).

There may still be reasons, even if one allows that the object of an emotion may be causally related to the emotion, for distinguishing between the cause (or occasion) of an emotion and its object. Any sophisticated causal theory will not claim that the object is *the* cause of the emotion (especially if one restricts 'causes' to events); perhaps the object will usually be at most 'causally relevant', so this will not be the ground of the distinction. And there are many things which can be causes of emotions, or causally relevant, without being objects of the emotions. Donnellan adumbrates a three-fold distinction between ordinary causes of emotions and a special sub-species of causes he calls 'producers of emotions', and between both of those and objects of emotions. (That 'objects' may be regarded as another special sub-species of causes is a complication that need not concern us at the moment.) He proposes two criteria for distinguishing producers of emotions from ordinary causes:

> First, explanations in terms of producers of emotions require for their force that the subject of the emotion be aware of them, whereas this is not necessary for ordinary causes. . . . Second, and perhaps more importantly, knowing the producer of an emotion 'rationalizes' the emotion as knowing the ordinary cause does not, and this is necessary also for its explanatory force (Donnellan, 1970, pp. 948–9).

Where Jones becomes afraid of what Smith will say next about him, after Smith has said 'Sometimes I wonder about you', and after Jones has been drinking (where, had he been sober he would not have found Smith's remark ominous): what Smith will say next about him is the object of Jones's fear, his having drunk too much is the ordinary cause, and what Smith has just said is the producer of the emotion. In fact, I suspect that separate 'producers' will materialize only for fear and hope, and perhaps a few other emotions, where the object – the thing feared or hoped for – need not be 'rationalizing'. The object would be mentioned in a complete statement of one's reasons for being in the psychological state, but it need not itself materialize. The 'producer' takes the explanation a step further back, to one's reason for holding the beliefs characteristic of the emotion (that the object exists, or did or will exist, or that the object has the appropriate properties, or all of these). We need not be concerned with the examples or the details. Even if producers are distinct from objects, they still exemplify the special dependence on thoughts that we are concerned with. Not all causes of emotions are producers, and not all causes of emotions are objects, but both producers and objects (whether or not they are themselves 'causes') mark points at which thoughts enter into emotions. It is because of the importance of thoughts in the classification of mental states as particular emotions that objects and producers enter (at their differing points) in the explanation of those states. Or rather, both producers and objects show that importance.

Appendix B
On Thoughts and Emotions

We have tried (in part I, section 11) to give thought its proper place in the analysis of emotion. We have tried (in Appendix A) to show that giving thought its place leaves room for causal connections. Perhaps a bit more should be said about the difficulty that can be raised by the allegation of tautology, and how it is met. On a causal analysis, it must be true that 'if I did not have the thought, I would not have the emotion'. The difficulty is over the force of the 'would not'. If the statement were 'if I did not think that the tickets are gone, I would not be vexed that the tickets are gone', the connection between thought and emotion would be analytic or tautologous. It is not enough to chop off the occurrence of the thought specifying the object, and simply leave the name of the emotion by itself (vexation, anger, fear . . .). Even where there are no difficulties of fine discrimination between emotions, specifying the object through the thought may be essential to specifying the emotion. For example, even if we simplify by regarding fear as composed of a desire plus a thought, 'if I did not think that is an unruly mob and that unruly mobs are dangerous, I would not be afraid' (leaving off 'afraid of the unruly mob') the statement would still be arguably tautologous because a desire to run does not constitute fear unless it is desire to run in a situation viewed as dangerous. To avoid possible confusion, the very general notion of a mental state, which may be unambiguously picked out or identified (as a state, not an emotion) in general terms or by emotional constituents excluding thoughts may be brought in.

But what if there are no constituents of an emotion excluding thoughts? In that case there would be no underlying description of the emotion and the causal theorist would be reduced to saying that the emotion causes itself. Are there any emotions which do not just involve thoughts essentially (which we argue all do), but are essentially just thoughts? Certainly there is, in general, a distinction between thoughts which produce emotions and dispassionate thoughts. And even a thought which is characteristic of an emotion can occur without its giving rise to the emotion. It can occur alone, or it can occur in conjunction with other necessary conditions but in the face of countervailing conditions (or just in the absence of sufficient ones – but part of the issue here is what constitutes sufficient conditions). Could an emotion consist of thought alone?

Not every thought-constituted emotion would be an embarrassment to the causal theorist. An emotion can affect the course of one's behaviour. Equally, it can affect the course of one's thoughts. The only effect of my jealousy may be to cause me to dwell on the faults of my rival. *These* thoughts do not cause, though they may in some sense constitute, my jealousy. (There may be nothing else to my jealousy but the thoughts on which, to use Thalberg's term, my emotion is 'founded'.) What Hume calls the 'calm passions' may be a source of difficulty for the causal theorist. Certainly they create difficulty for *his* causal theory. Mary Warnock suggests they are not really emotions at all. But I believe that her claim is mistaken (see part I, last section). However we settle that issue, the calm passions need not be *pure* thoughts. They may involve some agitation (though not much) and are known by their effects (on thoughts and behaviour – they may serve as dispositions or motives to action). So, even if it is allowed that they are emotions (which I think they indeed are), they are in any case more than mere foundational thoughts.

The hypothesis Thalberg discusses is 'that emotions with objects are effects of the convictions, doubts, or conjectures upon which these emotions are founded' (1964, p. 214). Where the thoughts are incidental or coloured thoughts, not giving the object of the emotion, they do not cause any more difficulty for the causal theorist than emotions with non-thought elements. Calm passions with weak affects, or dispositions to behaviour, are also not a problem. But there are cases where the emotion seems to amount to nothing more than a belief.

> Suppose that I truthfully say that I am frightened of German
> nationalism as a political force; I would in this case normally be
> taken to have revealed that I believe that German nationalism
> is in some way dangerous, unless I add that my fear is altogether
> irrational. The belief is the main constitutive element in the fear,
> which would disappear, or at least be modified, with the
> disappearance of the belief. If in this case the belief were
> abandoned, nothing would remain that would constitute fear. . . .
> Just because the thought is in the normal case an element in the
> state of mind, together with the affect, one can intelligibly speak
> of being frightened of German nationalism, when the thought of
> danger is present, without the associated disagreeable affect
> (Hampshire, 1965, pp. 84, 97).

These sorts of 'calm' passions may involve thoughts of different types and involve them in different ways. Where 'belief' is used with its full normative force (so the thought of danger is not merely a passing thought or a fantasy) what makes the state of mind an emotion is (mainly) that the belief can be part of a motive to action – which is more than merely informing action as a part of its background. Sometimes, however, the thoughts constituting emotions are not beliefs that I endorse. Even if a man dissociated himself from a thought, however, and even if there is no element in addition to thought, there may be features of the thought that make one count it as an emotion: how the thoughts occur, or their source, or higher-order thoughts about the source. . . . For example, an emotion may consist of *obsessive* thought: 'The man who is frightened of the dark may not believe that he is in danger; perhaps he knows that he is not; but at the same time he finds that the thought or idea of danger stays in his mind, and that he cannot rid himself of it' (Hampshire, 1965, p. 98). The state of mind may remain fear, despite the recognition of the irrationality of the relevant thought, but it is no longer *simply* fear; and one may now be in a position to operate on one's state of mind in other ways (i.e. now that one has gone as far as rational argument will take one – or perhaps there is always an appropriate object lurking behind the apparent inappropriate one, see Sachs, 1974). The thought of (though not belief in) danger is part of what makes the state of mind fear. But a difference remains between having a thought and having an emotion. It would be a mistake if, in recognizing the importance(s) of thought, one were to assimilate emotions to mere thoughts (which is not to say that *turbulence* is necessary for an emotional state). (The ranges of thought-dependence, both within particular emotions such as fear and among types of emotion such as fear and shame, are explored in part II.) It is arguable that in many cases, when one says 'I am afraid of X' and, even more, 'I am afraid that (e.g.) it will rain', the emotion word introduces a belief or attitude rather than an emotion. Partly because the emotion word is not always detachable in the way it generally is in more basic cases, i.e. 'I am afraid of German nationalism' may not imply 'I am afraid' *simpliciter*; and it seems at least awkward to regard the belief as giving the rationalizing (in Davidson's sense) object: i.e. when 'I am afraid that it will rain' I am not 'afraid because it will rain' (it may not) or because 'I think it will rain' (because that belief, in this case, would be my fear, and it cannot cause itself). So the causal theorist may well wish to confine his argument to cases where rationalizing objects are given, and separate off states with non-rationalizing objects, such as hope (and other forward-looking emotions – see Kenny, 1963, p. 72), desire that P, fear that P, wish that P. He might do this and still recognize the similarity of these states to basic emotions in involving pro or con attitudes, but also their even-more-important similarities to neutral (non-rationalizing) states such as expecting that, suspecting that, and believing that P. (It might also be worth investigating a problem parallel to that raised by Davidson for beliefs and attitudes in relation to action: 'a person can have a reason for an action, and perform the action, and yet this reason not be the reason why he did it. Central to the relation between a reason and an action it explains is the idea that the agent performed the action *because* he had the reason.' For thought, object, and emotion: can one be angry that P, and believe that P, and yet not be angry – hope, etc. – because P? Non-rationalizing desire may provide a model for mental states with non-rationalizing objects, and so suggest further reasons for regarding mental states which reduce to beliefs as distinguishable and distinct from emotions.)

Appendix C
On a Humean View of Fantasy

I have argued that the key to understanding emotions, conscious or unconscious, cannot be found in Hume. I have also claimed (part II, section 5, and Neu, 1973) that the key to understanding fantasy, conscious or unconscious, cannot be found in Hume. I would like here to do a bit more to sketch some of the arguments relating to fantasy hinted at elsewhere.

The difference between perceptions, memories and fantasies is not a matter of degree. They are all mental entities, processes or whatever (not to prejudge the nature of the mental), i.e. they are all forms of thought. They may have the same content. Given a thought, and only a thought, there is no way of knowing whether it is a perception, a memory, or a fantasy. The strength or vividness of the thought will not differentiate them. The simplest refutation of such a Humean (degree-of-vividness) criterion is that it is phenomenologically false. Perceptions, on this view, should be vivid, memories dimmer (the older the dimmer), and fantasies dimmest. In fact, however, each comes in all degrees of brightness (assuming it is clear what one is measuring when one is measuring 'strength' or 'vividness' or 'brightness', and that it is the same quality in each). On a conceptual level, using a Humean criterion, it becomes difficult to understand how we can have 'hallucinatory' fantasies or memories: that is, fantasies or memories which we take to be perceptions. It becomes impossible to describe the nature of the mistake involved, for to take a thought to be a perception must be (on a Humean criterion) to take it to have the force of a perception. But a thought has just the force we take it to have; what we think is the criterion here. So if we take a thought to be a perception, though we can make other mistakes, it must at least be a perception. If degree of force is what makes a thought a perception and we are the sole judges of force, we cannot have 'hallucinatory' fantasies or memories. At worst, we can be unsure of the force of a thought, in which case it is simply uncertain whether the thought is perception, fantasy or memory.

Other conceptual paradoxes arise. Most relevant to our (psychoanalytic) concerns is what happens in the cases of mixed thoughts. Is a 'memory of fantasy' brighter than a fantasy? The question goes right to the underlying assumptions about energy. It seems natural that a memory should be dimmer than a perception because loss, seepage, or fading of energy would occur with time. The energy of the thought comes from the original perception. But where would the additional energy come from needed to lift a memory of fantasy up to the level of memory? If a memory of fantasy is less bright than a fantasy, one wonders how one distinguishes a memory of fantasy from a fantasy of memory and the latter from a very faded memory of fantasy. At what point do thoughts fade completely? Would a fantasy of memory be possible at all? The most radical difficulty with a Humean criterion is that there may be no aspect of the thought to which a notion of 'degree' can attach. So far we have assumed and accepted the narrow treatment of fantasies and perceptions as involving 'impressions' (or 'ideas' or 'sense-data'), mental pictures, some 'mental content' in addition to thought-content. The content of a thought is what is thought, the 'thought that so-and-so' or 'of so-and-so' is identified by the content of the so-and-so. (Even this is not quite accurate, various other circumstances must be taken into account for 'she hates me', even thought by one person on two almost simultaneous occasions may once be the thought 'my mother hates me' and another time 'my wife hates me'. But the problems of propositional identity are notorious and not special to the cases which concern us.) The same thought may take various forms, e.g. it may consist of visual images or verbal representations. The same thought may even be embodied in different visual images, as when I twice remember going through a door on a particular occasion; one time from the point of view of me passing through the door, one time from the point of view of an onlooker watching me emerge. But I may just be telling a story to someone and say, 'and then I came through the door'. And here I am remembering, but there is nothing of which it makes sense to ask, 'is it more intense?' The question does not arise. Here the form of my memory is its audible expression (there need not be any mental event of which it is a report), and it is not true that the louder my statement the more vivid the memory. If we shift the question of intensity to the feeling with which I remember 'that P' we do then have something we can measure, but we have shifted the question and the answer will not reveal anything essential to its being memory rather than perception.

The difference between perception and memory (where it is a memory of perception and a memory not simply *that* one has perceived, but *of* the perception) can be simply though unilluminatingly stated: it is a matter of time. A memory is a repetition of a perception *after* the occurrence of the perception, and, in some way, because of that perception, and is not itself a perception. (The circularity in the last clause of the formula is not readily avoidable; for one can remember a scene, for example, while seeing that scene again, without it being a memory of – a rather different thing – having seen that scene. One may even call up a memory to check whether the scene has changed, or the scene may call up the memory. Think of the taste of Proust's madeleine.) There is no such simple formula (even an unilluminating one) for distinguishing fantasy from perception. The natural contrast to appeal to, truth *vs.* falsity, will not make the difference. A fantasy is not a false perception, it need not even be mistaken for a perception. A fantasy of perception might consist of thought of a pleasant experience of sexual intercourse. But the thoughts need not be false (in all ways), they may be of an actual pleasant experience of sexual intercourse. But is it not then a memory rather than a fantasy? Not necessarily. The recollection in this case may be more a reliving, and it is certainly itself pleasurable. Further, I may deliberately set myself to fantasize, and I may not be concerned about accuracy (as I would be if I had set myself to remember the experience), but then I may be (cf. certain masturbation fantasies). Note that I need not be deceived in any of this. It is as though I am having the experience now (that is why and what I have set out for), but I know both that I am not and that I have had the experience in the past. Otherwise, in this case, it appears that there need be little difference between a fantasy and an experience remembered with pleasure. (Perhaps the relationship in time of the thought and the content, and the role of this relationship is what is essential to a fantasy involving memory. Can one have a fantasy of an actual current experience?) From another direction, it is clear that there are many ways in which a perception can go wrong (be 'false') without thereby becoming a fantasy.

What of a fantasy of memory? That is, a current fantasy, projected back and given the status of memory. A fantasy of memory is not simply a false memory. Memories themselves admit of various degrees and kinds of error without ceasing to have the character of memory. One may make a simple mistake, for example, think one has left one's glasses on the table rather than on the desk. Here the thought retains the character of memory because it is about the past, about an actual event in the past known to one to have occurred, and the thought retains its reference to that past event because there is enough in the total situation to identify the event. (What, precisely, makes this so, like the problem of how I know to whom you have referred when you say 'she hates me', is a nest of further problems.) All that is wrong is that 'X' has been substituted for 'Y'. In another case of false memory, where error is motivated, for example, thinking that 'you apologized' rather than 'I apologized', the character of memory is retained for the same reasons. In this case, all that has been added has been an explanation for the mistake, but it is presumed even in the case of the simple mistake that there is *some* explanation. Where the error is more radical, where there is no identifiable event in the past which can be taken to be referred to by a thought, the thought must be regarded as, in a sense, an hallucination. So it is, in a sense, a fantasy. But it is so far unclear whether it would be a fantasy of memory or a memory of fantasy. The latter case is more or less straightforward. It is a memory of fantasy if the radically false thought (perception) occurred on some occasion prior to its present occurrence and its present occurrence is a (true) memory of that occurrence. The memory must, of course (if it is to be an hallucination) mistake the fantasy for a true perception.

Fantasy of memory calls for more in the way of mechanism than memory of fantasy. This is partly because questions about memory which have been sidestepped, must now be raised (though we will not be able to answer them here). One wants to know how a fantasy gets any reference to time (cf. part I, section 6, note 5). For example, if the fantasy is a picture of some scene, must the scene include a calendar? Even if it does, does that have to be the date of the thought-content? Not every thought about the past pretends to be a *memory* of a past event (e.g. 'Brutus killed Caesar'). Even where a fantasy includes the subject as a character in the tableau, even a child, need the age of the subject in the thought correspond to the date of the thought? What if the child is pictured as viewing some (actual) event in the subject's later adult life? Even in the cases of greatest interest to psychoanalysis, where the subject is included as a child in the fantasy as a participant in some event presumably taking place in his childhood (primal scenes), it is not always clear how the dating of narratives or recon-structions is achieved. The possibility of projection back of contemporary productions (i.e. of retrospective fantasies) is always open. And vivid 'screen memories' and even ordinary childhood memories tend to be distorted reproductions:

> In the majority of significant and in other respects unimpeachable childhood scenes the subject sees himself in the recollection as a child, with the knowledge that this child is himself; he sees this child, however, as an observer from outside the scene would see him. . . . Now it is evident that such a picture cannot be an exact repetition of the impression that was originally received. . . . It may indeed be questioned whether we have any memories at all *from* our childhood: memories *relating* to our childhood may be all that we possess (Freud, 1899a, pp. 321, 322).

Even 'relating' ideas (if viewed as images) to our past (or future) can be problematical.

In exploring the question of the nature of fantasy, I would connect it with notions of wish-fulfilment and certain forms of falsity and awareness of falsity. But that I cannot do here. I will turn now to a few remarks on a final issue connected with the question of the force of fantasy and unconscious fantasy.

The satisfactions of fantasy are not fleeting in genuinely psychotic states, where contact with reality is well and truly lost. According to the model of day-dream fantasy, one is (in day-dreams) in some sense aware of the contrast with reality. Hallucinatory wish-fulfilments are rather more like psychotic states. Are unconscious fantasies hallucinatory? As an approach, are infantile hallucinatory wish-fulfilments unconscious fantasies? Are they unconscious? It is not immediately clear what elements are and what elements are not unconscious. One must note that when Freud speaks of inhibiting the cathexis of a memory image, what happens on his *Project* model is that energy is kept from flowing into neurones. We are not aware of neurones and their energy states (as such). Consciousness has its own place in his apparatus. So when we inhibit the cathexis of memory and so prevent flow-back into the perceptual system, we are prevented (it would seem) from being conscious of the memory. There is, however, another mechanism by which we can become conscious of memories, i.e. perceive memories, without their becoming perceptions: attention. Freud treats the attention cathexis of consciousness as an organ of inner perception. But he also holds that there is no consciousness of energy shifts in the psyche, except as pleasure and unpleasure, until linguistic connections (*Pcs.*) are established (Freud, 1900a, p. 574). So in the case of the hallucinating infant it would seem that the memory is submerged except for its appearance as a delusory (hallucinatory) perception. So the fantasy is here conscious, but not as fantasy (because the infant is not aware of the falsity). So the hallucinatory wish-fulfilment is not a day-dream, but not obviously an *unconscious* fantasy either. The case of an adult hallucinatory wish-fulfilment would be still more difficult because it might bring in verbal connections and so consciousness of other elements. It is still arguable that in the case in hand we do have an unconscious fantasy. Perhaps one ought not to say that the hallucinatory perception *is* the fantasy and that the fantasy is therefore conscious. Perhaps the perception should be regarded as the manifestation of an unconscious wish, and it is that wish and not the hallucinatory perception which is the fantasy. We shall have to be prepared to distinguish unconscious fantasies from their conscious or visible manifestations, for it is only through such manifestations that we shall be able to come to know them. But at this point I think such distinctions and discussions can only confuse, and it is better to regard the sort of hallucinatory wish-fulfilments we have so far discussed as more like (conscious) psychotic states than unconscious fantasies.

The discussion of hallucinatory wish-fulfilment in terms of cathexes of energy might make it seem that Freud is offering (what we have seen to be untenable) a Humean criterion for distinguishing memory and perception by degree of intensity. But we should note that we are not aware of these differences in intensity as differences of intensity;

they provide the physiological background and explanation for what we are aware of: in the case considered, as hallucinatory perceptions. (Separate 'indications of reality' are what count.) A Humean criterion would be particularly unfortunate within Freudian theory, for Freud regards psychic reality as of equal importance with material reality in the aetiology of neuroses. A difference in strength or energy would be precisely the kind that should make an aetiological difference in Freud's model, and so would leave the equivalence unexplained.

Freud does seem to treat the distinction between memory and perception as one that can be upset by too intense memory. But one must be careful, for that an unwonted degree of energy can upset the distinction does not show that the distinction was originally made in terms of degree of energy. (Freud even suggests that high energy quantity is needed only on one occasion to establish the facilitation over which 'flow-back' occurs – Freud, 1950a, pp. 381–2). Specifically, a memory that becomes an hallucination by the addition of energy does not thereby become a perception in Freud's scheme, it is mistaken for a perception. The excessive energy explains the mistake, but if the distinction were in terms of energy there would be no mistake to explain. In any case, the 'mark of reality' is not 'intensity' but matching perception ('identity'), and later making disappear by action, that is, special 'indications of reality'.

Notes

I

Hume

1 . . . Had the essence but in one;
Two distincts, division none . . .

Property was thus appalled,
That the self was not the same;
Single nature's double name
Neither two nor one was called.

Reason, in itself confounded,
Saw division grow together,
To themselves yet either neither,
Simple were so well compounded . . .
(Shakespeare, *The Phoenix and Turtle*)

2 This is perhaps the most important point made by Cannon in his critique of the James–Lange theory of the emotions. It turns out that the same physiological changes occur in very different emotional states (e.g. adrenalin flows in rage, and fear, and joy). So emotion could not be, or at least could not simply be, the perception of those physiological changes. Put crudely, if all one had to go on were the tears, one would have no way of knowing whether one's tears were tears of joy or tears of sorrow.

3 These sorts of problems are raised and explored by Ryle, 1954a, Penelhum, 1956–7, and others. Ryle also points out contrasts in our methods for identifying feelings and sensations as opposed to our methods for identifying and describing pleasures. These contrasts are developed further by Gosling, 1969, ch. II. There is also a literature on the question whether pain is necessarily unpleasant, e.g. Gardiner, 1964, Pitcher, 1970.

4 They include such points as that enjoying something seems to require awareness of or attending to it, and that drawing attention to feelings while engaged in an activity can interfere with the enjoyment of that activity. The thesis is stated by Ryle:

The general point that I am trying to make is that the notion of *attending* or *giving one's mind to* is a polymorphous notion. The special point that I am trying to make is that the notion of *enjoying* is one variety in this genus, or one member of this clan, i.e. that the reason why I cannot, in logic, enjoy what I am oblivious of is the same as the reason why I cannot, in logic, spray my currant-bushes without gardening (1954b, p. 202).

The thesis is developed by Ryle, 1954b; Williams, 1959; Penelhum, 1964. For doubts, see Gosling, 1969, ch. IV.

5 Cf. discussion of problems of tensed ideas in Holland, 1954; and Pears, 1967, pp. 29–31. Even a picture (taking ideas as images) containing a calendar with a date next week circled, need not be a picture (or an *expectation* or *anticipation* or *prediction*) of an event next week. The problem here connects with certain difficulties raised for psychoanalytic theory by the problem of giving fantasies a reference to time. And how is one to distinguish memory of fantasy from fantasy of memory? We shall leave these problems for now.

6 Kemp Smith, pp. 185–6, says they are related causally, but this does not (cannot) mean that *the ideas* are associated through causation. In that case, the 'expectation' would be its own fulfilment. 'Causation' may find place, indeed a variety of places, in the analysis of emotions, but not here. We shall return to this point in the next section.

7 'The logical laws of thought do not apply in the id, and this is true above all of the law of contradiction. Contrary impulses exist side by side, without cancelling each other out or diminishing each other' (Freud, 1933a, p. 73).

8 I follow Árdal (1966, p. 97), as opposed to Kemp Smith, in my interpretation at this point: 'The calmness or violence of a passion, although determined by causes, is independent of the mechanism which brings it about, whether direct, indirect, primary or secondary . . .'

9 Ewing (in the same symposium, 1957, p. 73) is also puzzled by the supposed contrast between 'personal opinion' and 'objective statement of agreed fact'. He suggests that 'in regard to emotions, attitudes and actions alike we may use "justified": (1) in a stricter sense such that something is only "justified" if the facts are what the person in question believes them to be, or (2) in a sense in which they are "justified" if his belief is reasonable in view of the evidence at his disposal, even though it may be in fact false . . .' In any case beliefs and their grounds are at issue (and so present).

10 She continues her example: 'To justify my attitude towards the

Prime Minister would be to point out what I thought were the merits and demerits of his character, and to run through his activities, perhaps particularly emphasising anything that he has done to me personally. I must cite, that is, my view of the facts, the history and the value of the object, if I am called upon to justify my attitude.'

II
Spinoza

1 Wolfson (1934, II, p. 195) treats Spinoza's claim as one of a long series of recognitions of the first law. This despite the fact that he notices (1969, p. 199ff.) that Spinoza extends the principle beyond animals to the inanimate realm where it would seem to lack sense (or at least the sort of sense it has in its narrower, merely empirical, application), and that the *conatus* and the thing itself are, according to Spinoza, not distinguishable.

2 Particularly helpful in this connection are Joachim, 1901, p. 191ff.; Hampshire, 1956, pp. 58–9, 92–3; and Hampshire, 1960a, pp. 191–2.

3 Perhaps bodily sensations are the obvious model for ideas of modifications of the body. Still, one can feel a difficulty over the nature of the level of awareness which is short of full consciousness (ideas of ideas). But I do not think we need to be detained by that difficulty here. As Curley (1969, p. 126) points out, there is a mode of thought for every mode of extension, but 'Spinoza's statements that "all things are animate, though in different degrees", and "there must be in God an idea of everything" (*E*, II, prop. 13, note), does not imply that my watch has thoughts and sensations, any more than Aristotle's doctrine that plants have souls implies that flowers feel pain.' I think that Curley is right, even if we do not interpret the thoughts corresponding to inanimate (in the ordinary sense) modes as Curley does (i.e. as true propositions about corresponding facts). He says 'my body is a set of facts, my mind a set of propositions describing those facts; my mind must contain a proposition corresponding to every fact that constitutes my body, for the propositions simply are the facts, considered in a different way' (Curley, 1969, p. 127). One wonders how to make sense of the mind 'containing' a proposition. Perhaps one might get further by following Hampshire's notion that if you learn the physical basis of a thought, that thought is transformed into a perception of that physical fact (Hampshire, 1969). But in any case there is ample textual evidence that one 'perceives' but does not 'know' everything in the body. (See *E*, II, props 19 and 23.) That is, the mind does not know the body except in so far as it perceives itself or has ideas of ideas, or is conscious.

4 That there should be this ambiguity is understandable because of

the development of terminology from 'common notions' or ultimate ideas such as 'equality' – 'existence', 'duration' – to eternal truths or adequate ideas: e.g. 'things equal to the same thing are equal to one another'. See annotation to Spinoza, 1929, Letter IV, *Correspondence*, ed. Wolf, p. 377.

5 Some modern writers on the emotions (e.g. Sartre, Schafer) err by emphasizing the activity of the emotions to the exclusion of their passivity (for contrast see Peters). Once one recognizes the centrality of beliefs in emotions, the question of the relation of belief and will (see Price, 1954, and Williams, 1970) must be given a new prominence. Because of the importance of this question in understanding the gradations of activity and passivity in human life, the mechanisms of self-deception and the nature of unconscious fantasy may become the most pressing issues for philosophy of mind in our time, for it is in these two areas that the problematic character of the relation of belief and will (or decision) comes most clearly to the surface.

III
Thought, Theory and Therapy

1 Whether such parallels exist we still do not know. And it is not clear, even if such parallels exist, whether 'reductions' are possible. There is an enormous philosophical literature on the question of whether even 'sensations' could be 'brain processes'.

The importance of a distinction between 'reduction' and 'replacement' was first impressed on me by Alasdair MacIntyre.

2 I suspect that this is one of the things that is misleading about Lévi-Strauss's 'correspondences' – they seem to call for sameness of, mythological, meaning. But perhaps this too can be interpreted as sameness of reference (sameness of thing represented or symbolized).

In the discussion on pp. 123–4, I read 'the morning star' and 'the evening star' as descriptions rather than proper names. But in any case I do not think it is necessary for me to go into the depths of the theory of reference. My point is to deny *a priori* knowledge (an epistemological point), not to deny a necessary connection (a metaphysical point). So I need not get into the argument about the possibility of contingent identity statements (see Kripke, 1971).

3 E.g. Freud's neurological quantity 'Q'. It is important that this would just be another way of describing it, and not a direct vision of the naked truth. Knowledge must be mediated through concepts, we cannot grasp any *Ding an sich* (or underlying *reality*) through direct wordless intuition. (Which may connect with Freud's speculation about the unconscious being the realm of non-verbal 'thing

presentations' isolated from 'word presentations'. Cf. Eliot, *Sweeney Agonistes*: 'I gotta use words when I talk to you.')

4 Cf. Sartre's animus against the invisible, including microbes, described in Simone de Beauvoir's *The Prime of Life* (1960, p. 46).

5 That 'facts' (in general) are theory-laden has been a point familiar in philosophy of science at least since Duhem (1905).

6 Cf. Darwin on 'species' as genealogical categories. Even if a change in rationale does not change membership of categories directly, it can profoundly affect our approach. Consider the post-Darwinian discovery that changes are discontinuous (through mutation) and therefore species are clearly distinct. Cf. changes in psychoanalytic developmental theories, new emphasis on ego development, arrest and fixation points, etc.

Objects may be of the same kind on different rationales, but then the kind itself may have changed. (So it would be wrong to see kinds as sets, determined by their members – one might also say some ways of picking out sets do not pick out kinds, even if they pick out the same objects as would, on other grounds, constitute a kind.) See W. V. Quine, 1969.

7 Consider other cultures. 'Taboos' that to us may look like unreasonably exaggerated fears, i.e. phobias, may in another society be perfectly normal – given the rest of their beliefs – and not open to a 'phobic' explanation on either the behaviourist or the psychoanalytic pattern (at least internally). (But then, taboos too may be traceable to renounced desires.) But the point is more than a cross-cultural difficulty. One cannot 'read' behaviour (or other 'manifestations' of inner states) without a background understanding of beliefs, intentions, etc. It is not just that there may be cultural variations, even within a culture (see p. 138) there are ambiguities and so problems of interpretation. More is needed than the isolated action – one must know the *context*: not the actual context, but the context as understood by the agent; his beliefs and his desires and his intentions, that is, his *reasons* for action. (The discussion could easily be extended to understanding expressions of emotion in pictorial representations, though 'context' of a somewhat different kind is needed. See Gombrich on Mondrian.)

8 See H. Putnam's penetrating critique of N. Malcolm (Putnam, 1962b). He provides a well-reasoned discussion of the theory of 'meaning' change. (See esp. discussion of natural kinds for which criteria are good but not perfect indicators. E.g. multiple sclerosis and virus, pp. 218–20.)

Debates about the reality of 'schizophrenia' may be understood as disputes about whether it denotes a natural kind or an odd conglomeration of symptoms. Is there a common aetiology (e.g. chemical or double-bind) and so a common treatment (or at least a 'family resemblance' among schizophrenic aetiologies and treatments)? Different conclusions may be based on different predictions about the development of science.

9 Another case: Winnicott's treatment of a little girl whose symptoms began with the birth of a brother – no rivalry, fear of faeces, generalized fear of objects moving behind her – and disappeared with enlightenment. She no longer feared her own power, her competition with her mother.

10 *The Freud Journal of Lou Andreas-Salomé*, 1964, p. 75. She mentions a paper on Spinoza written by Victor Tausk as early as 1907. While the paper is now untraceable (Paul Roazen, private communication), there is a brief report in the *Minutes of the Vienna Psychoanalytic Society* for 24 November 1909 (Nunberg and Federn, 1967, pp. 328–30) of a presentation by Tausk on 'Theory of Knowledge and Psychoanalysis' in which Spinoza is mentioned.

Bibliography

Andreas-Salomé, Lou (1964), *The Freud Journal of Lou Andreas-Salomé*, trans. Stanley A. Leavy (London: Hogarth Press).

Árdal, Páll S. (1966), *Passion and Value in Hume's Treatise* (Edinburgh University Press).

Beauvoir, Simone de (1960), *Prime of Life* (New York: Lancer Books).

Bénassy, Maurice and René Diatkine (1964), 'On the Ontogenesis of Fantasy', *International Journal of Psycho-Analysis*, XLV, pp. 171–79.

Bibring, Edward (1941), 'The Development and Problems of the Theory of the Instincts', *International Journal of Psycho-Analysis*, XXII, pp. 102–31.

Binion, Rudolph (1968), *Frau Lou* (Princeton University Press).

Brierley, Marjorie (1937), 'Affects in Theory and Practice', in *Trends in Psycho-Analysis* (London: Hogarth Press, 1951), pp. 43–56.

Cannon, W. B. (1927), 'The James-Lange Theory of Emotion: A Critical Examination and an Alternative Theory', in *The Nature of Emotion*, ed. M. B. Arnold (Harmondsworth: Penguin, 1968), pp. 43–52.

Chomsky, Noam (1959), 'Review of B. F. Skinner's *Verbal Behaviour*', in *The Structure of Language*, ed. Fodor and Katz (Englewood Cliffs, N.J.: Prentice-Hall, 1964), pp. 547–78.

Curley, E. M. (1969), *Spinoza's Metaphysics: An Essay in Interpretation* (Cambridge, Mass.: Harvard University Press).

Davidson, Donald (1963), 'Actions, Reasons, and Causes', *Journal of Philosophy*, LX, reprinted in *The Philosophy of Action*, ed. A. R. White (Oxford University Press, 1968), pp. 79–94.

Descartes, R. (1649), 'The Passions of the Soul', in *The Philosophical Works of Descartes*, trans. E. S. Haldane and G. R. T. Ross (New York: Dover, 1931), vol. I, pp. 329–427.

Donnellan, Keith S. (1970), 'Causes, Objects and Producers of the Emotions' (Abstract), *Journal of Philosophy*, LXVII, pp. 947–50.

Duhem, P. (1905), *The Aim and Structure of Physical Theory*, trans. P. P. Wiener (Princeton University Press, 1954).

Erikson, Erik (1950), *Childhood and Society* (Harmondsworth: Penguin, 1965).

Erikson, Erik (1958), 'The Nature of Clinical Evidence', in *Insight and Responsibility* (New York: Norton).

Erikson, Erik (1964), 'Psychological Reality and Historical Actuality', in *Insight and Responsibility* (New York: Norton).

Erikson, Erik (1968), *Identity: Youth and Crisis* (New York: Norton).

Ewing, A. C. (1957), 'The Justification of Emotions', *Proceedings of the Aristotelian Society*, suppl. XXXI, p. 59ff.

Eysenck, H. J. (1965), *Fact and Fiction in Psychology* (Harmondsworth: Penguin).

Frege, G. (1892), 'On Sense and Reference', in *Translations from the Philosophical Writings of Gottlob Frege*, ed. P. Geach and M. Black (Oxford: Blackwell, 1960).

Freud, Sigmund (1893c), 'Some Points for a Comparative Study of Organic and Hysterical Motor Paralyses', Standard Edition, I. (All references are to the Standard Edition, *Complete Psychological Works*, London: Hogarth Press, 1955–74.)

Freud, S. and Breuer (1895d). *Studies on Hysteria*, II.

Freud, S. (1899a), 'Screen Memories', III.

Freud, S. (1900a), *The Interpretation of Dreams*, IV–V.

Freud, S. (1905d), *Three Essays on the Theory of Sexuality*, VII.

Freud, S. (1905e), 'Fragment of an Analysis of a Case of Hysteria' (Dora), VII.

Freud, S. (1909b), 'Analysis of a Phobia in a Five-Year-Old Boy' (Little Hans), X.

Freud, S. (1909d), 'Notes upon a Case of Obsessional Neurosis' (Rat Man), X.

Freud, S. (1910d), 'Future Prospects of Psycho-Analytic Therapy', XI.

Freud, S. (1910k), ' "Wild" Psycho-Analysis', XI.

Freud, S. (1913c), 'On Beginning the Treatment', XII.

Freud, S. (1915e), 'The Unconscious', XIV.

Freud, S. (1920g), *Beyond the Pleasure Principle*, XVIII.

Freud, S. (1923b), *The Ego and the Id*, XIX.

Freud, S. (1926d), *Inhibitions, Symptoms and Anxiety*, XX.

Freud, S. (1933a), *New Introductory Lectures on Psycho-Analysis*, XXII.

Freud, S. (1950a), 'Extracts from the Fliess Papers (1892–1899)' and 'A Project for a Scientific Psychology', I.

Gardiner, P. L. (1963), 'Hume's Theory of the Passions', in *David Hume: A Symposium*, ed. D. F. Pears (London: Macmillan).

Gardiner, P. L. (1964), 'Pain and Evil', *Proceedings of the Aristotelian Society*, suppl. XXXVIII, pp. 107–24.

Geertz, Hildred (1968), 'Latah in Java: A Theoretical Paradox', *Indonesia*, 5, pp. 93–104.

Genet, Jean (1949), *The Thief's Journal*, trans. B. Frechtman (Harmondsworth: Penguin, 1967).

Gombrich, E. H. (1962), 'Art and the Language of the Emotions', *Proceedings of the Aristotelian Society*, suppl. XXXVI, reprinted as 'Expression and Communication' in *Meditations on a Hobby-Horse* (London: Phaidon, 1963).

Gordon, Robert M. (1969), 'Emotions and Knowledge', *Journal of Philosophy*, LXVI, pp. 408–13.

Gosling, J. C. (1965), 'Emotion and Object', *Philosophical Review*, LXXIV, pp. 486–503.

Gosling, J. C. (1969), *Pleasure and Desire* (Oxford University Press).

Green, O. H. (1972), 'Emotions and Belief', *American Philosophical Quarterly*, monograph no. 6, pp. 24–40.

Hamlyn, D. W. (1953), 'Behavior', *Philosophy*, XXVIII, pp. 132–45.

Hampshire, Stuart (1956), *Spinoza* (London: Faber & Faber).

Hampshire, Stuart (1959), *Thought and Action* (London: Chatto & Windus; New York: Viking).

Hampshire, Stuart (1960a), 'Spinoza and the Idea of Freedom', reprinted in (1971a), pp. 183–209.

Hampshire, Stuart (1960b), 'Disposition and Memory', reprinted in (1971a), pp. 160–82.

Hampshire, Stuart (1960c), 'Feeling and Expression', reprinted in (1971a), pp. 143–59.

Hampshire, Stuart (1965), *Freedom of the Individual* (New York: Harper & Row).

Hampshire, Stuart (1967), 'Freedom of Mind', reprinted in (1971a), pp. 3–20.

Hampshire, Stuart (1969), 'A Kind of Materialism', reprinted in (1971a), pp. 210–31.

Hampshire, Stuart (1971a), *Freedom of Mind and Other Essays* (Princeton University Press; and Oxford University Press, 1972).

Hampshire, Stuart (1971b), 'Sincerity and Single-Mindedness', reprinted in (1971a), pp. 232–56.

Hampshire, Stuart (1971c), 'Spinoza's Theory of Human Freedom', *The Monist*, LV, pp. 554–66.

Holland, R. F. (1954), 'The Empiricist Theory of Memory', *Mind*, LXIII, included in *Philosophy of Mind*, ed. S. Hampshire (New York: Harper & Row, 1966), pp. 266–94.

Hume, David (1739), *A Treatise of Human Nature* (*THN*), ed. L. A. Selby-Bigge (Oxford University Press, 1888).

James, William (1890), 'Emotion', in *The Principles of Psychology* (New York: Dover).

Joachim, Harold H. (1901), *A Study of the Ethics of Spinoza* (Oxford University Press).

Kemp Smith, Norman (1941), *The Philosophy of David Hume* (London: Macmillan).

Kenny, Anthony (1963), *Action, Emotion and Will* (London: Routledge & Kegan Paul).

Kline, Paul (1972), *Fact and Fantasy in Freudian Theory* (London: Methuen).

Kripke, Saul (1971), 'Identity and Necessity', in *Identity and Individuation*, ed. Milton K. Munitz (New York University Press).

Kuhn, Thomas S. (1962), *The Structure of Scientific Revolutions* (University of Chicago Press).

Lévi-Strauss (1949), 'The Sorcerer and His Magic' and 'The Effectiveness of Symbols' in *Structural Anthropology* (New York: Basic Books, 1963), pp. 167–85, and pp. 186–205, chs IX and X.

MacIntyre, Alasdair (1971), 'Emotion, Behavior and Belief', in *Against the Self-Images of the Age* (London: Duckworth), pp. 230–43.

MacNabb, D. G. C. (1969), 'Review of Árdal', *Philosophical Review*, LXXVII, pp. 127–9.

Mullane, Harvey (1965), 'Unconscious Emotion', *Theoria*, XXXI, pp. 181–90.

Neu, Jerome (1973), 'Fantasy and Memory: The Aetiological Role of Thoughts According to Freud', *International Journal of Psycho-Analysis*, LIV, pp. 383–98.

Neu, Jerome (ms.), 'Hampshire on Reasons, Causes, and Counterfactuals', 1972.

Nunberg, H. and Federn E. (1967), *Minutes of the Vienna Psychoanalytic Society*, vol. II, 1908–1910, trans. M. Nunberg (New York: International Universities Press).

Passmore, John (1968), *Hume's Intentions* (London: Duckworth, Revised Edition).

Pears, David (1962), 'Causes and Objects of Some Feelings and Psychological Reactions', *Ratio*, IV, reprinted in *Philosophy of Mind*, ed. S. Hampshire (New York: Harper & Row, 1966), pp. 143–69.

Pears, David (1963), 'Hume on Personal Identity', in *David Hume: A Symposium*, ed. D. Pears (London: Macmillan), pp. 43–54.

Pears, David (1966–7), 'Desires as Causes of Actions', *Royal Institute of Philosophy Lectures*, vol. I, pp. 83–97.

Pears, David (1967), *Bertrand Russell and the British Tradition in Philosophy* (London: Fontana).

Penelhum, Terence (1955), 'Hume on Personal Identity', *Philo-*

sophical Review, LXIV, reprinted in *Hume*, ed. V. C. Chappell (New York: Doubleday Anchor, 1966), pp. 213–39.

Penelhum, Terence (1956–7), 'The Logic of Pleasure', *Philosophy and Phenomenological Research*, XVII, reprinted in *Essays in Philosophical Psychology*, ed. D. F. Gustafson (New York: Doubleday Anchor, 1964), pp. 227–47.

Penelhum, Terence (1964), 'Pleasure and Falsity', *American Philosophical Quarterly*, I, reprinted in *Philosophy of Mind*, ed. S. Hampshire (New York: Harper & Row, 1966), pp. 242–66.

Peters, R. S. (1961–2), 'Emotions and the Category of Passivity', *Proceedings of the Aristotelian Society*, suppl. LXII, pp. 117–34.

Pitcher, George (1965), 'Emotion', *Mind*, pp. 326–46.

Pitcher, George (1970), 'The Awfulness of Pain', *Journal of Philosophy*, LXVII, pp. 481–92.

Price, H. H. (1954), 'Belief and Will', *Proceedings of the Aristotelian Society*, suppl. XXVIII, pp. 1–26, reprinted in *Philosophy of Mind*, ed. S. Hampshire (New York: Harper & Row, 1966).

Price, H. H. (1969), *Belief* (London: Allen & Unwin).

Pulver, Sydney (1971), 'Can Affects Be Unconscious?', *International Journal of Psycho-Analysis*, LII, pp. 347–54.

Putnam, Hilary (1962a), 'The Analytic and the Synthetic', *Minnesota Studies in the Philosophy of Science*, vol. III, eds H. Feigl and G. Maxwell (Minneapolis: University of Minnesota Press).

Putnam, Hilary (1962b), 'Dreaming and "Depth Grammar" ', in *Analytical Philosophy*, I, ed. R. J. Butler (Oxford: Blackwell).

Quine, W. V. (1969), 'Natural Kinds', in *Ontological Relativity and Other Essays* (New York: Columbia University Press).

Rapaport, David (1942), *Emotions and Memory* (New York: International Universities Press, 1971).

Rapaport, David (1953), 'On the Psychoanalytic Theory of Affects', in *Psychoanalytic Psychiatry and Psychology*, ed. R. P. Knight and C. R. Friedman (New York: International Universities Press, 1954), pp. 274–310.

Rathbun, Constance (1934), 'On Certain Similarities Between Spinoza and Psychoanalysis', *Psychoanalytic Review*, XXI, pp. 1–14.

Richfield, Jerome (1954), 'An Analysis of the Concept of Insight', reprinted in *Psychoanalytic Clinical Interpretation*, ed. Louis Paul (New York: Free Press, 1963), pp. 93–111.

Ryle, Gilbert (1949), *The Concept of Mind* (London: Hutchinson).

Ryle, Gilbert (1954a), 'Pleasure', in *Dilemmas* (Cambridge University Press), pp. 54–67.

Ryle, Gilbert (1954b), 'Pleasure', *Proceedings of the Aristotelian Society*, suppl. XXVIII, reprinted in *Essays in Philosophical Psychology*, ed. D. F. Gustafson (New York: Doubleday Anchor, 1964), pp. 195–205.

Sachs, David (1974), 'On Freud's Doctrine of Emotions', *Freud: A Collection of Critical Essays*, ed. Richard Wollheim (New York: Anchor Books), pp. 132–46.

Sartre, Jean-Paul (1948), *The Emotions: Outline of a Theory* (New York: Philosophical Library).

Schacter, Stanley and Jerome E. Singer (1962), 'Cognitive, Social, and Physiological Determinants of Emotional State', *Psychological Review*, LXIX, pp. 379–99.

Schafer, Roy (1976), *A New Language for Psychoanalysis* (Yale University Press).

Shope, Robert K. (1971), 'Physical and Psychic Energy', *Philosophy of Science*, XXXVIII, pp. 1–12.

Spinoza, Baruch (1675), *Ethics* (*E*), ed. James Gutmann, trans. William Hale White and Amelia Hutchinson Stirling (New York: Hafner, 1949).

Spinoza, Baruch, *The Correspondence of Spinoza*, ed. A. Wolf (Allen & Unwin, 1929).

Strachey, James (1934), 'The Nature of the Therapeutic Action of Psychoanalysis', reprinted in *Psychoanalytic Clinical Interpretation*, ed. Louis Paul (New York: Free Press, 1963), pp. 1–41.

Taylor, Charles (1964), *The Explanation of Behaviour* (New York: Humanities Press).

Thalberg, Irving (1964), 'Emotion and Thought', *American Philosophical Quarterly*, I, reprinted in *Philosophy of Mind*, ed. S. Hampshire (New York: Harper & Row, 1966), pp. 201–25.

Thalberg, Irving (1973), 'Constituents and Causes of Emotion and Action', *Philosophical Quarterly*, XXIII, pp. 1–14.

Trigg, Roger (1970), *Pain and Emotion* (Oxford University Press).

Wallerstein, Robert (1965), 'The Goals of Psychoanalysis: A Survey of Analytic Viewpoints', *Journal of the American Psychoanalytic Association*, 13.

Warnock, Mary (1957), 'The Justification of Emotions', *Proceedings of the Aristotelian Society*, suppl. XXXI, pp. 43–58.

Watling, John (1973), 'Hampshire on Freedom', in *Essays on Freedom of Action*, ed. T. Honderich (London: Routledge & Kegan Paul), pp. 15–29.

Williams, B. A. O. (1959), 'Pleasure and Belief', *Proceedings of the Aristotelian Society*, suppl. XXXIII, reprinted in *Philosophy of Mind*, ed. S. Hampshire (New York: Harper & Row, 1966), pp. 225–42.

Williams, B. A. O. (1970), 'Deciding to Believe', in *Language, Belief and Metaphysics*, ed. Kiefer and Munitz (Albany: State University of New York Press, reprinted 1973), pp. 136–51.

Williams, B. A. O. (1973), *Problems of the Self* (Cambridge University Press).

Wilson, J. R. S. (1972), *Emotion and Object* (Cambridge University Press).

Wittgenstein, Ludwig (1953), *Philosophical Investigations*, trans. G. E. M. Anscombe (Oxford: Blackwell, 2nd edition, 1958).

Wittgenstein, Ludwig (1958), *The Blue Book* (Oxford: Blackwell, 1958).

Wolfson, Harry Austryn (1934), *The Philosophy of Spinoza: Unfolding the Latent Processes of His Reasoning*, vols I and II (Cambridge, Mass.: Harvard University Press, Schocken Paperback edition, 1969).

Wollheim, Richard (1966–7), 'Expression', *Royal Institute of Philosophy Lectures*, vol. I, pp. 227–44.

Wollheim, Richard (1967–8), 'Thought and Passion', *Proceedings of the Aristotelian Society*, LXVIII, pp. 1–24.

Wollheim, Richard (1969), 'The Mind and the Mind's Image of Itself', *International Journal of Psychoanalysis*, L, pp. 209–20.

Wolpe, Joseph and Stanley Rachman (1960), 'Psychoanalytic Evidence: A Critique Based on Freud's Case of Little Hans', in *Critical Essays on Psychoanalysis*, ed. S. Rachman (Oxford: Pergamon, 1963), pp. 198–220.

Woozley, A. D. (1949), *Theory of Knowledge* (London: Hutchinson).

Index

abreaction: in Freud, 137–40, 143–55; in Lévi-Strauss, 113, 119–20

actions: and appropriateness, 66; backward tautology, 160; and beliefs, 166–7; capability of, 98, 150; dependence on the self, 80; and desires, 42, 71, 74, 92, 99, 159, 161; and emotions, 56–7, 63–5, 100–1, 153; and intentions, 53; and thoughts, 76, 147

aetiology: *see* mental disorders: aetiology

affects: and abreaction, 137–8, 143; and 'calm' passions, 166; Freud's theory, 141; and ideas, 140; psychoanalytic theory, 146; sole essential constituent of emotions, 91; and thoughts in Hume, 1, 2, 36, 152; unconscious, 144; in Warnock, 61

Alexander, Franz, 111

ambivalence, *see* emotions: conflict

Andreas-Salomé, Lou, 150–1

anger: and accompanying ideas, 27; and beliefs, 1–2, 40; and calm passions, 57; in Descartes, 79; expression, 52; feeling, 99–100; and hatred, 55, 85, 96, 99; and jealousy, 41; justification, 61–2, 65; nature, 56, 63; object, 31, 38, 43, 139; scale, 60; and thoughts, 159

animals, 2, 44–5, 51–2, 153

anthropological problems, 131–2

anxiety, 128, 134, 139–42, 146, 150

appetite, 73–5, 100, 148, 153

appropriate: beliefs, 1, 41, 46, 59–60; emotions, 39, 65–7, 84–5, 89, 147; feelings, 61; objects of anger, 62, 139; objects of pride, 35, 37; thoughts, 36

Araucanian shamanism, 121

Árdal, Páll S., 10–11, 13–15, 17, 25, 37, 50, 53, 68

association, 3, 7–8, 11–12, 16, 18, 36, 87, 148–9; by contiguity, *see* contiguity; double, 9–10, 19, 21, 24, 28, 32, 34–6, 77, 152–3; of ideas, 5, 19, 24, 27–31, 34, 78–9, 85, 102, 139, 142, 144, 152–3; of impressions, 14, 20, 23–4, 28, 34, 56, 152; by resemblance, *see* resemblance

attention, 23–4, 27, 29, 31, 34, 37, 76, 78, 141, 173

attitudes, 3, 23, 39, 57–60, 62–3, 167, 168

aversion, 7, 21, 55, 77; therapy, 108, 132

beauty, 9–10, 20, 24, 53

behaviour: and calm passions, 54, 56, 140; differing from opinions, 63; and emotions, 36, 71, 76, 101, 103, 138, 153, 166; inference from, 50–52, 141; intentional, 53, 137, 139, 161; justification, 62; non-linguistic, 44; and stimuli, 109; and symptoms, 130, 132, 147; and unconscious fantasies, 145; without thought, 43

behaviourist therapy, 2–3, 107–12, 124–30, 133–4, 147, 154–5

beliefs: and actions, 167–8; in activity, 22–3; in animals, 51; and attitudes, 58–60; in behaviourist therapy, 109; and calm passions, 57; communication, 50; and desires, 45; and emotions, 1, 2, 37, 52, 63, 65–7, 78–82, 85, 87–9, 92–3, 95, 99, 118, 136, 147–8, 152–3, 157–9, 166–7;

and feelings, 3, 48, 55; as 'force and liveliness', 48–9; grounds, 96; object, 90; power of, 115–17, 135, 154; and state of mind, 36, 46; unconscious, 1, 3, 36; and vivid perceptions, 7, 24, 47

Bénassy, Maurice and Diatkine, René, 144

benevolence, 49, 54, 55–6

Bibring, Edward, 149

body: and external causes, 98; idea of, 74; and mind, see mind and body; modifications, see physiological responses; movement, 79, 130, 160; sensations, 20, 22, 64, 76; sensations in animals, 52

Brentano, Franz, 142

Breuer, Josef, 137–8

Brierley, Marjorie, 140

Burgess, Anthony, 108

Californian shamanism, 122

Cannon, W. B., 116, 175

catharsis, 138, 143

cathexis, 140, 141, 150, 173

causation, 8, 11, 17–18, 24, 27, 29–31, 56, 92, 163; of emotions, see emotions: cause; external, 30, 72, 76, 77–80, 82, 87, 96, 98, 101

Chomsky, Noam, 109

Clockwork Orange, 108–9

colour perception, 12–19

conatus, 71–3, 76, 82, 84, 97–9, 149–150, 153

conditioning, 108–9, 112, 125–6, 132–133, 147

consensus, 60, 114–17, 154

contiguity, association by, 11, 24, 27, 29–30, 78

criteria, defining, 130–1

cultural factors, 131–2, 155

Cuna childbirth myth, 118, 120

cure, 107, 110, 114, 117, 119, 121–2, 133, 134, 137, 154; rate, 111–12

Davidson, Donald, 163, 167

day-dreaming, 145, 173

death instinct, 149

degree, see scale of degree

depression, 40, 107

Descartes, René, 31, 79–80, 83, 87, 149

description-dependence, 44–5

desire: and action, 159–61; alteration, 111; as a basic emotion, 71, 76, 81, 93, 153; behaviourist definition, 109; and conatus, 73, 82, 99; conditional, 45–6; in Descartes, 79–80; as direct passion, 77; and emotion, 103; and fear, 165; and imitation, 102; as impression of reflexion, 7, 21, 23; and love, 41–3, 54–6, 92, 94, 100–1; non-rationalizing, 167–168; object, 85–6; as psychic energy, 148; repressed, 135–6; and thought-dependence, 43–5; unconscious, 73–4, 76, 153

despair, 21, 64

diagnosis, 124, 132, 134–5

Diatkine, René, 144

displacement of emotions, 11, 27, 102; psychoanalytic, 27, 126, 127, 134, 141, 143–4, 148, 155

distinctions of reason, see under reason

Donnellan, Keith S., 163–4

Dora, 115

drugs, see effects of drugs

effects: belief in, 48; of calm passions, 53–4; cause and, 56, 61, 64, 86, 153; of drugs, 22, 66, 107, 154; of emotions, 28, 38, 159; of ideas, 29–30; of pride, 34, 36

Eliot, T. S., 145

Elisabeth, 137

emotions, 1, 5, 7, 13, 16, 18–19, 24, 36, 57, 61, 77, 79, 90, 97–9, 118, 139–40, 152–3, 155–6, 167, 169; and action, 56, 101; active/passive, 46, 67, 72, 76, 79–84, 96–7, 148–9, 154; basic (primary), 71, 76–7, 86, 93, 153; cause, 8–11, 18–19, 21, 28–38, 48–51, 54–6, 60–1, 64–6, 77, 80–2, 85–91, 93, 96, 98, 109, 152–4, 157–62, 164, 165–6; chain, 11, 14, 16, 19, 20; classification, 1, 16, 37, 57, 60, 62, 67, 93, 118, 146, 152–3, 155; conflict, 32–4, 55, 63,

emotions—*cont.*
96–7, 100, 136, 140–1, 148–9, 153, 157; discrimination, 1–2, 16, 19, 69, 77, 85, 91–4, 118, 137, 142, 144, 146–7, 152–3, 155; and Erikson's 'forces', 123; expression, 36, 52–4, 56, 99–103, 137–9, 143, 153; and ideas, *see* ideas and emotions; identification, 2, 16, 42–3, 69, 85, 137, 141, 152, 161; and impressions, 49, 54; intensity, 17, 60; justification, 40–1, 58–62, 64–7, 147; nameless, 61, 93; object, 8, 14, 18, 21, 23–43, 45, 50–1, 54–5, 58, 60–66, 78, 80, 85–94, 152–4, 157–60, 163–6, 168; objectless, 91, 93; occasion of, 91, 158–9, 163; producers, 164; spectrum, 14; and thoughts, 1–3, 31, 36–47, 52–3, 57, 59, 62–4, 69, 77, 79, 87, 89, 91–3, 98–9, 118, 136–7, 140–1, 143, 146–147, 148, 152–7, 159–62, 164, 165–168; transformation, 2, 5, 37, 65, 69, 87, 93, 95, 97, 123–4, 128, 136, 139, 147, 152, 154–5; unconscious, 137, 139, 141–5, 155
energy, emotional/instinctual/psychic, *see* psychic energy
envy, 39–40
epistemology, 26–7, 74–5, 78–9, 81–82, 95
Erikson, Erik, 110, 115, 122–3, 135, 154
essence, 71–4, 80, 97–9
Eysenck, Hans, 108, 125

false beliefs, ideas, etc., 64, 80–2, 87–89, 90, 91, 95, 96, 158, 171, 172
fantasies, 2, 80, 92, 95, 139, 140–1, 147–8, 169–71; and memories, 87, 113, 143, 155, 172; physiology, 120–1, 154; unconscious, 36, 46, 145, 146, 155, 173
fear: in animals, 52; and beliefs, 166; and calm passions, 57; communication, 50; conditional, 46; conflictual origin, 33–4; and desire, 165; as direct passion, 77; as emotion word, 162; as impression of reflexion, 7, 21; object, 40–1, 80, 84–5, 126; objectless, 43, 56, 95, 141, 147; in others, 102; reasonable/unreasonable, 61, 64–6, 84–5, 135, 166; scale, 56, 91–2; and thoughts, 159; *see also* phobias
feeling(s): alien, 150; and beliefs, 48, 99; communication, 53; conflict, 33; and desire, 56; effects, 55; and emotions, 5, 14, 18, 36, 54, 59, 77, 90–1, 140, 144, 152; expression, 100; inferred, 51; normal, 61, 93; and pride, 35; strength, 60; theory, 49; and thoughts, 1–3, 47, 57, 76, 141–2; variation, 19
forces (Erikson), 122–4, 135
freedom: absolute, 81–2, 97; through knowledge, 2, 78, 136, 139, 147–8, 151–2, 154
Frege, G., 123
Freud, Sigmund, 133–51; and Breuer, Josef, 137–8; on emotions, 155; on ideas, 78; and Little Hans case, 124–9; on memory, 172–3; on neurophysiology, 119; on professional acceptance, 116; on psychic reality, 174; on the unconscious, 131; *see also* Spinoza compared with Freud
Freudian psychoanalysis, 2–3, 95, 110–12, 152, 154

Gardiner, P. L., 10
Geertz, Hildred, 131–2
Genet, Jean, 115
Gill, Merton M., 111
God, intellectual love of, 81, 85, 98, 154
Gordon, Robert M., 147
Gosling, J. C., 37–8, 40–2
gratitude, 40, 42
Green, O. H., 38, 157–9, 161–2
grief, 21, 49, 57, 59, 64, 77
guilt, 51, 146

hallucination, 169, 172–4
Hamlyn, D. W., 160
Hampshire, Stuart, 24, 43–4, 45–6, 66, 72–3, 91, 103, 148, 149, 151, 166–7

hatred, 8, 33, 54–5, 58–60, 62–3, 77, 85–6, 96, 99, 148

hope, 7, 21, 33–4, 60–1, 64, 77, 86, 93, 167

Hume, David: Topics listed below (and under Spinoza) categorize the dominant themes of the passages referred to. For treatment of specific subjects *see* the subjects (e.g. affects, anger, etc.). In this connection note that Hume is mentioned on the following pages: 1–38, 46–57, 61, 63, 65, 68, 73, 76–9, 85, 87, 90–1, 93–4, 99, 101–2, 141, 147–8, 152–154, 157, 163, 169–70, 174

    associationist mechanisms, 11–12, 14, 36; on belief, 46–9; on calm passions, 53–7; on cause, 8, 32–6, 38, 48, 151; on cause and object, 32–6, 157; on conjunction, 54–6, 153, 163; on emotions, 1–3, 5, 7, 11, 36, 76–9, 137, 152–3; epistemology, 26–7, 78, 141; on fantasy, 169–74; on feeling, 61–3; on indirect passions, 8; on love, 100–1, 153; on object, 26–37, 65; on object and cause, 32–6, 157; on pleasure, 20–4; on pride, 8, 10, 18–19, 26–8, 50, 153; on reason, 63–5; on self, 24–5, 37, 50; on simplicity, 12–17; sympathy principle, 49–53, 102; *see also* Spinoza compared with Hume

Hume's Classification of the Passions (diagram), 68

Hume's Square (diagram), 32

humility, 8, 11, 26–7, 32, 34, 37, 52, 55, 77, 94

hunger, 7, 38

Hutcheson, Francis, 7

hysteria, 119–21, 128–30, 132, 136–7

ideas, 1, 3, 5, 7–8, 23, 47–9, 55, 86, 96, 142, 152–3, 170; adequate/inadequate, 79, 81–4, 86, 92, 96–8, 148–9, 151, 154; association, *see under* association; of body, 74; and emotions, 78–9, 87, 140; enlivened, 51; of ideas, 31, 74, 76, 78; object

of, 90; as objects, 31, 52; of self, 25–7, 29, 50; simple, 12–17; unconscious, 76

identity, 25–6, 72

ideogenesis, 105, 120, 122

imagination, 7, 47, 55, 78–80, 82, 96, 147–8

imitation, 102

impressions, 1, 3, 5, 7–9, 11–12, 21, 23–4, 27–9, 33, 47–9, 54–6, 73, 76, 85, 90, 152–3, 170; in animals, 52; association, *see under* association; of pride, 19; of reflexion, 7–8, 10, 11, 16, 19, 20–4, 28, 35, 48, 50, 63, 77–78, 102, 152; of self, 25–6, 50–1; simple, 16–18, 137

incorporation fantasies, 46

induction, 162–3; Lévi-Strauss, 119, 122–3, 135

insight, 3, 113, 118, 133–6, 139, 141, 144, 155

instinct, 54, 73, 128, 134–5, 140, 142, 148–9

intensity, *see* vividness

intentionality, 46, 53, 78, 85–6, 91, 137–9, 161

James-Lange theory of emotion, 2

Javanese mental disorder (Latah), 131–2

jealousy, 40–1, 49, 62–3, 88–92, 146, 166

Joachim, Harold H., 73

joy, 11, 21, 28, 64, 77, 79, 81, 87

Jung, Carl Gustav, 149

Kemp Smith, Norman, 7, 10, 34, 47–9, 53, 68

Kenny, Anthony, 8–9, 37–40, 167

Kleinian pre-linguistic fantasies, 146

Kline, Paul, 112

knowledge, 144; liberating effect, 2, 78, 136, 139, 147–8, 151–2, 154; of mind, *see under* mental states; reflexive, 69, 75, 118, 147, 151, 155; self, *see* mental states: knowledge of own; theory, *see* epistemology

Kubrick, Stanley, 108

Kuhn, Thomas S., 113

language, 2, 44, 52, 143–4, 173
Latah, 131–2
learning, 15–19, 108–9
Lévi-Strauss, Claude, 112–14, 116–23, 135, 154
libido, 149
Little Albert, 111, 124–6
Little Hans, 111, 124–8, 133–4, 136, 141, 155
Little Peter, 111, 133
logic, 46, 82, 86–7
love, 8, 21, 33, 40–2, 54–6, 59, 62, 77–81, 85–6, 88, 92–4, 100–1, 146, 148, 153

MacIntyre, Alasdair, 53, 138
MacNabb, D. G. C., 77
Marxism on social change, 139
meaning, 20, 49, 132, 154
memory(ies), 2, 7, 25, 47–8, 140, 145, 148, 152, 169–71, 173–4; *see also under* fantasies
mental disorders: aetiology, 95, 105, 107–9, 111, 117, 122, 124–5, 128, 130, 134–5, 148, 155, 174; classification, 129–30, 132
mental states, 1, 3, 7, 31, 35–6, 38–40, 42–3, 45–6, 57, 60–1, 66, 69, 89, 91, 92, 118, 142, 160–1, 164, 167–168; active/passive, *see* emotions: active/passive; knowledge of others', 42–3, 46–7, 49–51, 92–3, 101–2, 153; knowledge of own, 5, 44, 48–9,64, 73–5, 92–3, 98, 147, 162
Mill, J. S., 2
mind, 3, 16, 26–7, 32, 75, 78, 80, 83, 93, 107–8, 139, 147, 149, 155; and body, 74–5, 80, 83, 90, 96, 100, 150–1; state of, *see* mental states
mobs, rationality of flight from, 84, 92, 97–8, 165
Moore, G. E., 15
Mullane, Harvey, 141
myth, 112, 114, 117–19

Navaho shamanism, 121
Neu, Jerome, 44, 113, 134, 137, 148, 169

neurosis, 110, 112, 119, 130, 134–5, 149, 174; *see also* mental disorders
Newton, Isaac, 5
nosological issues, 124, 128, 130, 132, 155

Oedipal conflict, 124, 126, 132
opinions, 50, 57–60, 62–4
Othello, 88–92

pain: as basic emotion, 71, 76–7, 85–6, 93, 98, 150, 153; and belief, 94; cause, 88–9, 96, 99; and instinct, 149; perception, 102; and pleasure, *see* pleasure and pain; in sickness, 118, 122
passions, 3, 7, 18, 21–2, 26–7, 31, 46–51, 54–7, 63–4, 67–8, 79, 91, 100, 136, 153; calm/violent, 53–4, 56–62, 91, 140, 153, 166; circle, *see* emotions: chain; conflict, *see* emotions: conflict; direct/indirect, 8, 20–1, 24, 53, 77; strong/weak, 54
Passmore, John, 12–13, 15, 17–18, 26–7, 30, 50
patients, 115–17, 122, 136–7; selection, 111–12
Pears, David, 13, 25, 38, 59, 159–60, 163
Penelhum, Terence, 22, 25
perceptions, 7, 12, 27, 30, 48–9, 87, 94, 98, 102, 169, 170–1; in Descartes, 79; false, 172; liveliness, 47; and memories, 145, 148, 170, 173–174; and pleasure, 90–1; and self, 24; simple, 17–18
phobias, 112, 124–30, 132–4, 155
physiological responses, 2, 31, 43, 54, 56, 74, 90–1, 93, 96–7, 99, 102–3, 117–23, 151, 154, 156, 161, 174
Pitcher, George, 27, 64–5, 78
pity, 40
pleasure, 23–4, 29, 81, 86, 150, 152–3, 173; as basic emotion, 71, 76–7, 86, 98–9; and love, 78–80, 92–3, 101; object, 88; and pain, 7–8, 18, 20–2, 33–4, 48, 78, 102, 149; and pride, 9–11, 18–19, 28
poetry, 1, 53, 119

Price, H. H., 47
pride, 8–11, 18–21, 24–9, 32, 34–7, 50–2, 55, 77, 152–3
Proust, Marcel, 171
psychic energy, 123, 135, 139–40, 148, 170, 173–4; discharge, 120, 136–40, 143, 146, 150, 155
psychoanalysis, 2–3, 49, 76, 110–14, 116–19, 121–5, 128–30, 132, 136–137, 139, 147, 150–2, 154–5
psychological states, *see* mental states
Pulver, Sydney, 140–3
Putnam, Hilary, 131

Quesalid, 113–14, 116–17, 154

Rachman, Stanley, 125–8, 133
Rapaport, David, 140–1
Rathbun, Constance, 149
reason, 3, 53–4, 57, 63–4, 78, 91, 95, 136, 147, 153; distinctions of, 14–19
reasonableness of emotion, *see* emotions: justification
reasons, 37, 40–2, 44–5, 64–5, 67
reflexion, 17; impressions of, *see under* impressions
regret, 14, 19, 46, 86, 93
Reider, N., 110
remorse, 14, 19, 39, 51
repentance, 94
repression, 49, 73, 135–7, 141–3, 149
resemblance, association by, 11–15, 24, 27–30, 34–5, 51, 78, 126–8, 152
responsibility, 51, 93
Richfield, Jerome, 144
Rimbaud, Arthur, 119
Rousseau, Jean-Jacques, 50
Russell, Bertrand, 144
Ryle, Gilbert, 22–3

Sachs, David, 167
Saussure, F. de, 144
scale of degree: of ideas and impressions, 47; of simples, 13–14, 16–17, 22
Schachter, Stanley and Singer, Jerome E., 66
self, 8–10, 21, 24–9, 32, 34–5, 37, 50–51, 152–3; consciousness, knowledge, *see* mental states: knowledge of own; maintenance/preservation, 71–4, 76, 82, 99, 149, 153; perceiving, 7, 24
sensations, 2, 7–8, 18, 20–4, 33–5, 37–38, 48, 61, 64–5, 76, 82, 101, 161
sense and reference (Frege), 123
sexuality, infantile, 125–6, 133
shamanism, 112–24, 134, 150, 154
shame, 51, 77, 93–5, 167
Shope, Robert K., 140
Shorter, J. M., 161
simplicity, 12–20, 22, 28, 35, 77, 100, 153
Singer, Jerome E., 66
Spinoza, Benedictus de: *See note under* Hume. Spinoza is mentioned on the following pages: 1–3, 31, 46, 57, 67, 69–103, 118, 135–6, 139, 142, 147–56
   on belief, 87–90; on cause, 86–8; compared with Freud, 2–3, 73, 78, 87–8, 103, 142, 147–51, 152, 155; compared with Hume, 1–3, 31, 57, 73, 76–8, 85, 87, 90–1, 93–4, 99–102, 147–9, 152–3; on *conatus*, 71–73, 149; on desire, 73–6, 100–1, 103; on emotions, 1–3, 57, 67, 70, 80–1, 84–6, 92–4, 96–100, 118, 148, 152–4, 156; epistemology, 78–80, 95; on ideas, 31, 78–9, 82–3; on pleasure and pain, 76–7; theory of imitation, 102; on thought, 46, 90–92; view of mind, 69, 118, 139, 142, 147, 150–1, 155
states of mind, *see* mental states
stimulus generalization, 126–8, 155
Strachey, James, 145
structuralism, 117–23, 154
sun's distance case, 82, 88
symbols, 112, 117–22, 154
sympathy, 25–6, 49–51, 53, 77, 102
symptoms, 107, 110–12, 114, 130–2, 137–9, 143, 147, 155

Taylor, Charles, 109
Thalberg, Irving, 67, 89, 147, 159–160, 166

therapy, 110, 112; aversion, 108, 132; behaviourist, *see* behaviourist therapy; (psycho)analytic, *see* psychoanalysis; role of thought, 105, 108–9, 112, 119, 121, 134, 154–5

thoughts, 1, 14, 30–1, 36, 75–6, 90, 142, 147, 169; alien, 46, 88, 137; and emotions, *see* emotions and thoughts; mixed, 169–70; obsessive, 47, 88, 167; in therapy, *see* therapy: role of thought; unconscious, 3, 36, 92, 105, 138–9, 141, 143–6, 148, 155

time, 2, 52, 143–4, 171–2

transference, 113, 139, 145, 148, 150

Trigg, Roger, 22

turbulence, 29, 33, 53–4, 57, 59–61, 153, 167

unconscious, 49, 73–4, 87, 131, 136–7, 141, 143–5, 149, 155; made conscious, 135–6, 148, 151; *see also under* desire; ideas; thoughts

vividness, 7, 15, 18, 24, 47, 169, 173–174

Wallerstein, Robert, 110–11, 124

Warnock, Mary, 57–63, 153, 166

Watling, John, 45

will, 57, 79–80, 83, 87, 90, 100–1

Williams, B. A. O., 22, 25, 157–8, 162

Wilson, J. R. S., 31, 38, 39, 43, 66, 159, 162–3

wish-fulfilment, 140, 172–3

wit, 20, 24

Wittgenstein, Ludwig, 2, 52, 95, 129–131

Wolf, Abraham, 87, 90

Wollheim, Richard, 44, 46, 53, 138

Wolpe, Joseph and Rachman, Stanley, 125–8, 133

Woozley, A. D., 75

Wordsworth, William, 2

Zuni witchcraft, 115